A BOY
FROM
NOWHERE

VOLUME TWO

by
David Mitchell

Published by

MELROSE
BOOKS

An Imprint of Melrose Press Limited
St Thomas Place, Ely
Cambridgeshire
CB7 4GG, UK
www.melrosebooks.com

FIRST EDITION

Cover designed by Tanya Fukes

ISBN: 978-1-906561-13-0

Printed and bound in Great Britain by:
CPI Antony Rowe, Chippenham, Wiltshire

CONTENTS

PREFACE

In Volume One I described the early part of my life in the East End Docklands where I was born in the slums and backstreets of that area. Yes, that is where it all began during the so-called 'roaring twenties' – in 1928, to be exact. I arrived in this world just in time to welcome in the Great Depression, which occurred in 1929.

The effects of the Great Depression were felt all over the world. It was a time when millionaires became beggars overnight, having lost their fortunes in the crash – some even committed suicide as a consequence. Of course, Britain was affected during most of the 1930s too, and the situation manifested itself in much hardship and unemployment because the majority of businesses went into a nosedive; many people found their services were no longer required and lost their jobs. Although almost everybody was affected, it was the working classes that took the brunt because, quite simply, no work for them meant little or no food for many back then. Older readers will know that in those days the generous handouts to the unemployed that apply today were not then available.

As an unskilled worker in the docks, my father was one of the first to be laid off and so was often unemployed. I believe he received the princely sum of 17/6d per week to pay the rent and buy food for the family – the equivalent today of just 87.5p! Of course, values were quite different then, but even so, 17/6d was not much on which to feed a family for a week.

I have been asked a number of times why I call my book *A Boy From Nowhere*, and I reply that it is because the East End of those dark and difficult days was a kind of 'nowhere' place to be and to live. Generally speaking, people resigned themselves to lives of poverty and slum conditions, little money and poor food, and they saw little hope of their quality of life improving. Yes, people dreamed their dreams of a better life, but in their heart of hearts they knew they were but dreams. And we all know that many dreams do not come true – not unless your name is David Mitchell! I was extremely fortunate, for all mine came true.

And so in Volume One I describe how although I sprang from the heart of the East End, I managed to obtain a position in business in the City, and the story plots my advancement in the commercial world despite the many handicaps I had to overcome and the fact that because the war had completely disrupted my education, I possessed neither educational qualifications nor any skills whatsoever. I left school at fourteen years of age, as most working-class lads did, and all I had was a burning ambition to succeed and a willingness to work hard and learn.

Nevertheless, I took full advantage of the opportunities that came my way and succeeded to the point that I was appointed managing director of a Czech-owned firm that was responsible for the sale and distribution of all Czechoslovak confectionery products in the United Kingdom – I was charged with the task of establishing new offices, employing staff etc, and I was at that point twenty-eight years of age. The responsibility I had taken on my young shoulders was considerable and I describe my adventures and experiences along the way.

Before that, in Volume One, I described my shock when as a young man of only twenty-four years, I first set foot in Prague in January 1953 and saw a communist state in action. I had never known any other way but to live the free and democratic way of life that we enjoy in the UK, but too often take for granted. I gazed and listened to everything so that I could report all this to my family back home, and several members of them hardly believed me when I explained what I had seen and heard.

In Volume Two I also explain the reasons why I eventually decided to resign my position with the Czechs. This was not an action that I wished to take, for I had made many friends in what Neville Chamberlain, our Prime Minister before the outbreak of war, called 'That far-away country of which we know nothing'. I occupied a position that was unique and to all intents and purposes I was my own master. I loved my work deeply, but I knew I had to go for the sake of my family and myself because eventually, like every ambitious businessman, I wanted to establish and run my own business. I had tired of making money for others – I wanted the opportunity to make money for the benefit of my family and myself.

And I eventually achieved this ambition as well. Volume Two describes how I managed to start my business from absolutely nothing, the kind of problems I experienced in setting it all up and the way I overcame them and so went on to develop a successful business importing and distributing confectionery products from manufacturers in the UK as well as abroad.

But in 1984 circumstances occurring in our business lives contrived to make my wife and I consider early retirement. We therefore decided to close our business down, build our dream villa in the sun and retire to the Costa Blanca to live for as long as we wished. We actually stayed for nine wonderful and very enjoyable years. I describe our lives in Spain and why we decided eventually to return to England to live after a period of time in which I believe that perhaps we saw the very last of good old Spain. For after they joined the EU in 1990, the situation and atmosphere which made Spain such a popular venue began to alter and there is no doubt about the fact that many changes began to slowly take place. Some were for the good but others affected that special Spanish atmosphere which we enjoyed so much when we first went to live there.

We were confident that it would probably not take long to sell our villa and so finally we returned to Devon to live in the delightful village of Cheriton Bishop, and here we shall stay.

This book, therefore, covers the period from the late 1950s, when I had been appointed director of sales, marketing and distribution of all Czechoslovakian confectionery products in the UK, up to the point when we return from Spain to live in England once more.

1

MEETING JACK COHEN SOCIALLY – DEVELOPING THE SUPERMARKET BUSINESS AND OTHER EXPERIENCES

Having now returned from our adventurous and extremely interesting trip behind the Iron Curtain, which involved the whole length and breadth of what was then Czechoslovakia, I of course resumed my duties at my office immediately, as I was anxious to deal with any problems that may have arisen in my absence. However, I had endeavoured to keep in contact with my secretary, Joan Gloster, as much as possible during the time I was away and she had kept me fully informed. So I found there were no serious issues which demanded my urgent attention.

Earlier in the year I had placed orders with the various factories for what we called 'current lines', i.e. items which sold the whole year round, and also items which comprised our Christmas range. The forward buying was a responsibility I retained but I had passed over the task of administrating sales and deliveries via our twelve agents throughout the country to my sales manager Bob Warrior, because I personally had a potentially greater programme before me, i.e. the further establishment and development of our supermarket programme. Bearing in mind that I had a whole industry behind me, and remembering the reluctance of British manufacturers back then to supply supermarkets for fear of price cutting and consequent disruption within the confectionery trade, our prospects for success were very high in my view and also in the view of Sydney Eagle and his son Geoffrey, about whom I have commented in Volume One, and with their connections I felt that with their full cooperation the doorway to the supermarket trade was wide open to us. We were not proved wrong at all in that confident outlook.

I have to say that Sydney kept to his word with regard to Jack Cohen (later Sir John Cohen), the founder of the Tesco empire, and arranged a dinner meeting at the Eagles' apartment, which was situated by Regent's Park. One can imagine what kind of apartment it was when I say that the floor below the Eagles was occupied by Joe Loss, the famous bandleader of that era and before, whilst the floor above was occupied by the Russian Ambassador. It was a very large apartment containing a large number of rooms – much more spacious, I would say, than the ordinary four- to five-bedroom house. My wife Lynne was, of course, invited too, and as we entered the apartment we observed an amazing oil painting on the wall immediately facing us. It was a scene of a rather ornate lounge and on a table in the centre of the room stood a tall glass or vase which reflected the French windows, and through the windows a lovely garden could be seen. The garden, with all kinds of colourful flowers and plants, was depicted in every beautiful detail; it is indeed hard to imagine how an artist could paint such detail in this minute but perfect way. When I later asked him about it, Sydney told us that it was a painting he had recently bought and that his purchase was reported in an art magazine, which he showed to us. I believe he paid quite a lot of money for this painting – something over £30,000, if my memory serves me correctly, and although that is a lot of money today, back then it was a small fortune. But why not? Sydney was a very wealthy man and what is the point of having money if you can't spend it on things you like?

I believe we were the first to arrive and were offered a cocktail, which was very pleasant. After a while the others arrived; the dinner party included Jack Cohen and his wife Cissie, Geoffrey Eagle and his wife, the daughter of Sydney together with her husband, Lynne and myself and, of course, Sydney and his wife. We were all introduced and I was very pleased indeed to meet Jack Cohen, because in our supermarket programme we hoped that in time Tesco would also become interested in what we had to offer. It was a very pleasant meal, but we did not discuss business in any way whatsoever, as far as I recall; this was a social evening and introducing business into the conversation would have been very impolite.

I noted that Sydney and Jack Cohen spoke to each other very intimately, like two brothers, and Geoffrey spoke to Jack Cohen like an uncle – in fact he called him 'Uncle Jack'. The relationship was obviously an extremely close one – it was more like a family atmosphere between the Cohens and the Eagles. After dinner the gentlemen retired to another room to light their cigars, recharge their glasses and play bridge, whilst the ladies went into the lounge and continued to chat with each other. I was also invited to play bridge, of course, but unfortunately I have never been a great card player and so never learned to play this intriguing game; therefore I diplomatically declined and expressed my wish to watch the others play. I didn't mention it at the time as I didn't want to boast, but I was, of course, a dab hand at snap and won against my children every time! But somehow the elegant game of bridge had eluded me. Never mind, I found that watching this card game was a very entertaining experience – even better than a Morecambe and Wise performance, because during the whole period in which they played bridge, Sydney and Jack Cohen chided each other, using typical Jewish humour and expressions, for making what they each thought were obvious mistakes. Standing there and observing in the background, I was indeed highly amused at their exchanges.

It is worth a comment about this brotherly relationship between Jack Cohen and Sydney Eagle. According to the story I was told, by Sydney himself, these three young Jewish boys served in the army during World War I. They were all from the Whitechapel/Stepney region, which back in those days was an area heavily populated with Jews, and they were Sydney himself, Jack Cohen and a third chap whose name was Michael Burzin. When they were demobbed after the end of World War I they used their discharge allowances wisely. Jack Cohen opened a small place in Middlesex Street, better known as Petticoat Lane, selling everything, but mainly groceries. I was told he made a point of obtaining and selling items with superficial damage, such as dented tins, and later specialised in a disinfectant product as well. I was told later, but not by Sydney, that everything did not go too smoothly for him and he experienced some financial difficulties. The word 'bankrupt' was mentioned to me but I am not aware if this was true or not. But let us say he had his difficulties and problems. However, he was a fighter and so battled his way back. It may surprise the younger readers of this story of mine to know that supermarkets were not always in existence. In days gone by everybody bought their groceries in the small family shops we came to know so well. But it is a fact that Jack Cohen pioneered supermarket trading in this country in the 1950s after he visited the USA and saw it in operation there; and what a terrific success he made of this development in the UK. Without doubt he was regarded in the early days as being the king of supermarket trading in this country.

He lived to see Tesco reach the number two position after Sainsbury, who were once the leaders because of their greater number of stores, but I am sure he never realised just what he had given birth to and what an enormous, international organisation Tesco would grow into. It was already large before his death but in the following years it mushroomed into the gigantic company it is today. He was, of course, already proud of what he began and had developed to a point, but he would have been even more proud of the way in which it was expanded, for it is now, as everybody knows, a virtual commercial empire, existing not only in this country but in a number of other countries too.

Jack Cohen was a simple man, and emotional, but he was also very astute and knew a good business deal when he saw one. He was a terrific buyer with a very pleasant and humorous manner which made it difficult for those selling to him to resist. I know; I was one of them! His motto was 'pile 'em high and sell 'em cheap', and that is exactly what he did. In the process he made a fortune and having recognized the all-important factor of being in a position to buy big, he embarked on a take-over policy of other smaller supermarkets and stores, which whilst also establishing new branches, helped to make Tesco the giant it is today. By so doing he could almost dictate his own buying terms.

He was in a position to be very generous to various charities – and he was. In recognition of his services he was knighted and then became Sir John Cohen. What a great honour for a man of such great achievement, for a man from such humble beginnings, and how very proud he must have been when kneeling before the Queen at Buckingham Palace to receive his knighthood. Whether or not he shed a tear or two before Her Majesty I am unaware, but it would not surprise me in the least to know that he did, for, as I have already remarked, he was a very emotional man. In fact, I would bet my bottom dollar that at some point he did succumb to his emotions.

Turning now to Sydney Eagle, he used his money to open a confectionery shop in The Cut in south east London and blossomed out into substantial wholesale trading not only of confectionery items but many other varieties of merchandise; with all his valuable friends and contacts throughout Britain he became a big buyer and distributor. He invested his fortune wisely and also became a very wealthy man.

The third man, Michael Burzin, eventually became 'The Nottingham Mystery Man', and at first he specialised in buying lace remnants from the many factories in the Midlands that were producing lace goods. He would then travel around to the various street markets, open the back of his vehicle and stand there with a mask over his face selling these remnants off cheaply – hence his nickname. Later on he established and developed Burnard's Stores, a chain of mainly grocery stores which was later taken over and absorbed into the Tesco empire that Jack Cohen was building.

He had earlier also absorbed Victor Value, another smaller supermarket chain. Jack Cohen certainly became very big in the takeover world. It is most important to mention at this point that from the early years he was very ably assisted by Daisy Hyams, a lady that I, and a great many others, did not take to very much. She was a bully to almost all who tried to sell to her and did not care what she said to anyone – her words were often impolite to the point of rudeness to those who were endeavouring to sell to her. Whilst we all had to respect her position as a very substantial buyer, I think few people, including yours truly, looked forward to sessions with her. She was a hard buyer who was accustomed to getting her own way and would brook no nonsense once she had made up her mind what she wanted and nothing, but nothing, would deter her from her target – she would settle only for one's agreement to her price demands.

I had one or two disagreements with her – I could not, and would not, allow myself to be pushed around or bullied by Daisy. She was not accustomed to people standing up to her – that was plain. But on the other hand, neither was I used to such rudeness and I would not take that from anyone, no matter how important she thought she might have been! When I started my own business and began to buy in large quantities I followed the example of Jack Cohen, i.e. by being pleasant and humorous in negotiations, and it is surprising what you can achieve when adopting that stance. What a great pity it was that Daisy Hyams never followed the example of her boss.

She had two under buyers helping her, one of whose name was Dipple, but I cannot, for the moment, remember the name of his colleague. They were nice chaps and all of us tried very hard to deal with them rather than Daisy; however, when negotiations were in full flow, and going along very well, out would come Daisy to join in the discussions and convert what were pleasant talks into something else. And so when you exited the Tesco offices you experienced a considerable sense of relief at having got out of there in one piece! But in selling one has to use what cunning one has and I always had a card up my sleeve in the form of Sydney Eagle, and if ever I got into a fracas with Daisy, I would ask Sydney to get Jack Cohen to intervene. He did and I am happy to say that served to calm Daisy down very noticeably; I think Jack Cohen was the only one who could handle her. I believe thereafter that she took a dislike to me. But she of all people should realise that in business one has to use every weapon one can in the face of adversity – she did!

I should also mention that when Jack Cohen took over Burnard's Stores he also had to take over a certain other lady – Mrs Carrington (called

'Carrie' in the trade). She was to Michael Burzin what Daisy was to Jack Cohen, but a much nicer person – although when she had her dander up she too could be a fearful character to handle. Of course, those of us who knew both ladies forecast with much certainty that there would be great fireworks if these two attempted to work in harmony together. In such a confrontation there could be but one winner – Daisy! And so it was, I believe, that Carrie left Tesco within a matter of weeks following the takeover. What happened was inevitable between these two ladies who both had very strong wills and who were very fiery. I always wondered, though, what kind of people these 'ogres' were when at home. I rather suspect that they were 'pussycats' in the presence of their own families and that their commercial reputations were but an act.

Well, time went by and both Sydney Eagle and I were getting impatient to see a start to our supermarket programme and wanted to get things moving. So in negotiations with him I urged him to start the ball rolling by placing an order with me for 1lb boxes of chocolates for which we had developed a very acceptable box design. He agreed to buy a first lot of sixty tons, but with the strict proviso that I match his price – not a penny more. So I sent a telex to Prague with an outline of what was required, but decided that it would be better to go personally to Prague HQ and deal with any problems. My secretary, Joan Gloster, made all the necessary arrangements for flight and hotel etc, for she was excellent in conducting such tasks, and confirmed everything to my colleagues in Prague. So I duly arrived there and immediately hit trouble – the price Sydney wanted to pay was too low. It just didn't work out.

I discovered that the difference was not a very large one, but every penny counted. So at HQ I asked for a specimen box to be brought into the conference room and we laid every chocolate on the table. I then requested them to be divided into cost categories so that we could determine which were more expensive, which were average and which were cheaper to produce. And only by juggling around, subtracting one or two pieces here and adding there, did we get to a level which would enable the business to go ahead. At last we had reached an acceptable compromise, but it was a struggle. Now all I had to do was to return to London and convince Sydney that the changes had been necessary and the only possible way to reach his price. In this instance, and I make no bones about it, we had to sacrifice a measure of quality in order to reach Sydney's price requirements. As a matter of fact, I made such a policy quite permanent whenever I had price problems with Sydney – I always forced him to make a sacrifice too. Our relationship, therefore, was full of compromises, a situation well supported by his son Geoffrey, who I found to be a very reasonable and fair young man. I returned on the Friday evening and during the flight back to London (direct flights between London and Prague had now been reinstated) I mused over the events of the past days and knew that I was at the beginning of a very exciting development indeed, and the more I thought about it the more enthusiastic I became. I just could not wait to get back to my office.

On Monday I went to my office and on the following day disaster struck when we heard that Selwyn Lloyd, the Chancellor of the Exchequer at that time, had decided to apply Purchase Tax to confectionery products. These had hitherto been exempt from this tax as it was classified as a food item (all food items were exempt from Purchase Tax). This tax was later substituted with VAT, and the same situation, with the exclusion of actual food products, applies even today. But by deciding to exclude confectionery items as food products, in one fell swoop this man, Selwyn Lloyd, had destroyed all the efforts I had put into this important contract, because the imposition of Purchase Tax would, of course, affect the consumer price which was so important to Sydney Eagle. I of course immediately phoned Sydney and he agreed we should meet urgently. I explained to him the difference in price that this tax would result in and he was very dubious about buying such a large quantity of goods on a now totally different basis. His mind was tuned to the retail-selling price of five shillings; this new tax would make that impossible. He recognised, of course, that it was not our fault, nor his, and we both silently, or maybe not so silently, cursed Selwyn Lloyd. I did manage to rescue something of the contract I had flown to Prague for and I believe we ended up at around twenty tons or so; an order not to be sniffed at, but not the contractual quantity we had discussed and which I had used to fire the enthusiasm of the people at HQ and also at Diana in Decin, the factory which was to produce this item for us.

Of course, the confectionery trade slowly became accustomed to the new price levels made necessary by the application of Purchase Tax and so in time, when the dust had settled, I was able to resume negotiations with Sydney Eagle in an effort to build up a range of products, all of which might be suitable for supermarket trading. These negotiations went ahead quite rapidly; I put my thinking cap on and suggested a number of variations of confections that one or other of our factories in Czechoslovakia could make and which could be placed in a box.

I had already developed a number of ideas during my working holiday tour of the factories in 1960 and in time these ideas came to fruition in the form of finished boxes, so at last we had the framework of what we called our supermarket range to offer, and at last a proper marketing job could be done. But in the process of developing this range I encountered other problems, such as design work. The artists in Prague had still not got the hang of what I was after, which was, quite frankly, to dress these boxes up in such a way that they looked as English as possible, because for various reasons, foreign confectionery in general was at that time not all that popular with the public – a situation that has changed very considerably today. However, we did of course go to extensive trouble to ensure that we abided very strictly by the letter of the law and so the country of origin was clearly marked on every box, as required by the regulations at that time.

So I thought about this problem of design and decided to tackle it by asking Rapid, the State Advertising and Publicity Organisation, if they would object if I used part of our advertising appropriation to cover the costs of having the designs effected here in the UK. They agreed and so I used the services of a young group of commercial artists in London. Thank God that I managed to secure this agreement, for it became far easier and a much simpler way to get our designs done in the way that we wanted. I have to say that if I had been forced to have box and packaging designs done in Prague I doubt if we could have put such an attractive range together. But I worked very closely with the lads I retained to perform this task and explained to them basically what I was looking for. They would then render sketches which I would in turn discuss with the Eagles, and from these negotiations we selected our rough designs which were then produced as proper artworks ready to be sent to the printing factories in Czechoslovakia for production. I know that Sydney Eagle in particular loved being involved in these kinds of negotiations, because to take an idea and then develop it into a finished article for sale took a lot of work, especially, if I may say so, on my part. But I treated Sydney and Geoffrey Eagle as partners of a kind, and I think they appreciated the way that I consulted them in every part of that development. So they felt rather proud that they too had made a valued contribution in building this excellent range of merchandise.

I also learned that the *Daily Mirror* in Holborn had an extremely wide selection of photographs and colour negatives of every type and description which they were quite happy to hire out at, I think, about £10 each and which would be more than useful as designs for some of our boxes. There were very attractive negatives of animals and pets, children, country and village scenes, maritime scenes – everything one could possibly imagine.

I was sure that I could find suitable scenes for chocolate boxes there and if so that would be terrific. So I went along to Holborn and spent hours and hours, and not all in just one day, looking at their massive collection. I eventually made a selection and took them away to show and discuss with Sydney and Geoffrey Eagle and, between us, to choose those we liked. They were very enthusiastic about some of the negatives, which we later used in actual production.

The negatives we selected were sent off to Prague HQ for processing and those we didn't require I returned to the *Daily Mirror*. In this way we developed the very attractive range of boxes of various sizes and contents that I have described. We also produced a very attractive catalogue incorporating information about the Czechoslovakian confectionery industry, pictures of the Board of Directors in HQ in Prague, a page about Eagle Bros. Ltd, and photographs of Sydney, Geoffrey Eagle and yours truly. I dedicated a full page to describing the excellent relationship that my company, Sugosa Ltd, had together with Eagle, and colourful details and photographs of the full range. This catalogue was then posted to wholesalers and supermarkets, big and small, all over the UK and where we could, we followed up such mailings. In this way we introduced more and more customers to our supermarket range; not all of them were supermarkets, of course, as our boxes were more than suitable for other types of outlets as well.

And so by using these and similar methods we developed the supermarket business to a very substantial extent and were soon shipping some thousands of tons of finished merchandise for delivery to the supermarkets and other outlets. However, in business one must always try as best one can to prepare for ugly surprises and events that slowly, or sometimes suddenly, creep up on you. And so yet another major tax problem then confronted us in the form of what was called the Sugar Surcharge. I cannot now, after all these years, recall the exact details of this tax, but if my memory serves me correctly it was a tax on sugar and had something to do with using the revenue to subsidise the colonial sugar growers in various parts of the British Empire and Commonwealth from whom we bought and imported sugar, and by so doing to guarantee them a minimum price for their products – even if world prices fell. So the Government decreed that this tax should apply to any item which contained sugar, which obviously included all confectionery whether made in Britain or imported.

However, the tax was not a straightforward or fixed amount, for it depended totally on the world price of sugar, and as that price fluctuated so did the subsidy and so did the tax. Strong representations were made to the Government of the day about the impracticality of a system which made accurate advance costing of products, whether home produced or imported, absolutely impossible. How could anybody place substantial orders for goods in advance without knowing exactly what those goods were going to cost? All our confectionery lines were based upon agreed retail or consumer price structures – that was the nature of the British confectionery trade. But, as usual, the Government was totally deaf to the entreaties of the various trades and industries which used sugar in their products and refused to listen to the valid arguments and pleas for reason which were placed before them.

So our stupid politicians had placed before us a problem for which we really had no answer but which we just simply had to face up to. Of course, I gave the matter very serious thought and eventually found the answer. I realised we had to find a means of being able to adjust the contents of a box to match the price we wanted to pay and on the basis of which this new tax could be taken into account. I gave a lot of thought to how this might be done. It was obvious that we had to find a way of adjusting the weight of the contents and to be flexible in the matter, for even reducing a box by 1oz gave a substantial reduction in overall costs. However, reducing the weights of the actual individual chocolates would have been an almost impossible task for our factories, and equally impossible, it seemed, to adjust the overall contents by total weight.

The answer came when I saw, quite by accident, an advertisement for this vacuum forming machine, which was quite new then. A metal mould of a tray shape would be placed in the machine, then a layer of plastic was placed over the mould and a strong vacuum drew the plastic over the mould producing a finished and perfect plastic tray. I reasoned that we could pre-prepare a variety of tray moulds, each adjusted to contain various weights; this would be an absolutely flexible method and we would then be able to control the final costs accurately, despite the Sugar Surcharge. Even so, the problems during production would be quite considerable. We were told that we could see such a machine in action at the premises of G.F. Lovell & Co. Ltd at Newport, South Wales.

The machine manufacturers arranged it so that I and my colleague Antonin Belina, from the HQ in Prague, who was Export Manager at HQ and who was in London at that time, could go to see it. We did so and recognised it as being the probable answer to our problems, for according to the level of the surcharge at any time, with such a machine we could adjust the weight of the contents very quickly in order to keep our retail price structure in place. I did not know it then, but that visit to G.F. Lovell at Newport was much more than useful and in fact became invaluable to me later on in another respect, which I write about in a future chapter. The directors, including Mr Lovell himself, gave us a splendid welcome and entertained us to lunch, despite the fact that at that time we had only come to look at the machinery. They were very hospitable and their hospitality was very much appreciated by Antonin Belina and myself.

However, during our return journey from Newport to London Antonin advised me that there was a major problem and that it would be very difficult indeed, even virtually impossible, to obtain the foreign currency necessary to purchase this machine, and in any case, it would take ages to come through even if an application was eventually successful. However, we were all aware that our needs were very urgent and so we had to try to overcome that problem too.

So having found the answer to our problems we could not take advantage of it because of the shortage of foreign currency in Czechoslovakia! In all of these discussions and thoughts on the problem, as I have explained before, I worked closely and in harness with Sydney and Geoffrey Eagle, and I believe that they had never been brought into such discussions about designs and various other issues with any of their other suppliers, and, as I have said before, I do think they appreciated that kind of relationship and actually enjoyed becoming so involved. I am confident that I had developed just the right kind of cooperation with Sydney and Geoffrey. Therefore, during discussions I took a chance and made the suggestion that it would be even worth our while to buy this machine, record it as a supermarket cost and present it as a free gift to whichever factory was selected by HQ. They could then produce these moulded plastic trays on behalf of themselves and any factory in Czechoslovakia with a similar problem. There was no question that it would help us enormously to overcome a very difficult situation which could quite easily threaten our supermarket development. I was delighted when Sydney and Geoffrey both agreed with this proposal wholeheartedly and so, to cut a long story short, I purchased the machine and it was shipped off to Prague. It is so easy to write those words but they mask a whole host of smaller problems I encountered before the machine left our shores, including overcoming our Czech Managing Director who was against the idea. He was fearful about the financial consequences, but I managed to convince him that it was my responsibility and that all would be quite OK.

The inclusion of such vacuum-formed plastic trays became universal in the confectionery industry in time, but I do believe that Lovell's, and shortly afterwards ourselves, were among the pioneers in the UK for this form of packaging. Firms like Cadbury and Rowntree etc began to use plastic trays well after we did. One final word on this vacuum forming machine – I did believe that the use of the machine was so versatile that many machines might be required and ordered, subject to foreign currency being made available, by other Czech factories in various industries. But to my knowledge only the one was ever supplied and I rather suspect that someone ordered it to be copied and eventually produced in Czechoslovakia.

Perhaps the reader would allow me to make some further comment on Antonin Belina. As Sales Export Manager for HQ he and I of course spent many hours working together. In any Western business he would have held the position as Export Director, but in the Czech system every organization had but one director, although the State export conglomerations did have one or two so-called Deputy Directors. Originally, Anton was a sales representative for the Lidka factory – a wonderful factory that specialised in very high-class confections of various kinds. It doesn't exist any more, for it was considered that the output of this wonderful factory could be concentrated by having Lidka items produced by other factories some distance away. Now, Lidka employees were very highly skilled and positions there went from father to son and mother to daughter, thus creating a unique passing of skills down through the generations. The Lidka factory was indeed a golden jewel of the Czechoslovak confectionery industry. All this was lost in the silly communist attitude of enforcing production concentration and centralisation. When this most unpopular decision was brought into effect, Antonin was asked if he would agree to a transfer to the Ceskeslovenske Cokoladovny HQ at Modrany near Prague, and he accepted this new role; that is how I came into contact with him once again, having met him previously when visiting Lidka.

I must explain that Anton was a card. He was funny, he was mischievous and he was highly amusing. I developed a close relationship with him over the years. He was a great help to me, although from time to time something of a defeatist: he thought every problem was a disaster. He made the time pass much more pleasantly during our many trips together to various parts of his country when visiting factories, and also here in the UK. Sometimes, as I have quite a keen sense of humour, he made me absolutely split my sides with laughter. Many is the time I would come away from a business conference at which Anton was present to find that he had slipped a few sweets into my coat side pockets just for a joke; I was not very pleased when I discovered that some of them were of the sticky type! I am not really 100% sure about his capabilities, or whether he was super efficient, but he was well liked by everyone and I think that maybe that is how he held his job down. It did mean many trips to the UK for him and whilst he was here I did my best to be hospitable towards him. He visited my home on a number of occasions and knew all my family. I also visited his home on the outskirts of Prague and met his family too.

When after the Prague Spring was broken by the invasion of Czechoslovakia by the Warsaw Pact nations in August of 1968, communism returned with full force with all its evil facets – and I write more fully about this very sad situation in the next chapters – and following the invasion all the new conditions which had so improved life in Czechoslovakia for some months during the Prague Spring, which had been brought in by Mr Dubcek, were cancelled. It became much worse than before because Moscow insisted upon retribution against not only all those who had sided with and supported him as the originator of the new attitude towards state bureaucracy and which had led to the relaxation of many controls which were stifling the public, but even against communist party members who had apparently stood by and done little or nothing to oppose him. So, quite understandably, many people began to be rather nervous once more, and I am sad to say that Anton was one of them. I did meet him in London subsequent to my resignation and departure from Sugosa, but I knew him well and I was quite sure he was getting too nervous to continue to be in contact with me. You see, I was no longer 'one of them' following my resignation, and so our friendship, which had lasted so long and which was so close, gradually diminished and finally faded away, despite a number of efforts on my part to continue contact with him. I was very sad indeed to hear a few years later that he had not survived an operation in Prague and had passed away. When the news reached me I wrote a nice letter of condolence to his wife, whom I also knew. I shall always remember Anton. I was very pleased to have known him and to have had the pleasure of working with him. I regarded him as a friend of mine and I retain many fond memories of the times during which we worked so closely together.

I should have mentioned that by this time my company, Sugosa Ltd, had come to a financial agreement with Eagle Bros. Ltd. I made a proposal in order to solve the problems of uncertainty of levels of costs in general which existed with the supermarket programme. I proposed, and they agreed, that although we would continue to operate and keep our records and responsibilities independently, the very nature of our business together made it more than advisable for us to amalgamate overall turnover receipts as well as overall costs, but only those attributable to our mutual supermarket business, of course, and work on a shared profit basis at the end of each financial year. All of this could be calculated and checked by our respective accountants. It meant some changes in both our and Eagle's accounting and records systems. It also meant that Sugosa would share some risk factors, which were previously the exclusive domain of Eagle Bros., and that we would need to have considerable trust in each other. On the other hand, Sugosa would also share in final profits and almost certainly gain. This agreement was my brainchild and we celebrated the signing in style by holding a grand dinner, which was very much appreciated by Sidney Eagle in particular.

I apologise to the reader for describing the foregoing in detail, but I wanted to do so in order to bring home the wide responsibilities I had and that the solving of problems was chief among them. Not only did I have to be a good salesman but an accurate buyer, in addition to being well versed in design, advertising, shipping matters, storage of our goods and distribution methods, plus office administration, and also be a good negotiator of business strategy too. In other words, I really had to be a Jack-of-all-trades. All this I had to pick up and learn from experience myself – nobody taught me. And, if I may say so, I fitted into this versatile role quite well. It certainly would not have been easy for my Czech principals to find someone else capable of carrying out all those functions in an efficient manner. No doubt I made a few mistakes along the way – we all do – but I cannot remember any that were to any extent serious.

It was around this period that I received a call one day from our company solicitor Christopher Vowles. Mr Vowles attended to legal matters on behalf of the Czechoslovak Embassy and most of the Czech companies in London, of which there were quite a few. Anyway, Mr Vowles told me that he and his wife were giving a dinner party for a group of people, most of whom would be Czech, and including a number who did not speak English. Therefore, as he understood I was getting on very well with my learning of the Czech language he would appreciate it if Lynne and I could come along as well. I replied that we would be delighted to and on the appointed day I went home a little early to ready myself. It was normal dress so I didn't have to trouble too much. Mr Vowles lived in a very nice house in Wimbledon and we found it without a lot of difficulty.

Some of the guests were already there by the time we arrived. Introductions were made all round, but as is usual at these affairs, five minutes later we had forgotten the names of most of them, if not all. After a drink or two we were called to the table and noted that there were place cards at each position at the table. Lynne usually likes to be next or near to me on such occasions and I prefer to sit by her; but in this instance we were not seated next to each other, although she was only three or four places from me. I remember that to my left sat a Czech lady who spoke almost no English whatsoever, so I was able to put my rapidly improving Czech into practice; I didn't do too badly – she said she was surprised, especially with my accent. Immediately opposite to me was a gentleman in military uniform and I remembered that we had been introduced to him over drinks; he was Major Macek, who, he informed me, was from the Military Attaché's office. And it was Major Macek who occupied my attention for most of the evening, although I did my best, for the sake of politeness, to pay spasmodic attention to the lady sitting to my left.

Major Macek spoke to me about a whole variety of subjects; he showed particular interest in my hobbies. At that time I was very much wrapped up in, and very enthusiastic about, the vexed game of golf. As soon as I mentioned golf he latched on to this like a terrier and would not shut up about it. He said that at the Embassy they have a whole range of sports equipment, including golf clubs, and that he would very much like to try the game some time, as he had never played. Well, I never needed to be asked twice, for I had somehow developed an interest in demonstrating and teaching the rudiments of golf to those very new to the game and enjoyed the experience of helping such learners along.

So I invited Major Macek to play a game with me at my favourite spot at that time, Betchworth Park Golf Club, which is in the lovely Box Hill country not far from Dorking in Surrey. As usual, I advised Mr Mantell, the steward there, that we would be coming and once more he and his wife were excellent hosts. I was quite surprised how quickly the Major took to the game and we had a very pleasant nine holes, followed by lunch and then the remaining nine holes. This was to be the first of such meetings and looking back, I could not come to any other conclusion than that I had been deliberately set up at that dinner party. It was no accident that I was placed opposite the Major at the dinner table. But at that time I was innocently encouraging this new friendship and suspected nothing; we played golf now and then and he even visited my home with his family on a few occasions – always bearing gifts; one time it was a case of Pilsner beer, and then on another visit perhaps a bottle of whisky.

On one occasion he was kind enough to invite Lynne and myself to the very special Embassy-owned apartment in Cadogan Square. I am certain that this special place, which was truly delightful and wonderfully superior in every respect, was used by the Ambassador himself when he wanted to hold receptions or meetings away from the Embassy. It was furnished with excellent and exquisite taste and Bohemian cut crystal glass seemed to be everywhere. The light coming from the crystal chandeliers sparkled and shone just like multi-coloured diamonds. To my surprise, Major Macek had a colleague there with him and we were introduced; he was Captain Vokac and he had come over to London for a visit as, in time, he was going to replace Major Macek when the latter was recalled to Prague.

We had a drink or two and chatted generally and then got down to the real reason for our meeting there, which was to view a 32 mm film which had been taken of my family and myself when we visited Czechoslovakia by car and I shot a wild boar near Ruzova. Once again, on that occasion, I had to 'lie in wait', which meant sitting in a hide built in a tree. We were sitting there for hours and as we saw nothing and it was getting rather dark, we decided to alight from the hide and return to the hunting lodge. On our way back we walked through a number of fields and my hunting colleague stopped at the edge of each one to look through his binoculars (special binoculars which reflect light even though it may be rather dark) to see if anything was there. But after we negotiated a number of fields and saw nothing he tired of doing that and we just walked on without taking any care to be especially silent. Suddenly, from the forest to our left we heard a noise and a dark shape appeared in the gloom. It seemed to hesitate, go back and then appear once more. I was told afterwards that this is the habit of wild boar; they are very nervous creatures and it is up to the male, but sometimes the female, to make sure there are no enemies when they exit the forest. We froze and my colleague looked through his glasses and then nodded to me to shoot. I raised the rifle and tried to view the boar through the telescopic sight but it was so dark that I just could not get my visual bearings. Meanwhile, the boar, sensing that something was standing there before him, began to snort and paw the ground with his foot. Realising that to wait much longer might be very dangerous, I simply decided to look along the barrel of the rifle, line it up against the black shape before me and fire. Fortunately for both my hunting friend and me it was a good shot and the boar lay dead in the grass.

Once again, I could not help that tinge of regret as we looked at the beast – he was a big boy, but he did not have any tusks. However, it was explained to me that in the first instance these wild boar cause an immense amount of damage to growing crops – they are certainly no friends of the farmers as they can easily uproot a whole field of seedling potatoes or other plants in one night; secondly, they are very prolific breeders and thirdly, they now have no natural predators (bears and wolves do not exist in this area any more). Thus the culling of wild boar is an absolute necessity, and for this reason there is no closed season on wild boar. After hearing this I felt a little better but I still had some feelings of guilt. Then followed the unpleasant part of gutting the animal and there was no other choice but to leave the carcase there until the following day. I have often recalled that adventure and speculated what might have happened if my shot had only winged the animal. Normally, wild boar will not attack you and will run away if you disturb them, but when they have young, or if they are wounded, they can be very dangerous indeed, especially the big boys with large, fearsome tusks. But even without tusks they can be more than a handful if alarmed or upset because they also have a vicious set of sharp teeth. So in my case, if the wild boar had turned on me it would have resulted in a running contest between me and it. I have absolutely no doubt at all in my mind that in top gear I would have broken all speed records – and won!

Anyway, the following day the boar was brought back to camp and we were encouraged to re-enact the hunting and shooting of the boar and it was filmed. I had mentioned this film to Major Macek, explaining my problem as 32 mm film was rather an unusual size for normal usage – I know very little about sizes of film as such, but as I understand it, 16 mm was more normal – and therefore I had no means of viewing it. Immediately, he said it was not a problem and he would arrange something, as they had a 32 mm projector at the Embassy – and that really was why we were invited to this very special apartment. The film was duly shown and it was like a Charlie Chaplin episode, for we all had rather jerky movements; whether that was the fault of the film or the projector I have no idea, or perhaps it was us! But we all laughed and laughed at it, for it was very comical. It was a very pleasant evening and Lynne and I enjoyed it very much.

One sequel to the wild boar story that I must tell: they asked me in Decin if I would like to have the boar's head as a trophy. Well, I imagined that they meant the head would be specially prepared and mounted, perhaps on a polished wooden plaque, and I could just visualise it on the wall of my lounge. So I answered in the affirmative. They said they would send it on to the offices of Koospol, the Foreign Trade Corporation, in Prague where we held most of our discussions when not at the HQ in Modrany or in the factories.

Some days later in Prague they handed me a brown paper parcel which had arrived from Decin for me. At first I was puzzled, but then remembered about the boar's head. But just at that very moment we were in a terrible hurry as we had been invited to the Ministry of Foreign Trade offices, which were formerly the HQ of the Gestapo during the German occupation. They knew I was very interested in matters concerning war history and so this invitation was arranged. We arrived in a street quite close to the Ministry and I parked my car nicely in the shade. We went inside the Ministry and were given a VIP tour of the whole premises, including the torture room in which a leather chair still existed at that time. The upholstery of this chair was heavily stained with blood from former victims and in a glass case one could see the various torture instruments used by the Gestapo when questioning people. It is almost unbelievable that such things could happen in the twentieth century and that human beings could be treated in such a cruel manner, but they did and in that very room, in that very chair.

Our tour was very interesting to me if not so much to Lynne and our children. At the end of our visit I thanked the people there very much indeed and we proceeded towards our car. But although I had left my car in the shade earlier it was now in the very hot sun (I had forgotten that the sun moves around – or rather that the earth does) and as we approached it the most awful stench met us; it got worse as we drew nearer. It could only be one thing – the boar's head. It seemed that the foolish people in Decin had just had the head cut off, wrapped it in brown paper, tied it with string and sent it to me in Prague. What a daft thing to do and what on earth could I do with a boar's head in that condition? I just had to get rid of that object from my car somehow and so I had no alternative but to pick the parcel up gingerly and look around for a waste bin. In the street where we had parked there wasn't one, but there was one immediately outside the Ministry from which we had just come. So I just placed it in the bin and walked away as quickly as I could. I just wonder what the bin man must have thought when he emptied it the next day and found that parcel – it must have been quite a shock for him!

In the weeks and months that followed, Major Macek and I met on frequent occasions. He asked me if I could introduce him to my friends and acquaintances. I did so until I began to smell a rat and realised that the Major was using me to get introduced to as wide a number of other people as possible. And that is how they work; the object was to go from person to person, meeting all their friends, and so on until they reached that one person who could be helpful to them in their aim, which was simply to gather as much information as possible, whether political or commercial, that might be useful back home. Of course, if they came into contact with someone useful to them in the military field that would have been a big achievement for them. In turn, such contacts would have been turned over to specialists who know perfectly well how to cultivate such people. I began to feel decidedly uneasy and so I thought it would be wise to reduce my number of meetings with the Major and eventually try to cut them out altogether. However, he continued to bombard me at my office with calls and I continued to make excuses as to why I could not accept his invitations to lunch, etc. At last he got the message and tried to contact me less often. As time went by and I had not heard from him at all I began to feel somewhat relieved, until I received another call, this time from Captain Jan Vokac, who explained that Major Macek had been recalled to Prague quite suddenly and that he had been sorry that he had had very little time to say his goodbyes to all his friends, but he had left a bottle of whisky for me as a small gift. When and where could we meet so that he could give me this bottle? Well, having met Captain Jan Vokac before, I recalled I rather liked him and also that his political views were much more reasonable than the arch-communist Major Macek.

So I agreed to meet him at Trafalgar Square. I immediately recognised him and we went somewhere nearby to have a drink and a chat. We met frequently after that. Like the Major, John, which was what I called him, was keenly interested in golf and football, which I loved too, so we had much in common. Neither did he pester me, as Macek had done, to introduce him to a wider circle of friends. But Macek had used the traditional way of 'passing on' in the spy world, for each person occupying that position at the Embassy had a duty to refer his replacement to known contacts and pass them on for further development. I suppose my use to them was connected to the fact that in those days I knew an awful lot of people. The bottle of whisky, or slivovice or whatever, was used only as a pretence and was the main method for new people or replacements to make the first contact. The departing Deputy Military Attaché never said his goodbyes; such people vanished mysteriously, turned up in Prague and you and others, as contacts, were then duly passed on in the way I have described. I will tell of the fate of Captain Vokac later on and how he too fell victim to the strange and evil displeasure of the Communist regime.

2

MY FURTHER ADVENTURES IN CZECHOSLOVAKIA, HUNTING, AND WORLD CUP WILLIE IN 1966

My family were enjoying living at Old Coulsdon very much indeed. It was so different from living in London and very refreshing. We were almost in the countryside and yet we were able to enjoy all the facilities of London. We were only seventeen miles from the centre and yet within a couple of hundred yards from our house you could enter the woods and continue walking in countryside for miles and miles. We took good advantage of all this at every opportunity, but mainly on Sunday afternoons we went on family walks, enjoying the surrounding area. And then, in September 1963, we were blessed with another daughter – little Debbie. She was the apple of our eyes and all the family fussed over her, of course; she was much loved, as indeed all our children were, and caused us much happiness.

Meanwhile, as far as business was concerned, we were going ahead by leaps and bounds, but it definitely was the supermarket programme which showed very considerable promise and great opportunities. By now it was also providing the greater part of our sales and turnover. And then my car, which was private and paid for by me, broke down once more and I was told that if it was reliability I was after then it would be better to renew my main means of transport.

Our Group Managing Director at that time was Josef Dolezal, a very nice man and easy to discuss matters with. Therefore, I discussed the matter of a car with him, pointing out that the vast majority of people in my position who have to travel around with a substantial sample range, normally have a car supplied to them by the company. I further pointed out that this was the second car, fully paid for by me, that I had virtually worn out on business and that I was not in a financial position to purchase a new one. I told him that in order to further progress our supermarket business a car was essential to me and that I had made some investigations and found that long-term car hire/rental contracts were being offered at quite reasonable rates. Mr Dolezal agreed with what I had said, for being there on the spot he was able to understand the situation so much better than those people sitting in Prague, most of whom had never even been to Britain or to any Western country. However, such a proposal would need the sanction of Prague because it was completely unknown for one of their employees, director or not, to have a car supplied to them. With their very parochial minds and bearing in mind that many of them had never been abroad in their lives they had no conception of conditions or practices in the West. But Joseph Dolezal did and when he sent his recommendation to Prague that I must be provided with transport in order to carry out my duties properly I can well imagine one or two of the people there having kittens at the very idea.

Anyway, Josef Dolezal sent a telex off to Prague with the proposal and his recommendation and we waited for the reply. When it came not only I but even Mr Dolezal burst out laughing, for it said something along these lines: 'In Prague we come to work by tram – Mr Mitchell should do the same.' Such was the ignorance and stupidity of those people in Prague whose task it was to make decisions on such matters. But what could one expect of lowly paid civil servants who were quite ignorant of conditions in the UK – to such people the very idea that anyone working for them should be provided with a car in order to carry out their duties and responsibilities was quite preposterous; to have a car in Prague was only a dream and so they compared my situation to theirs. Mr Dolezal quickly sent a reply back telling the people in Prague that there were no trams in London and neither were there any such connections between London and Birmingham or Manchester or Newcastle, for example, and asked how I was expected to board a bus or a train with a sample range consisting of up to ten to twelve small suitcases. Those in Prague realised they had made a rather foolish error and agreed with the proposal, even if somewhat reluctantly. I believe I was the very first foreign employee of the Czechs ever to receive a company car – it was really quite unheard of. And so rather quickly I equipped myself with a brand new vehicle with a contract/hire company, and since I needed plenty of space for my samples I chose a Ford Consul, which had a large boot. It was a very nice car which attracted many an envious glance when I was often motoring in Czechoslovakia.

A further word or two about Josef Dolezal: as Managing Director of our group in London he must of course have been a party member. Such a position would not possibly have been offered to anyone who was not. When he first arrived in London it of course took us a little time to get used to him, and he to us and his task whilst in London. But I always found Joseph to be friendly, easy to talk to and a delight to have as a colleague. He also had something very rare with so many communists – good, sound commonsense and recognition of good commercial propositions which was never tainted by political influences. I recall one occasion when I saw in Borough High Street, just south of London Bridge, a very large wide-fronted shop premises which was for sale. The property was on three floors and at the rear were parking spaces plus a small warehouse with a delivery bay. To my mind, and Joseph completely agreed with me, such a building would not only be a wonderful means of advertising many Czechoslovak foods and produce but it would also house offices for our three companies as well as a number of other Czech companies. In other words, if Sugosa could buy these premises we could let offices out to such companies in a manner which would mean that Sugosa would possibly exist on a rent-free basis and possess an excellent investment. Not only that, but parking spaces were becoming more and more difficult to find in London. Add to that the warehousing and delivery bay facilities, which would have been invaluable to my company with its new involvement with the supermarket trade. The price of those premises was £250,000 at that time because the explosion of City and even near-City properties had not yet taken place. As this property was sited so close to London Bridge itself, my view was that one day it would be worth a lot of money. Of course, those idiots in Prague rejected the proposition even though it was strongly supported by Josef Dolezal and myself. Imagine how I felt when many years later, in 2002/3, I saw in the property section of the *Daily Telegraph* a photograph and advertisement of the very same premises, which were once again for sale, but now the value quoted was £25 million! Such a wonderful proposition, and one on which we could not lose, rejected by fools who had no proper understanding of commercial affairs.

Josef Dolezal eventually returned to Prague and although he was given a managerial position at Koospol, the Foreign Trade Corporation,

I am afraid I lost touch with him. Sadly, I heard that he passed away at quite a young age – I think it was cancer. But Josef was a very pleasant man and quite easy to get on with. However, after his death I heard through the ever-existing grapevine that when he returned to Prague from London he too had to appear before the usual committee to answer some questions about his stay in the UK and that he was somewhat criticised because, they alleged, he had succumbed too much to my influence. What a ridiculous allegation to make. I spoke with Josef, as our Managing Director, quite frequently and any proposals I put to him were those which I considered sound and advisable. He did not always agree with me and there were occasions when I was not able to persuade him. Therefore, such an allegation was absolutely ridiculous and probably the brainchild of one of those communist fanatics who tried to feather their own nest by pretending that they were good interrogators and by attaching untrue rumours to returning delegates from abroad. And that, incidentally, is one of the great dangers of communism – it encourages people to inform on others and so ingratiate themselves with those above them. Such allegations may be totally untrue, especially if someone held a grudge against you or perhaps coveted your job.

Even in London there were ugly situations born of the communist system and I recall one instance which will give an idea of the kind of things that went on. One of the commercial delegates at the Embassy, a very nice gentleman named Veroslav Holub, invited me to lunch one day. We went to a Chinese Restaurant in Edgeware Road, which was supposedly the favourite restaurant of Cliff Richard, the well-known singer. It was a very pleasant lunch and we discussed various commercial matters and some non-commercial matters too. We parted company after lunch and I thought no more of the matter. But about two or three weeks later Karel Jiracek, who was at that time our Group Managing Director, asked me if I had been to lunch with Veroslav and I confirmed that I had. A little later I discovered that Veroslav had been hauled over the coals at the Embassy when submitting his expense account; apparently, as I worked for them, I was not on the list of people who may be entertained at the expense of the Embassy. Jiracek, who liked to enjoy lunches and dinners himself, told me it was quite OK to have lunch with Veroslav, but I should pay the bill. In other words, it was better that such occasions be covered by my company, Sugosa Ltd, and not by the Embassy.

Some time went by, during which I invited Jiracek to join me together with customers of ours for a golf match when I hoped to resolve a rather serious matter which had developed – it was my practice to discuss difficult matters in pleasant circumstances and so I organised this golf match. As I had no partner I invited Jiracek to join us and make up a foursome – I have written about this elsewhere so I shall not repeat myself. Suffice to say, the day was successful – the golf match was exactly the right way to achieve our aims. But about ten days later Jiracek asked me if I had informed Veroslav Holub about the golf match we had played and I told him that I had not. Apparently, Jiracek had neglected to put this occasion down on his reports and now he was being hauled over the coals. He was trying to find out who had been so 'kind' to report him maliciously to those above, but as I had no knowledge of anything like that I was unable to help him. However, I was intrigued by this occurrence and so made it my business to investigate. It transpired that during my absence from the office Veroslav Holub phoned me; my secretary, Joan Gloster, quite innocently told him that I was dealing with a very important matter indeed over a game of golf and that Mr Jiracek was with me. There was no reason why she should not say what she did and in my view she acted perfectly correctly. But Holub, remembering that it was almost certainly Jiracek who informed against him and got him into some trouble at the Embassy for taking me out to lunch, now saw an opportunity to get his own back and did so by informing on Jiracek. I didn't know this for absolute certain, but when I met up with Holub in Prague much later on he admitted all to me – but with a wink and a smile on his face. I believe he was over the moon to have succeeded in getting one back on Jiracek. But I warned him; Jiracek was a dangerous person to have as an enemy.

It was also around this time that Rapid, the state advertising organisation, sent a film unit to Britain. Their task was to travel around the country filming shops that were stocking any food items from Czechoslovakia and, hopefully, British people buying them. That is a very difficult task whatever the product, because although Czechoslovak exports to the UK were quite substantial, running into many millions of pounds, they were as a flea bite to the overall total of similar goods in distribution. Eventually, these film people came to see me at my office and explained that they would like to film Czechoslovak confectionery products on sale to the British public. I explained the position and said that it would be easier to 'manufacture' a venue.

On that note I requested them to leave the matter with me and told them that I would contact them at their hotel as soon as I had made arrangements. First of all I contacted one of the wholesalers towards the southern part of London and explained what I wanted to do. They recommended to me a small shop in a village in Kent who was one of their customers.

I then went to the village, spoke with the owner of the shop and asked her if she would lease her shop to us for a few hours whilst we made a film. At first she refused vehemently and said that she could not possibly close her shop to her regular customers, but when we began to talk about money she began to soften somewhat. In fact, I offered her far more in cash than any profit she would ever have made by staying open and on that basis we made an agreement. I informed the film unit and gave them the address, and it was arranged that we would meet at the shop the very next morning. Meanwhile, I got my staff busy preparing Czech confectionery lines taken from our sample room, which we transported down to the shop where we got busy placing many Czech items on display. We put them in the window, we put them on the counter, we put them in the display cabinets, we put them everywhere we possibly could so that by the time we had finished the shop looked like one which might have been seen in Vaclavske Namesti (Wenceslas Square) itself!

The film people were very pleased at what we had done but now they were in a small group outside the shop talking animatedly amongst themselves. I saw the leader of the group look at me and then he came over with a smile on his face and said that everything was fine but they needed someone now to be filmed walking along, looking into the shop, entering and expressing much pleasure at the wonderful display. I could tell from the look on his face that he had me in mind and so I immediately protested. "No, no, no," I said, "I have not minded at all arranging all this, but I am no film actor!" But he pleaded with me saying that there was nobody else and that it should be an Englishman; and so in the end, for the sake of harmony, I agreed to do it. After all, what could I lose? Only my reputation as a film star if I did it badly!

So the leader of the group and one other man told me what they would like me to do. I had firstly to be filmed strolling along towards the shop – then, 'Cut!' Then they took a film of me stopping, obviously very much attracted by the excellent display of goodies in the shop window – then, 'Cut!' Now the cameras moved inside the shop and I had to enter. Then I had to show exceptional delight at the display and speak to the owner of the shop, who agreed to stand behind the counter serving. And so, in my best Clark Gable manner, I did so, but what I was actually saying to the lady owner was absolutely nothing to do with confectionery. I told her that very shortly now we would soon be out of her hair and she could re-open as normal, and I apologised to her for the length of time it was all taking. But I was speaking with a big smile on my face all the time and pretending that we were discussing the assortment of confections. I then had to select one or two items and pay for them, and the cameras followed me as I left the shop. After two or three hours of this the film was finally finished; we packed up all our samples, leaving a goodly share for the shop lady to sell to her customers, and then we departed.

The film was shown all over Czechoslovakia in picture houses and on Czech television. It was reported widely in the newspapers and I was invited on my next visit to Prague to come to the film studios, called Barandov, just outside Prague. I did so and they showed me the film as well as the large studio and invited me for lunch. It was a very interesting few hours I spent there and I would like to say that the film made me famous all over Czechoslovakia, but sadly it didn't. I obtained more fame from my various broadcasts on Czech radio when I spoke in a mixture of Czech and English. I even received two letters from listeners who admired the fact that I was trying my best to speak Czech – and not for the first time I was complimented on my accent, and I felt good about that. But as far as film acting was concerned, I don't think Clark Gable had anything to worry about!

And whilst I remember it, there was another quite amusing occasion that occurred in the early 1960s. I had been introduced to a Jewish chap who, for some reason, especially liked Englishmen and wanted to be introduced to me. I liked him too and met him several times when visiting Prague. On once occasion he invited me to a large hall where he and many of his Jewish friends were celebrating some special Jewish holiday, but I cannot recall the name of it. The occasion was honoured by the presence of the Israeli Ambassador and the first part of the evening was rather sombre because we had to listen to speeches by various rabbis, terminating with a speech by the Ambassador himself. And then, quite suddenly as if everybody had been waiting for a signal, all those present broke up and formed a number of friendly circles where they sat talking with each other. The atmosphere had changed in a flash. Now the music began with a frenzy and it was clear that a jolly time was going to be had by all. The circles became smaller as people got up to dance with each other and as far as my circle was concerned, it also diminished as couples joined in the merry dancing. What a contrast it was to just half an hour ago! Anyway, I looked around me and to my horror I found that I and just one girl were the only people still sitting there from our group. What should I do? I could not dance to that music and in that frenzied and very energetic style! On the other hand, as we were the only two people left it would have been very impolite of me not to invite her to dance. I dismissed immediately an idea that came into my head, which was to tell the young lady that I had just discovered that at that very moment I had developed a broken ankle! And so, very reluctantly indeed, I said to her the magic words, "Smim prosim?" – which means, "May I please?" – and to my great disappointment and embarrassment she responded, "Dekuji – ano," which means, "Yes – and thank you." At that point she arose from her seat and if I were to tell you that she could not have been less than 6'6" tall, please believe me when I say that it is completely true. In fact, she may even have been taller. Now, I am only a rather short chap – about 5'6" at the last count and shrinking. She was a whopper and when I saw how tall she was, towering at least a foot over me, if not more, I was tempted to sit down again. I just prayed for a big hole to open up and swallow me – anything to take me away from the terrible situation I had got myself into. But it was no use – I just had to dance with this giant of a girl. As we approached the dancing area people began to titter and when we began to dance it must have been a very comical sight. People were laughing at us all around. But I am proud to say it didn't faze me – if someone began to laugh at us I began to laugh with them and make comical faces as if I couldn't care less. After careful consideration I thought that was the best reaction in the circumstances. The girl with whom I was dancing then suddenly had a fit of the giggles as she too saw the funny side of it. I think we probably looked like a couple dancing together and having a lot of very good fun. In future, I said to myself, make a rule to never, ever go dancing without taking a tape measure with you! Looking back I rate it as one of the most amusing experiences of my life. But – oh boy! – I do get myself into some scrapes!

I continued to visit Prague whenever it was considered necessary, and also the various factories which were situated all over the country, and as I did so more and more ideas came to us and new lines were developed from these. It was obvious to all and sundry that my visits to the factories were more than useful. By now our supermarket range was taking shape very well. But for some reason, which I cannot remember, I had to go to Prague in 1961 or 62 on some urgent mission and I went by plane, but it was winter. Normally, I tried to avoid going there in winter as much as possible, but there were occasions when I could not avoid the winter months completely. My colleague in the Foreign Trade Organisation in Prague was a chap called Franticek Grepl – I called him Frank. The people I worked with in Prague changed very often – many of them went abroad, if they had behaved themselves, as commercial delegates, and so Frank was my current colleague.

Anyway, we had to go to a town called Liberec rather urgently and Frank told me that the only train we could catch left Prague at 6 p.m. or thereabouts. I asked him if we should get something to eat before catching the train but he said it was not necessary as the train we were catching was an express coming in from outside the country and that there would certainly be a restaurant car. We had, however, to change trains at a town called Turnov. We duly boarded this train, but the first thing I noticed was that there were only individual carriages. How could we eat in the restaurant car if we could not get to it? Frank smiled, as he always did when he made a mistake, and said that we would get something in Turnov. The train did not leave at 6 p.m. – it left after 7 p.m. And then it went so slowly – I could have walked quicker – and made many stops.

By the time we arrived at Turnov it was very late and we were very hungry and thirsty. We alighted and Frank quickly found a lady in railway uniform. They jabbered away and I could tell from Frank's face that the news was not good. In fact, our connecting train had already left Turnov and there would be no further connection to Liberec until the morning. Meanwhile, the temperature had dropped very noticeably.

Not realising what conditions I may be subjected to, I had only a light overcoat on and I began to shiver. Frank went to make some enquiries and returned to say the temperature had fallen to -16 °Celsius! Such were East European weather conditions. No wonder I was cold. He also said he had tried to phone for a taxi and that they promised to send one to us as soon as one became free. But the time went by and it seemed to be getting colder and, of course, no taxi. So Frank went to the stationmaster in his nice warm office, who agreed that we could take refuge from the bitter cold there. We did so, but looking back, if that stationmaster had not agreed to assist us I think we would have frozen to death or at least suffered from exposure. The hours went by but no taxi came; eventually, at about 5.30 a.m., a taxi duly arrived and we were very glad indeed to see it.

The journey between Turnov and Liberec was not a great distance – maybe 30 km or so – and so we were soon at our hotel, Hotel Zlaty Lev (Golden Lion), in Liberec. But after checking in we only had one hour or so of sleep before having to get up and be in time for our meeting at the factory. I doubt I was on top form that day, but at least we had the chance of a warm drink and something to eat. After that experience I resolved never to undertake such a trip again by plane if I could avoid it or be at the mercy of public transport in Czechoslovakia. Therefore, I decided to come by car in future when I could be master of my own destiny and be able to move around without relying on unreliable train services and being caught out like that again. Gradually, over the years, the road conditions in Czechoslovakia became better and better. Today you can drive from any

Western coastal point to Prague by motorway or autobahn and never stop; but I pity such motorists these days who never get to see the villages and small towns that we did, which made our trips so much more enjoyable and interesting.

Just a further word about 'Frank' Grepl: he was one of those Communist Party people who came from a factory somewhere in Moravia. He was a communist through and through and chaps like him had only to voice their wishes and ambitions and someone in the Party would see that something was done, for he was regarded as a loyal and trustworthy man. In the factory he was a political attachment and his function was to hold meetings of the workers, make speeches to them about the glories of communism, to describe the awful conditions and deprivation which existed in Western countries, tell them how very lucky they were to live in a communist state and generally urge them to work harder and more efficiently. In other words, Frank was, if you like, a commissar and steeped in communism from head to foot. At some point Frank must have expressed a wish to his superiors to become involved in foreign trade, which was attractive because such people travelled abroad and were in a position to earn foreign currency, plus they could see foreign places, and that was exactly what Frank wanted to do – hence his appointment at Koospol, the Foreign Trade Corporation, and how he came to be my colleague in the confectionery department.

I shall never forget Frank's first visit to the UK. I am not certain, but I am fairly sure that this was his first visit ever to a democratic country and I believe that his communistic principles were shaken to the very core – but he dare not admit it. I am certain that his communist teachers had convinced Frank that life in the Western capitalist countries was very grim and there is no doubt about it, he was shocked when he saw at first hand that those teachings were quite untrue. Frank and I had many political discussions in the time we worked together, for despite his beliefs, he was a nice fellow. I found him easy to talk to and he had a sense of humour. Most of the time he lost the argument and then his eyes would twinkle, a grin appear on his face and he would end the discussion by saying that I had the advantage over him because we were talking in English and he implied that if we could discuss the same mat-ters in Czech I would most certainly be on the losing end. Of course, my Czech was not good enough really at that stage to conduct a discussion like that. But I would like to make it clear that I never attempted to change Frank's political views; that would have been a stupid thing to do anyway, for one had to be so very careful not only with whom but also how one discussed politics. In such a strange atmosphere it was so easy to make a mistake.

However, these conversations occurred quite naturally with Frank, for as I have said, he was an easy chap to talk to. When he came to London I met him at Heathrow Airport. It was quite early and I asked him what he would like to do that afternoon. He said he would like to go to a super-market – they were unheard of in Czechoslovakia then but somewhere he must have heard about them. So I duly took him to one of the major supermarkets, which was quite huge, and as Frank walked around I could see that he was very impressed indeed, coming, as he did, from a land of shortage and especially a severe lack of choice. But Frank being Frank, and no doubt feeling the need to voice some criticism or another, he said to me, "David, why do you need to have eight or nine different kinds of butter? Surely you only need one, as in our country. Isn't it a waste of resources to have so many kinds?" He and I had already discussed the need in a free market of competition and I reminded him of that. He looked at me, lifted his eyes to the heavens and shook his head as if to say, "How can one understand a system like this?" I think that from his first visit to the UK Frank was well on the way to changing his mind about communism – but would not dare say it, of course.

In the course of time Frank and I became good pals and on one visit to Prague he even took the risk of inviting me to his flat, and that was a big risk, for his political reputation would have been somewhat tarnished if this innocent invitation had been discovered. I had the pleasure of meeting his wife and we had a very pleasant evening. They had a piano and I played a little for them. I knew Frank over a couple or more years and got to know him well; I always liked him.

But then he used his political influence to obtain a semi-permanent post in Tokyo just in time for the Olympics, which were being held there. He told me about this very excitedly and how much he had always wanted to see the Olympics live. When he left the Confectionery Export Department to take up his new post I am afraid I lost touch with him, but some years later I learned that after his return from Tokyo Frank fell ill and died a relatively young man. I was very sad indeed to hear this news, for com-munist or not, he was a nice chap and I liked him very much. I am almost certain that given another year or so I may have shown or demonstrated the further advantages of capitalism, which in turn may have succeeded in changing his political views – not that I would specifically want to try – but in the normal course of discussions between one friend and another I obtained the clear impression that a change in his attitude was occurring, which was already apparent to me but evidently, and hopefully, not to his communist bosses.

I shall always remember Frank when I was in Czechoslovakia with my wife Lynne and two young children. He came with us as our tour involved stopping off at a couple or more factories. But Frank made the trip much more interesting by proposing small diversions to see this castle and that. Sometimes these places were closed. But that did not deter Frank and he would go to find someone in charge – and would you believe the whole place was opened up just for us so we were able to see a number of sights that ordinarily would be closed for visitors. I have no idea what means of persuasion he used; for all I know, Frank may well have been a member of the secret police; if so, their word was law and you dare not cross them. But there was an element of magic or mystery about Frank's ability to achieve the almost impossible. I noticed that people were rather subservient towards him when he spoke to them. But he always spoke to these people just out of my hearing and so I have no idea what he said to them. Maybe my suspicions about Frank are right and maybe he was something more than he pretended to be. No matter – whatever he was I still liked him a lot.

Back home, around 1964, Lynne and I decided to take our children to Pontin's Holiday Camp at Brixham in Devon. The very thought of going to a holiday camp filled me with horror, for I was getting quite accustomed to the very nice hotels and restaurants I had been visiting over the past years. Was I becoming a snob? What? That little chap from the back streets of London's East End Docklands? I hoped not. For the sake of the children I agreed to go. As a matter of fact, it wasn't nearly as bad as I thought it might have been and we had a very nice and enjoyable week. We went on a fishing trip to catch mackerel and caught so many we just couldn't eat them. So we threw them onto the roof of our chalet where the seagulls soon polished them off. But my main memory of that short holiday was our darling little daughter Debbie, who was only twenty-two months old and whom we entered in the fancy dress party they held for the kids. Lynne and our eldest daughter Jackie had the idea of putting her in the competition as Pebbles, and the small son of some people we had befriended as Bamm-Bamm – both from the TV cartoon *The Flintstones*. Little Debbie looked a darling and was perfect with a little grass skirt and a necklace of peanuts round her neck. Despite being so young she and the little boy took their parts very well – and they won first prize! The children had a great time and I was very glad we went on this holiday.

In the meantime I had been visiting Prague and other places many times – wherever the factories were situated. At weekends, as I usually did, I made tracks to Marianske Lazne where I had friends and where very often my artist friend from Prague, Jiri Trnka, could also be found on the golf course or in the clubhouse where he loved to lecture his friends and colleagues on the rights and wrongs of life in general.

But on one trip in October 1963 my hunting friend Slavek told me that a big cull of deer was ordered and he invited me to take part. Not in an organised group but by our two selves. However, on the Saturday when this was to take place I had already accepted an invitation from another friend, Mr Mozna, a director of the Pilsner Brewery, to visit him at the brewery in Plzen, about 40 km distant. I was told that the brewery is the best place of all to drink perfect beer. So I asked Mr Mozna if it would be all right if I brought a friend along, to which he readily agreed.

On the day I picked up Slavek at his flat and off we went to Plzen. We of course knew where the world famous brewery was and I drove to the huge gates, which, on the instructions of Mr Mozna, were opened for me. I drove in and parked my car and Slavek and I were shortly greeted by Mr Mozna, who took us on a tour of the brewery and showed how the famous beer was made, which was very interesting. Then he invited us to the special Director's Room. I am sure that I cannot do full justice with any description of this room in mere words, but it was carved entirely out of wood. The floors, the walls, even the ceilings were all made of wood on which there were numerous carvings by artists and technicians, long since dead in all probability, because it was very old indeed. Even the tables and chairs were hand carved and the whole effect was magical. I have never seen such a room in my life. It was truly beautiful and I doubt very much if a room like that could be produced these days. Evidently, it was a room that was reserved for the guests of the directors.

Well, there we enjoyed a foaming tankard of that delicious beer and sitting there it was confirmed to me that there is no place better to drink than there in the brewery. Mr Mozna asked us if we would like another tankard each and we readily accepted. There are many who copy so-called Pilsner beer (it is not a lager); however, none can match the original, which is more correctly described as Plzenske Pivo. But when we had finished that second tankard I felt it was time for us to go, because we had a planned hunting trip to go on. So we bid Mr Mozna goodbye and Slavek and I drove out of the gates.

However, we had only proceeded for about thirty yards when Slavek asked me to stop, because in the pub, which was almost adjacent to the brewery (I do not think it is there any longer), he wanted to take the opportunity to talk to some colleagues in the forest organisation who frequented it. He said he would very much like to discuss something important with them. So I stopped and we walked the few yards to the pub. Sure enough, Slavek's friends were there and a serious discussion followed. Slavek explained to me later that he wanted to invite them once again to help in the cull of deer that was now taking place in his area in return for an invitation for him to visit their area, where apparently it was very good for pheasants. Apparently, these two chaps had already visited Slavek in his area but after several days they had no success and he wanted to invite them to try again.

The foresters do this sort of thing frequently and in that way they exchange the possibility to take part in various forms of hunting. Of course, when talking I knew that Slavek would want another beer, so we had one, and maybe another. But then Slavek looked at his watch and realised we had overstayed our visit to Plzen and that therefore it would probably be too late now to go hunting. But he suggested we should go back to Marianske Lazne and try. I would have had to go back to my hotel anyway to change my clothing. So we said our goodbyes to the foresters and they in turn wished us 'lovu zda'r', which means 'good hunting', and returned to Hotel Esplanade. There I quickly changed and we immediately set off to reach a place called Lazne Kynzvart, about 14 km distant.

We entered the forest and quite soon we found a clear spot where I could park the car. Slavek looked again at his watch, then looked at me, and I could see he did not feel this hunting trip was worth the trouble – it was too late and nearly dusk. But he decided that as we were there we should at least make an effort and try. Just at the moment we got out of the car a great forest lorry came trundling down a hill nearby creating such a terrible noise. Slavek again looked at me and said something to the effect that firstly we were too late, then there was all this noise and there would not be any deer around for miles. He was resigned to the fact that it was hopeless.

But as I was beginning to learn, hunting is an unpredictable affair and so he gave me his gun. I put it on my shoulder and off we walked with me trailing Slavek. We had not walked 100 yards when Slavek froze, and I naturally did the same. He pointed and there by a tree, about sixty metres from us, was standing this magnificent stag. I was told later that it was between two and three years old but well developed. Slavek looked at it through his binoculars and I did the same. Then Slavek motioned me to shoot. Normally, this animal would have been allowed to live because such a specimen would be very good for the herd, but this was a cull and so normal practices did not apply. I took careful aim, fired, and the animal crumpled to the floor. It was a clean kill straight through the heart; the deer knew nothing about it. Slavek said later that it was one of the best shots he had seen. I was much flattered but I think it was more luck than judgement. Once again, as we stood over the carcase and the unpleasant task of gutting the animal was performed by Slavek, I could not help feeling that tinge of regret that I always felt after a kill. I am not sure my heart and soul was in hunting, although I did enjoy the camaraderie and bonhomie that were an essential part of it all. Also it got one into the fresh air and was an opportunity to see and explore the wild forest. I accept that culling is, sadly, a necessity, but I think I now prefer to leave that to the forest experts.

As a matter of fact, it was said to me later that the deer I had shot was well known and recognised by a doctor who belonged to a hunting club in the area. He was from Plzen, actually, and he had been observing this particular deer for some time. He was waiting for the clubs to be given permission to join in the cull, which had been much discussed and anticipated. Apparently, he was quite annoyed to learn that he had been beaten to the punch and that 'his' stag had been bagged by some stupid English visitor!

Another experience that stays in my mind was in the same year. Slavek invited me to accompany him to a town to the east of Prague called Podebrady (the birthplace of the famous composer Smetana) to go pheasant shooting. I had never tried this form of hunting before and so I gladly accepted. It would be a new experience. But beforehand, Slavek took me into the forest where I could practise a little with a shotgun, for I had never fired one of these in my life. He threw bottles up in the air and I had to try to hit and smash them. I seem to recall that I was not very successful. He also took me to a small place where they shot clay plates up in the sky – I wasn't very good at that either. On the day we were to go to Podebrady, Slavek came to my hotel very early in the morning and off we went in my car. Slavek knew the way and so it was an easy journey – I believe Slavek drove us there whilst lucky me dozed in the back. We arrived just in time for the parade of hunters when you must all line up and be inspected by the police and by a director of the forest organisation in that district. After this had taken place everybody then retired to the pub close by where we all drank two large glasses of beer, one for each arm, they said, and a dish of a kind of goulash soup, which, although a bit strange as a breakfast, was truly delicious; in fact it was much more than that because we had left Prague so early it was not possible to have breakfast and so we were rather hungry. When we had finished in the pub off we went to find some pheasants. They had dogs there to flush out the birds. It was indeed great to have the opportunity and experience of going on a pheasant shoot, but I am definitely not good at shooting the type of gun needed for pheasants, i.e. shotguns. It was all too quick for me; a bird would break cover but by the time I was ready to shoot the damned thing was miles away! I got better as the day wore on and I think my bag was three and a half pheasants for the whole day – I claim the half because two of us shot at the same bird simultaneously, so we good-naturedly decided to share the honour. However, there were experts there who bagged over twenty and maybe even thirty or more pheasants during that day.

Well, the hunt went on all day long and by the late afternoon I began to feel absolutely ravenous once again. There was nothing I could do so I trudged along hoping that the hunt would soon come to an end so that we could get something to eat and drink when suddenly I spied a tree. Well, this tree was totally devoid of leaves, this being October, but on it was one, just one, apple. I looked around; nobody else had seen it, so I walked over, plucked the apple from the tree and greedily ate it. I have to say that it was the most delicious apple I have ever tasted in my life. It kept me going until they called a halt and everybody returned to the pub – where else would you go when you are with hunters?

As I entered the pub, a man stood by the door and he was asking everybody who entered some small details about themselves. These were gladly given and when it became my turn I told him that I was English, I came from Old Coulsdon in Surrey, and that I was there in Czechoslovakia to buy confectionery. When we were all seated and beer had been served, this man picked up a small accordion, but not one with piano keys – it was a button-type accordion – and then he began to sing – and you must believe me, dear reader, when I tell you that he sang a song about every man in that pub, including me! This was an amazing feat of memory such as I had never witnessed before, and to this day I have no idea how he did it – once again yet another new experience.

Of course, it was very jolly in the pub and there was much joking and kidding going on between the chaps there. But the time came to think about going and I assumed we would be going back to Prague. But then Slavek said that we had both been invited to the farmhouse of one of the hunters to have 'veceri' (supper) there. Well, whether it was the fresh air or whatever was causing it I know not, but I did know that once more I was hungry! After all, I reasoned, Slavek and I had only had a bowl of soup first thing in the morning and, in my case, that most wonderful apple. So I think we had a right to feel hungry and the invitation was, therefore, music to our ears.

So we went one or two kilometres to the farmhouse and there, already prepared, was a large table sufficient to seat maybe twelve people – and every seat was occupied. We were then given a glass of beer and shortly afterwards the lady of the farmhouse brought in a very large tureen, which was steaming hot. She placed it in the middle of the table and invited everybody to help themselves. As a guest from England I was given first opportunity to partake of this wonderful food and looking into the tureen I saw that it was filled with delicious-looking pork cutlets with all kinds of vegetables swimming around in a gravy sauce that smelt really fantastic. I helped myself to just one cutlet but the lady of the house urged me to take another. Well, what could a starving man say? So I took another. The cutlets had evidently been braised for a long time as a kind of goulash with plenty of paprika and some garlic and they were so tender they melted in one's mouth. I have to say that I include that meal as one of the memorable ones I have had the pleasure to experience in my lifetime and I have never forgotten it. When we departed we of course thanked everybody for their very kind hospitality and soon we were on our way back to Prague; me to my hotel and Slavek – well, I am not sure where he went, but if I know him well I am certain he would not be without a warm bed that night. All in all it was a very nice and very enjoyable day. However, I don't think I shall ever go pheasant shooting again. I am glad I tried it but that one experience was enough for me. But should I ever be persuaded and suc-cumb I will most surely take some sandwiches with me.

Back home once again and in the office things were going well. Then in 1964 I read something about the preparations being made for the World Football Championships, which were going to be held in England in 1966, and that the Football Association was having a character developed which would be used in marketing products for the occasion. This character, I read, would be a cartoon-type lion wearing a Union Jack football shirt and his name would be World Cup Willie. I thought about this and an idea came to me – what if we were to put Willie into a giant picture lollipop? That would surely be a winner.

First of all I had to find out if we would be able to obtain a licence from the Football Association, and from previous experience I knew it would be better to approach the matter via one of the agents dealing with copyright characters. What better than to approach Walter Tuckwell & Associates, through which I had negotiated the Noddy contract and others? I was very pleased to find out that they were handling matters for the Football Association too. They confirmed to me that no licence existed or had been issued for lollipops and so I gave instructions to Bob Warrior, my sales manager, to get the name of the artist who designed Willie, contact him and ask him to draw up some sketches for me to send to the factory. I was very busy on the supermarket side of things so I left the matter in Bob's hands. A few weeks later I asked Bob how the 'Willie project' was going. He seemed a little embarrassed and answered that he intended to deal with it immediately. A further ten days went by and I repeated my question to Bob, but even now it was not under way. I was determined not to lose this exciting opportunity so I told Bob not to worry about it any more – I would take over the project myself.

I immediately contacted Walter Tuckwell and was pleasantly surprised to learn that the artist who made the original design of Willie was known to me and had carried out some work for us on box designs a year or so earlier. I remembered him as a chap who loved Pilsner beer, of which I always had an ample supply in my office. I asked Walter to request the artist to contact me; he duly did this and we made an arrangement to meet. He knew I always had access to a goodly stock of Pilsner beer and so I didn't have to ask him twice! I outlined my idea to the artist, who thought it was great, and I explained what I needed from him, i.e. designs of Willie with few or even no protruding contours as sharp contours only make for problems in production. He promised me designs within a few days – and he kept his promise. He insisted upon delivering the designs to me in person and I knew why – he wanted to continue his renewed acquaintance with Pilsner beer!

The designs were excellent and I arranged for them to be sent to Prague via the diplomatic bag by the Czech Embassy together with a letter describing what I had in mind and with the request that they should forward these designs to the factory in Trnava, Slovakia, with a personal request from me to Mr Sloboda, the director, to prepare prototype samples for me, and further that I planned to come to the factory in two weeks to collect them myself. I have explained earlier in Volume One that Mr Sloboda, the Director of this particular factory, was our guest in the UK and how we took care of him. Mr Sloboda owed me a favour or two and now I was cashing in. I thought then that every opportunity to get the various factory directors on our side by spoiling them on their visits would be an excellent strategy and would pay dividends in due course. This was an opportunity to see if I was right and so I duly travelled to Prague and then on to Trnava, which was situated in Slovakia. Mr Sloboda gave me a good reception; he was very glad to see me once again. A little later, in his office, he showed me the prototype samples of our World Cup Willie lollipops – they were absolutely perfect.

But of course, carefully prepared samples are one thing, but what about actual production, for, as I explained, it would be necessary to avoid distortion of Willie during the manufacturing process. Mr Sloboda assured me that quality control in his factory was very good and that I had no need to worry about this issue. It had been my own wish to try to reach a retail price of our giant lollipops at 6d each; at this popular price level the line would fly out, of that I was absolutely certain. It was difficult, but with the help and intervention of Mr Sloboda we got there. My plan and the way we had spoiled him when he visited the UK was a splendid strategy.

I flew back to London with the precious prototype samples quite elated and could not wait to get back to my office to get matters progressed. I was sure that with a winner like this we would effect a very substantial business and that it could do nothing but good for Sugosa. But, unknown to me, disaster unfortunately awaited.

When I arrived back at my office an urgent message awaited me that I should ring Walter Tuckwell immediately. I did so and he gave me the news that the Football Association had withdrawn the option they had granted us for World Cup Willie Lollipops. The reason they gave was that G.F. Lovell & Co. Ltd of Newport had objected on the grounds that their licence covering boiled sweets also covered lollipops. Well, of course this was a ridiculous argument, for on that basis all sugar confectionery would be covered by such a description, so why use specific descriptions as applied for by Lovell's and granted by the FA? Through Walter Tuckwell I tried to argue our case and they were very sympathetic and supportive, but the FA were quite adamant; they simply did not want to risk the possibility of any legal claim against them, saying it would be very bad publicity at a time when they just did not want anything like that occurring which might spoil the whole atmosphere of the World Cup administration.

I thought the matter over and I was absolutely determined not to let go of this wonderful opportunity. I therefore considered it would be best if I directly approached the chairman of Lovell's, Mr G. Lovell himself. After all, he was a gentleman I knew as a decent chap and someone with whom one could negotiate; I was sure he would remember our visit to Newport when we came there to study their vacuum forming machine. The next day I phoned Lovell's but Mr Lovell was not there. They invited me to phone later. I did so – Mr Lovell was still not there. It was explained to me that in addition to his many duties he was also a local Justice of the Peace and was extremely busy almost all of the time. They recommended I keep trying and even gave me his home number when I stressed the matter was very urgent. I phoned his home and left a message there to the effect that I was in my office and that I would stay there until he called me back. I waited and waited – he finally called back shortly after 9 p.m.

I introduced myself and I was glad he remembered me from my visit with Anton Belina a couple of years earlier. I explained the situation from our point of view and I listened patiently to him whilst he explained Lovell's point of view. He said that his company had invested a lot of time and money in World Cup Willie confectionery lines and that he just could not allow anyone to introduce any confectionery items which might compete against his company. I tried everything I knew to convince him that our lollipops would in no way interfere with or influence the sale of his World Cup range. After twenty minutes or so I could see I was getting nowhere and suggested to him that I make the trip down to Newport and talk the matter over face to face. Mr Lovell agreed with this quite reasonable suggestion.

As the matter was so urgent I went the following day and in his office at Newport I once again pleaded with him to allow our application for World Cup Willie picture lollipops. I showed him the samples and I could see he was very impressed. But that appeared to make him even more adamant. And so, partly in desperation and partly because I could think of no other alternative, I said to Mr Lovell that it would be a tragedy to let such an opportunity go, for I too, on behalf of Sugosa, had invested time and money in the project; therefore, would he consider Lovell's adopting the line and carrying out sales and distribution themselves? Mr Lovell thought that over for the moment and then asked about price details. I stuck my chin out and quoted him exactly the same price we would have ended with on a net basis, i.e. after deducting all expenses. I suggested to him that a retail price of 9d would be very reasonable for such a line and he seemed to accept that. Obviously, I had to forget completely my original intention to market the line at 6d, which, of course, I didn't mention to Mr Lovell during our negotiations. He replied that in principle he would agree to this idea subject to his people costing the quotation I had given him, and with that we went to lunch.

After two days Mr Lovell called me to say that he accepted my offer. I was very pleasantly astounded, for I had anticipated some troubles in this respect. But Mr Lovell confirmed that they would indeed have to sell the item on the basis of a consumer price of 9d each. Well, that I had of course to leave to him; we had got our price, thus guaranteeing a very handsome profit on the transaction and we shipped 3,500 cases of World Cup Willie lollipops, not far short of 100 gross tons. Of all the World Cup Willie confectionery lines, our lollipop was the second best seller – even at the increased price. But my God, what a winner it would have been had we been able to go ahead ourselves on the consumer basis of 6d each; I am sure we would have at least doubled sales. And when Mr Lovell offered to have his own vehicles pick up the merchandise from the docks – well, I was over the moon. This was like a well-earned bonus because delivery costs were a considerable part of the overall costs and I had, of course, built this into our selling price. Actually, Mr Lovell rued the day he made that offer, for we were using Horseferry Wharf in the Pool of London (a Czech-owned and well-known wharf at that time) for shipments and storage at that time and Lovell's lorries had many difficulties negotiating the very narrow streets, not to mention the queues that formed there. I had to intervene on a couple of occasions and speak to Mr Graham, the director of the wharf, when serious problems occurred.

To say I was elated would be an insufficient description of my feelings then. We had obtained a fantastic order which kept the factory very busy and we had made a very handsome profit on the transaction. I have to hand it to Lovell's for the PR arrangements they made to publicise the whole World Cup Willie range. They held a party at the Hilton Hotel in Park Lane and a lot of celebrities were invited and attended. They even managed to persuade Sir Stanley Rous, President of FIFA at that time, to get up on the small stage and pictures were taken of him pretending to bite one of our lollipops, which were printed in the national press the following day. Johnny Haynes, the former England captain, was there and a number of other well-known footballers and other celebrities. It was a big success and it demonstrated to me that Lovell's really meant business.

But I wanted some PR for Sugosa out of this exercise too. So after giving the matter some thought I formed the idea in my mind of organising some tickets for those matches to be held at Wembley Stadium, realising that very probably all England matches would be held there – in that I was fortunately correct. Then, I reasoned, I could invite some selected good customers to join us and watch some entertaining football. But how to get the tickets? The Czech Embassy was my best bet and so I contacted Captain Vokac, the Deputy Military Attaché, who by now had replaced Major Macek. He told me that he was in contact with a particular friend he had made at the office of the FA and he noted what I wanted. I believe I asked him for thirty tickets to every Wembley match and eventually he came up with twenty, with which I was more than satisfied.

I then decided it would be very nice to hold receptions for the last two matches, which we knew would be the semi-final and the World Cup final itself. But what we did not know at that time, however, was which teams would be participating. My dream was that England would qualify, and as we all know, my dream came true. The parties were held at the old Brent Bridge Hotel, which was quite near to Wembley – a hotel that in previous days was used by the England team when matches were held at Wembley. Others now joined in the organisation of that day, especially our publicity people, and when the offer came that the ladies at the Embassy would be willing to prepare the food for these occasions I was extremely pleased and gladly accepted. This rather unusual arrangement was agreed with the hotel management and in fact the lady responsible for all of the food preparation was Irena, the wife of our financial director Alois Zich; they remain good friends of ours to this very day.

Of course, we could only invite twenty people to see the matches, which got me into quite a lot of trouble, because when England qualified for the semi-final and then, after beating Portugal, qualified for the final itself I was positively bombarded by customers of ours all wanting me to supply them with tickets. I tried to obtain more but it was quite hopeless. It seemed as if the whole of England had become football crazy. So I tried to pacify them with an invitation to our receptions at Brent Bridge. Coaches were organised to take our guests from Brent Bridge to Wembley and the whole operation went very smoothly indeed.

I should mention that the display of food, which was prepared at the Embassy by Mrs Irena Zichova and then transported to the hotel on covered trays, was truly magnificent – an absolute work of art. Everyone, but everyone, including the staff at the hotel, was tremendously impressed by the wonderful variety of trays of various food assortments. There were different hams, salamis, sausages, Russian eggs in that wonderfully delicious Czech mayonnaise, and many, many different delicacies, all prepared in a very artistic way. It looked an exquisite picture. In fact people remarked what a pity it was to spoil the display by eating it. It was a truly wonderful display that could not fail to impress and I must say that the preparation of this wonderful food went a long way to making both receptions so very successful. We owed Mrs Zichova a substantial debt of gratitude. The reception we held before and after the semi-final was terrific. Everybody had a good time before, of course, but when England won through to qualify for the World Cup final itself – well, one can imagine the tremendous swell of excitement that everyone felt – including me.

For the final, when England played Germany, our party was even better. We had a number of celebrities there including Mr Silhavy, the Czechoslovak Commercial Counsellor, who honoured us with his presence, Jan Marko, manager of the Czechoslovak National Team, others from the Czech equivalent to our Football Association, then Mazopust, Pluskal and Urban, that famous Czech halfback line who fought so valiantly against Brazil in the preceding 1962 World Cup final losing 2–1, Johnny Byrne, the England centre forward of earlier days, Victor Railton of the *Evening News* and probably the most feared football reporter of those times, Mrs Cissie Cohen, wife of Jack Cohen, and her grandson, and others whose names I cannot now recall. Jack Cohen himself was to have been our Guest of Honour but found out from his secretary that he had accepted too many invitations – so his grandson came to our reception in his place. The atmosphere before the match was very tense, but after England won everybody let their hair down and had a good time. I was satisfied that the whole affair had been an excellent PR exercise. A full display of our products was there of course, and there were a lot of enquiries afterwards – but not too many from those valued clients to whom I had to refuse tickets! However, I am glad to say that, in time, they got over it. Sadly, the Brent Bridge Hotel no longer exists as it was demolished to make way for further development.

I should remark that at no time had I sought permission from Prague to organise our World Cup tickets or our receptions. My personal position was getting stronger and stronger as UK Director and in any case, the cost of the whole operation was met from just a small proportion of the excellent profits we had made from our transaction with G. F. Lovell and football lollipops. Therefore, I thought it would be a good idea to demonstrate a little independence of action for a change, which is a good thing when you are being controlled by faceless people from abroad. However, as a matter of courtesy I kept the Czech Group Managing Director, Antonin Vavra, fully informed of my plans and intentions and he raised no objections; as a matter of fact he became quite enthusiastic about our plans. Anton did not want to go to the final; he was not especially interested in football. But I told him I had especially reserved a ticket for him and I managed to persuade him that it would be a great atmosphere which should not be missed. Afterwards he thanked me profusely because whether one is a football fan or not it was truly a wonderful occasion and, in football terms, even a historic occasion. Wembley Stadium (the old one, of course) came very much alive on that great day and few of us who were there to witness it will ever forget the tremendous singing of 'When the saints come marching in'. But apart from Anton thanking me for persuading him to come to the match I never received a thank you or a single word of praise from anyone in Prague for a business venture which had been so successful whichever way you wanted to regard it. I am bound to say that, like any other human being, I like to receive a word or two of encouragement and I began to think about such things over the coming months quite seriously. I really loved my position and my work as UK Director and never thought the day would come when I wanted to leave it. But I was beginning to realise that I had a thankless task and that no matter how well I might do it would be as well not to expect anybody in Prague to recognize success, even if it stared them in the face.

Just a word or two about Antonin Vavra: Antonin was our Group Managing Director. His background was in the food retail sector and, once again as a strong member of the Communist Party, he eventually obtained a position with Koospol, the Foreign Trade Food Export Organisation. I had met him during visits to Czechoslovakia and found him to be an affable and quite pleasant fellow but he always smelled as if he had been drinking alcohol. I imagine he was very happy to receive the post of Managing Director of the Pilsner Urquell Group of companies in London, which meant that he, of course, had to live in London with his family. This gave him, and all other Czechs occupying a similar position abroad, the possibility of accumulating foreign currency, which was more than useful back home in Czechoslovakia. To gain such a position he had to have a very strong political affiliation with the Communist Party. These coveted positions were not made available to non-party members as a general rule.

Looking back on those few occasions when he accompanied us on visits to the factories whilst I was in Czechoslovakia I recall that he quite often left the meetings which were going on. He disappeared for twenty minutes or so and then returned. As he returned with a somewhat flushed face I had my suspicions about why he disappeared from our meetings, but later on I knew why and it did not take long after his arrival in London to realise that Antonin had a drink problem – a very serious drink problem. It is very hard for me to describe the difficulties that seem to arise on a continuous basis when one's MD is an alcoholic. They were complicated problems and sometimes very embarrassing. On one occasion I had invited an important client to my office and asked Antonin if he would care to join us to discuss some problems we had at that time; he accepted my invitation quite enthusiastically. At the appointed hour I was sitting with my client but – no Antonin. We waited and waited but he still did not come. So

I excused myself for a moment, went into Antonin's office, and there he was fast asleep, snoring and very evidently under the influence of drink. I awoke him, he blinked his eyes, went a little unsteadily to a cabinet, poured himself a stiff drink and, unbelievably, within a minute or so he was as right as rain. It was a remarkable transformation. Anyway, he soon followed me back to my office and we were able to conduct the meeting with our important client.

Antonin knew that I kept a small amount of alcohol in my office for the purpose of entertaining clients and so he began a practice of coming in quite early in the morning, rubbing his hands together and saying with a smile on his face, "Well, David, shouldn't we start the day right with a small drink?" At that time in the morning the very last thing on earth I wanted was to drink alcohol. But Antonin could be a funny man and easily offended. He was my MD and to that extent I had to respect his position and try not to get into a situation whereby we fell out with each other. So what does one do in those circumstances? Believe me, I have thought about this problem many times and wondered what I should have done. I found myself in an impossible situation, for I was being slowly drawn into his habits, of which I most certainly did not approve – but how to extricate myself without offending or upsetting him?

Whether I was right or not I do not know to this day, but I decided for the moment to humour his request; little did I realise that this would become a regular occurrence and on those days when he was in the office he came to me almost every morning for a 'pick-me-up' and I found it very difficult, in fact impossible, to break him from this daily happening. It became a big worry for me, as I had no idea how to get out of this predicament. It seemed to me, perhaps wrongly, that the people in Prague would certainly back him rather than me if I registered a complaint, and then my relationship with him as well as the people in Prague would have been completely spoiled for all time.

Eventually, Antonin was recalled to Prague and because, as a strong communist and member of the party, he still had quite an established position at Koospol they gave him a managerial post there. I am unaware if anyone arranged medical treatment for his addiction to alcohol but the plain fact was that he became even worse as time went by and, so I am told, could be found at his desk at 10 a.m. sometimes almost unconscious. I was also told that he began to frequent the bars in the large hotels where tourists from the West would be found and where his main objective was to make friends and persuade people to buy him drinks. Be that as it may, it was an explosive situation, a very sad one and one that obviously could not go on.

One day Antonin's son came home from school and found him sitting at the table, apparently unconscious but quite dead. Before him on the table was a burnt match, a cup with some coffee grounds in it, the gas ring full on and a saucepan of water on it – but the gas ring was not lit. To all intents and purposes it looked as though a dreadful accident had occurred and that Antonin had fallen asleep whilst making himself a cup of coffee. But I am not at all sure about that; Antonin was no fool and it is certain that he knew he was causing his wife and family much grief and unhappiness. If he were indeed seeking a drastic and tragic way out of his awful predicament then he would have thought it out very carefully. If that were so then he would have realised that if it seemed obvious he had committed suicide then his wife and family would be affected financially from the pension point of view. It is a possibility – and I put it no stronger than that – that he came to the conclusion that it was totally impossible to conquer his alcoholism. Or maybe, in his alcohol-soaked mind, he came to the conclusion that to live and to have a life without ever having another drink would be completely intolerable. Who knows how such people think when they are confronted with such a terrible choice? So the question is, and remains, did he plan the details of his suicide to make it appear as though it were a terrible accident? Or was it really an accident? Nobody knows and nobody ever will know because Anton took his secret to the grave with him. And so thus ended poor Antonin Vavra – a good man, a nice man whose heart was in the right place, but one who could not avoid falling victim to the demon drink.

3

THE MID 1960S, OUR VISIT TO MAJORCA AND THE PRAGUE SPRING

With the return to Prague of our Czech MD, Antonin Vavra, we waited with bated breath to find out who would replace him in London and therefore who our next MD would be. His replacement was a gentleman named Jaroslav Riha. I had never met him before, but then Koospol was a very large organisation and there were many different departments. I had always enjoyed good personal relations with the various MDs of our small group of companies, each of whom tended to change after a couple of years or so. This was always a difficult situation for us resident staff, especially for me, because it took perhaps the best part of a year to get to know a new MD reasonably well and learn how to work with him, and then, after a further year of good cooperation, that person left and it was necessary to start all over again with somebody new.

In the case of Mr Riha, however, I found it not at all easy to get close to him. He was a very cool person and acted in his post as MD in a very rigid and proper manner. He had very little sense of humour and seemed to go out of his way never to develop a more intimate relationship with me, or anyone else as far as I know. He was a very formal type of individual. He was, of course, a strong member of the Communist Party, otherwise he would never have been appointed to the position of MD in London. He always addressed me as Mr Mitchell and I always addressed him as Mr Riha. We never once got to Christian name terms, which is most usual among co-directors. Thus I found that conversations with him were somewhat stilted, stiff and uncompromising. Personally, I never found that such a relationship produced the best results, but that was only my opinion. Well, the next year or so would prove that to be the case, but I am jumping the gun a little so let's go back a while.

I have related how I had taken the family to Pontin's Holiday Camp at Brixham, Devon, and there is no doubt about it that for the children they were excellent places to go. And I have to admit that Lynne and I, after some misgivings, also enjoyed the week we spent there. However, in 1965 we raised our sights and Lynne and I decided to take the family to Majorca. We had been recommended a travel agent that specialised in organising holidays for Civil Service people and which had a very good reputation. So we had no hesitation in booking through them. I remember that for the return flights and full board in a very nice hotel – not a 5-star hotel, but a hotel of a very acceptable quality – the cost was £50 per person and I believe in the case of little Debbie we received a reduction. Today that is almost unbelievable, but quite true. Anyway, the day arrived for our departure from Gatwick Airport, which was very conveniently only about thirty-five minutes or so by car from where we lived. Back then there was no problem about parking the car at Gatwick, or any airport for that matter, for a fortnight or so and it didn't cost a fortune either.

Although both our older children, Jackie and Philip, had flown once before when we flew the car from Southend Airport across the Channel to Ostend, this was the very first proper air journey they had undertaken, and the same applied to Lynne. I should also mention that the airlines had not yet introduced the reservation of seats option when booking in at the airline reception desk. At the gate it was a free for all once you were given permission to board the aircraft. However, they made an exception for those with young children and so as we had little Debbie we were allowed to go first and choose our seats, which meant that we were all able to sit together. In those days Gatwick was relatively new and furthermore the airport was not afflicted by overcrowding; neither did one see those self-ish louts who, because presumably they are waiting for flights, lie down, occupying several seats, and just sleep. In fact, one could say that back then travelling was a pleasure. People were not treated like cattle and with a lack of consideration, as they are from time to time these days.

I, of course, had flown quite often backwards and forwards to Prague, but the flight to Palma was an exciting event – a first experience in fact for the children and Lynne, and as I was with my family, for me too. We were all looking forward to a great holiday together. At the other end we landed at Palma to be met by a blanket of heat when we exited the plane – it hit us like a shock wave. Palma Airport was quite crowded, as I recall, for it was a very much smaller airport in those days; but after clearing customs we were allocated a coach number to take us to our holiday destination and we found this without any problem, despite the fact that there were many coaches lined up waiting for their passengers. Then off we went in the direction of our resort, which was a very attractive place called Cala Millor to the south west of the island.

The coach journey, however, took us over hills and small mountains and sometimes, it seemed, by such narrow roads that if our coach had met another coming in the opposite direction I am not quite sure what would have happened. But driving on the right, when we looked out of the window we saw on occasion a sheer drop of many feet into ravines etc, so we were obliged to place our trust in the driver who evidently didn't believe in going at any rate of forward movement except fast. However, to my great surprise, he got us all there in one piece and we finally arrived at Cala Millor. When we saw our hotel we were very pleasantly surprised and even more so when we were shown to the two rooms that had been reserved for us, i.e. one for the children and one for Lynne and myself. Both had excellent verandahs which looked out over the swimming pool and sunbathing area immediately below. Beyond that was the beach and the blue Mediterranean. I would say the distance from the hotel to the beach was no more than sixty yards or so. We were very satisfied, happy and extremely comfortable in that hotel. It was clear that we had made an excellent choice.

After unpacking and freshening ourselves somewhat we went down for dinner and were allocated a table, which we retained for the whole fortnight. We were mostly served at the table by a nice young Spanish waiter named Jacinto, who looked after us extremely well. The food was varied and well cooked and, as far as I can recall, we all enjoyed eating there – even the children. My only criticism was connected with the butter, which in the heat always seemed to be melted within its little silver foil wrapping and sometimes even a little rancid; evidently they were short of refrigeration space.

We made a point of taking coach trips to see other places of interest too, for example Formentor, the holiday venue of royalty, film stars and other famous people. We also visited the Porto Christo caves where you boarded small boats and slowly navigated the various cave channels; in one spot was a grotto where a small orchestra was playing and this, combined with hidden lighting of a light shade of green which illuminated the nooks and crannies of the caves, made for a very pleasant experience. In the evenings at our hotel they had a nice lounge with a very good group playing the sort of pop music that even I did not dislike. The youngsters could dance if they wished – and they did! I am not a fan of pop music as such, but this group played excellently and I would be the first to admit that as they played and sang they entertained us all every evening. Therefore, most evenings we tended to retire to the lounge after dinner and sit there enjoying a drink or two and listening to the group playing. On some evenings we would get chatting to other guests and all in all it was very pleasant and relaxing. But on a few occasions we decided to take in the warm, balmy evening Mediterranean air and go for a stroll along the sea front.

Sometime during our first week there I happened to hear that El Cordobes (also known as El Beatle for the way he wore his hair), the famous young, handsome matador of that time, was fighting in the Palma Arena that coming Sunday. I had read much about El Cordobes, as his bravado and very courageous and daring displays had also been widely reported in English newspapers. So I was very curious to see this young chap if it were at all possible. First of all I asked Lynne, who was very nice about it and said that she didn't mind me going at all.

But firstly I had to get a ticket for this corrida from somewhere and wondered what the chances might be. I tried extremely hard to obtain a ticket; I went everywhere – to every travel agent, ticket office, hotel and even some likely looking shops, but nowhere could I buy a ticket. Also nobody knew where I could get one. They seemed to be more rare than hens' teeth!

So I returned disconsolately to the hotel and at dinner that night my disappointment must have shown because the waiter, Jacinto, said to me, "Senor, not happy this evening?" So I explained to him why. He nodded and went away, but just as we were about to finish our meal he returned with a big smile on his face and said, "Senor, it is good. I have one ticket for you to see the great El Cordobes tomorrow at the corrida!" Well, I can only imagine that my face must have lit up like a beacon to be told that! Jacinto gave me the ticket and would not take a penny more than the face value, despite the fact that I am sure he could have sold it on at a much higher price had he wanted to do so, for they were much sought after. Jacinto was a nice boy. He advised me to have an early lunch the next day and then go to the front of the hotel where I would find a coach which would take me and others to the corrida in Palma.

I would like to make it clear at this point that I hold no brief for bullfighting whatsoever. Perhaps it is a spectacle which belongs to the past and should be buried there. I read that there are movements afoot to eliminate it. Today I would not go to a bullfight free of charge because I think there are aspects which cannot be described in any other way than cruel. But I am writing about the 1960s when it was still very popular and well attended. I was also young and keen to exploit any new experience and that was my only reason, or, if you like, my weakness for wanting to witness this spectacle myself. Therefore, I hope that my words will in no way be taken as being words of praise or of encouragement of bullfighting; I am simply describing what I saw.

Anyway, I had an early lunch as recommended by Jacinto, went to the front of the hotel and there found not one but three coaches. I boarded the first one, but as I did so I could see there was no free place – every seat was occupied. So I alighted and tried the second coach, but here a number of people were standing in the aisle and it was almost impossible to determine if there was a free place or not. So I went to the third coach and there a large German man kept saying to me, "Deutche – no English," and as he was bigger than me discretion played the better part of valour and I got off. After getting off, though, I made my feelings very clear to the huge German, but from a safe distance of course! At that point I supposed that if these coaches were only for Germans then maybe there would perhaps be a coach for the English coming a little later and so I decided I would wait inside the hotel, out of the heat, for something to happen.

Well, the three coaches went on their way and I waited and waited and waited, but nothing came. Looking at my watch I was getting a bit desperate now. So I went to the young lady at the reception desk and explained my plight, at which she looked aghast and said that I should have taken one of the three coaches that were there earlier. I explained to her why I didn't and she nodded sympathetically as if she understood. She looked at the clock and then said to me that the only way now to get to Palma in time would be to go by taxi. I gulped at that because surely to hire a taxi to take me all the way to Palma and then wait for me for the return journey would cost an arm and a leg.

But then I thought, to hell with it; I have a ticket and I was quite prepared to move heaven and earth to get there. So I ran to the taxi rank, which was not far from the hotel, and the first taxi driver was fast asleep. But he heard me approach and awoke. I asked him if he could take me to the corrida in Palma; he looked at his watch and then nodded. To be quite sure what I was getting myself into I enquired about the price and I was pleasantly surprised, for it was not as much as I had feared.

So off we went, but we had only been travelling for 10 or 15 km when the car began to play up very badly. The driver had no alternative but to stop and he did so just a few yards short of a small village. He got out, lifted the bonnet, looked at me and gave me a look as if to say that it is now going to be very difficult. But he motioned to me to stay there and went off in to the village. When I saw him enter a crowded bar I then thought that was the end of my hopes; no doubt he would get a little tipsy in there and I would never reach Palma. But no – in just a few minutes he came out of the bar with two other men, and with me still sitting inside pushed the car to a kind of tin shack where they opened the doors. I have no idea what the problem was or what they did, but within ten minutes or so the car was OK again and so we resumed our journey. The driver put his foot down, despite the risky bends at high points (I just crossed my fingers and hoped we would not meet one of those coaches coming from the airport! It would have been a disaster had we done so). Finally we arrived at Palma and not too far from the Arena. The taxi driver motioned that he would wait for me in the same spot and that I should hurry otherwise I would miss the beginning of the corrida. As I did so I briefly reflected: could such a thing like that happen on a hot Sunday afternoon anywhere else but Spain? The Spain of that era, of course. I am not sure it would happen today.

I found my seat and just as I sat down the Grand Parade began. The three matadors, wearing their large cloaks around them, entered the arena followed by their banderillos and assistants, and then the nasty picadors on their well-padded horses. All marched towards the centre of the bull-ring and proceeded towards the President's box, which was situated up high. In unison, all three matadors lifted their hats to salute him whilst he acknowledged them with his snowy-white handkerchief and many smiles and bows in their direction. Then everybody disappeared behind the very sturdy wooden barrier which runs all the way round the arena. There were four entrances to the arena guarded by a wooden shield through which a man could pass, but not, hopefully, a bull – although I have seen pictures showing occasions where the poor terrified bull had jumped over the wooden barrier. In a sense it was very funny to see bodies ejecting themselves out of harm's way by popping up as the bull wended his way around the ring, but on the wrong side of the protective barrier. It would have been quite serious if the bull had caught one of them.

And now there was an eerie silence – it was a silence of nervous anticipation. Then, suddenly, a single trumpet sounded, very dramatically, and the crowd began to buzz; at once the gates were opened to allow the first bull into the arena. Out the great beast came, snorting and running around, obviously in a very angry mood without doubt, because he had been tormented into being even more angry. He was ready to charge anything that moved and he was played a little by the banderillos and sometimes by the matador too, but at the least sign of danger they ran back behind the barrier. I am convinced, however, that these acts of fear were performed to create drama. Eventually, the first matador came out with his large cloak and began to test the bull and his assistants lingered in the background ready to interfere if things got a little out of hand. He was trying to learn how the bull would react to various moves, which way he would turn, what to look out for, and so on. Then followed another distasteful part of the procedure, i.e. the sticking of darts into the back of the bull, the pain of which annoys the poor tortured animal even more. This is done mostly by the banderillos but on occasion, to prove to us all how brave he is, the matador himself joins in. The poor thing must have been driven to distraction with the pain from these darts in its back and upper neck.

Now, another burst by the trumpeter and the gates were opened to allow the picadors in, usually two sitting astride large, well-padded horses. These are not at all popular, even with the aficionados, the true and regular fans of bullfighting. The banderillos then urge the bull to go towards the horses, and when the bull charges, the picadors do their dirty work by sticking their sharp lances in the neck muscles of the bull, the object being to sever the neck muscles and make the bull lower his great head; but in so doing the poor old bull loses a lot of blood, which weakens it even more. The horse is protected by thick padding which the bull is not supposed to penetrate, but the horse is not always so fortunate. The crowd is booing now – they do not like this part of the procedure at all.

Finally, the matador signalled that the picadors should finish their nasty work and leave the arena, which they did to more boos from the crowd. The matador then began to play the bull more and more, trying to wear down its resistance, and when he thought it was the right time he went to the barrier where a banderillo handed him his small red cape and his sword. At that point the matador could, if he wished, dedicate the bull to either the President or perhaps to a lovely lady in the audience wearing a mantilla; in the event that the dedication is to a lady the matador usually throws his hat to her. The dedication may occasionally be to the audience itself. Of course, playing a bull with only a small cape is a much more dangerous task and the matador tried to get closer and closer to the bull as he carried out his passes – usually, if the passes are graceful and dangerous, the crowd cries out, "Olé, olé, olé," in a rising crescendo as each pass is achieved. When the matador felt the bull had little fight left in him he prepared to perform the final act. He went to the barrier where he was handed a different sword – this is the sword with which he would kill the sad and by now quite dejected bull, who looked quite fed up with the whole situation. Sometimes the kill is quick and decisive and the poor bull slumps to the ground; but on other occasions, when the matador's aim is not so exact, the scene becomes ugly, but I prefer not to describe those incidents.

The first fight was good but nothing spectacular; the second fight was about the same, I think. But then El Cordobes entered the arena to wild and loud cheers from the audience. Evidently, many of the people had seen him before, knew him and respected his bravery, skill and daring. When Cordobes began to play the bull with the large cloak even I, as a raw beginner watching the spectacle in awe, could tell he was in a different class to the others.

He made pass after pass, coming closer and closer to the bull all the time and the crowd loved it – the cries of 'Olé!' rang through the arena as if they would never stop. When he changed to the small red cape and was handed his sword he went immediately to the edge of the barrier, picked out a lovely lady (he was quite a fellow with the girls, I believe) who was wearing the traditional mantilla, dedicated the bull to her and then threw his hat to her. It was an excellent aim and she caught it very cleverly. I would say that Cordobes did not allow the picadors to do a great deal of damage to the bull, although it was bleeding but not to a great extent; but when he started to play the bull he got so close to the animal in the passes that he had quite a lot of blood on his tights. So the animal was fresher, less disabled by the picadors and represented more danger as a consequence; the crowd was well aware of that. However, it in no way prevented him from taking risks that the other matadors either were not capable of or were not willing to take – but Cordobes was.

I am no expert in bullfighting, but I could not help but judge that it was an excellent performance of skill and grace coupled with courage that at times was almost foolhardy, and when, at the end before the kill, he knelt before the bull, staring him straight in the eye to show the bull and the crowd who was master, the crowd erupted, wildly applauding his bravado. The poor bull was, by this time, quite exhausted and just stood there panting – just a sorry shadow of the magnificent beast that had entered the arena just twenty minutes or so ago – and then the kill took place, which was mercifully accurate and quick. But I found it impossible to do other than respect, or maybe a better word is admire, a man who was willing to take such obvious risks for the so-called 'entertainment' of others. Then followed the triumphal parade of Cordobes, escorted by two or more of his banderillos as he proceeded around the whole arena. Many ladies threw him flowers or other small gifts and then someone from the crowd threw in the old traditional wine container, which he then held up over his head, squeezed into his open mouth and then threw back to the audience. That happened a few times I recall during his triumphant parade.

When he had finished his parade he then stood before the presidential box and the President began to get the feel of the crowd to judge what they wanted to happen next. The crowd, completely won over by this great and brave display, cheered and cheered and the sound was almost deafening when it built up to a crescendo. The President then signalled his award by placing white handkerchiefs over the rail of his box. I cannot recall now the number of handkerchiefs he displayed but I think it was three, which meant that the award was two ears and a tail. Such awards, I was told, are only given very, very infrequently and only when the fight has been judged to be a heroic contest between man and beast. I considered that I was very fortunate indeed to witness a great occasion which, I imagine, has possibly been entered into the history of bullfighting – most certainly El Cordobes has and will be found there. However, the fate of the animal in every corrida is a foregone conclusion, and no matter what else I witnessed, I could not help feeling very sorry for the bull.

When it was all over I returned to where my taxi driver friend said he would wait for me and there he was, just as he had promised. Thank goodness the return trip was without incident and my family were pleased to see me back at the hotel and to hear all about my big adventure.

Apart from the fact that we had such an enjoyable holiday I cannot recall any other experience there which is worthy of special comment – we simply had a wonderful time and it was very nice to be together. The whole fortnight had gone very well and everyone had enjoyed themselves. In fact, so much that we decided there and then to repeat our holiday in every detail, except for the bullfight, the following year, 1966.

Let us now return to Czechoslovakia where by now the political situation, whilst still ruled by the Communists, was thawing a little. This was because in Moscow Josef Stalin had died and, to the surprise of everyone, Mr Kruschev denounced him as the evil dictator that he was to the nation and the whole world. He was now First Secretary of the Communist Party, which meant he was very much in charge of the Soviet Union. However, evidently he did not fully support the harsh conditions which had been visited upon the Soviet public under Stalin, so the strict control of the public was continued, but not quite so harshly. As I have remarked before, what happened in Moscow followed very shortly in the satellite countries, of which Czechoslovakia was, of course, one. And so one began to notice that previously suspected or even convicted people were being 'semi-rehabili-tated', or to put it another way, were being 'half-pardoned', right, left and centre. All such people were promised that if they behaved themselves and kept their noses clean they would, in time, be 'fully rehabilitated'. Semi-rehabilitation meant that they could return to a somewhat more normal life but still be subject to some restrictions, and full rehabilitation meant that their situation was more or less completely back to normal and there would be no further restrictions upon them – except for the standard restrictions that applied to all citizens under the Communist regime.

This thawing process eventually gave rise to the advent and the advancement of Mr Dubcek, a Slovak Communist leader whose attitude towards communism, encouraged by the new atmosphere introduced by Mr Kruschev in Moscow, differed somewhat to those of many of his colleagues. He believed in socialism and communism but, as he put it, he wanted 'communism with a human face'. He did not see why it was not possible to have a Communist government without being so strict on the people, allowing them to travel abroad if they wished (subject to them receiving an allocation of foreign currency, which was not easy to obtain), and trying to improve their general living standards, plus not imposing so many rules and regulations on them. After many years of deprivation and lack of freedom the public welcomed such a change, and so with popular public demand on his side, Mr Dubcek became a great favourite of the people and was eventually appointed First Secretary of the Czechoslovak Communist Party, and as such he also assumed the post of Prime Minister. This period began the so-called 'Prague Spring'.

Now, as his position strengthened, Mr Dubcek began to impose his thoughts and wishes on his colleagues. However, this situation placed many Czechs and Slovaks in a very difficult position. In the crazy system invoked by the ruthlessness of Communist control, survival or success under the Communists was, as always, connected to supporting the right people. So when any change took place it was very necessary for you, as an individual, to choose carefully, but above all to be accurate and try to forecast who was going to win over the others and who, therefore, one should support. Some people, like our old friend Karel Jiracek, had an uncanny nose for such situations, almost as if he had a crystal ball and could see ahead. Others were not so fortunate and backed the wrong horse, and such people lived to rue the day. I knew a number of people who unfortunately made the wrong choice and in one way or another paid a price for that mistake. The secret was to wait and wait until the position between opponents was getting somewhat clearer, then jump. Meanwhile, keep your mouth shut and above all avoid being trapped into any conversation or discussion where you might be asked who you favour. That was the only way to survive under communism.

Later on, in the case of Mr Dubcek, many Czechoslovaks were worried that Mr Brezhnev, who by now had succeeded Mr Kruschev, and his Politburo, who were all hardliners, by the way, in Moscow would not allow him to go too far in the changes he wished to make and indeed he had already begun to make. If he did, would the Soviet Union simply look the other way? I know for a fact that Karel Jiracek had never once, in my hearing at least, openly stated his support for Mr Dubcek, and there were other staunch communist die-hards who acted similarly, although neither did he say anything against him, not at that point anyway. Those who came down heavily in support of Mr Dubcek and the changes he recommended lived to regret their decision and I shall explain more about that later. Suffice to say, for the moment, that this atmosphere caught on among the Czech people – this period built up to what was called the Prague Spring, as I have mentioned earlier, and the lightheartedness and happiness of the people was there for all to witness. The atmosphere in Prague and other cities and towns was quite wonderful and all friends of Czechoslovakia and the Czech people were very glad to see it. However, there were those, including myself, who were very concerned because these nice people could not possibly see how, now that a hardliner was in control in Moscow, the Czechs would be allowed to continue with such policies. And so, taking into account the rumblings of discontent that were going on in Poland and East Germany etc, it was clear to some of us that we could expect fireworks at some point in the near future. Those of us who felt like that were correct, as we shall see a little later on. But a great many Czechs seemed to be blind to the dangers threatening them – they were in a state of denial. They would soon learn that the Russian bear would pounce on them before long and put their ideas of 'communism with a human face' theories promptly to bed.

During the 1960s there were occasions on my many trips to Czechoslovakia by car when Lynne and I thought that it would be a good education, as well as a nice experience for me, to take one or other of the children with me. Jackie, my eldest daughter, was the first one and she stayed in Marianske Lazne with my hunting pal Slavek Svinger and his very charming wife Jarka. They had two small daughters at that time, Diana and Inge, and so that was rather nice for Jackie. I left her in Marianske Lazne in the care of my friends whilst I went on to Prague and elsewhere to carry out my business obligations. She had a nice time but I think she was glad to see me when I returned to M. Lazne to collect her and take her back to Prague with me. There she met my friends and at the time the great communist display of youth and gymnastics called the Spartakiade was on. This culminated in a terrific parade which marched through and down the great and historic square, Vaclavske Namesti. With the help of a good friend I was able to obtain a room at a hotel in the monstrous square and so she and I had a wonderful view. As our room was almost opposite the stand where the Communist leader, Antonin Novotny, was to take the salute, our room was visited by the State Security Police, who checked out the room – and us. Evidently they were satisfied. We were even asked by reception if an elderly American couple could come to our room in order to get a good view of the parade. I agreed of course, and they promised to send me copies of a few of the photos they were taking – I gave them my address in England but I regret that they did not do so.

The next to come with me was Philip and on this trip he had been invited to stay at a small place called Svit, which nestles down at the foot of the mountains – the Vysoky Tatry (part of the Carpathian range) – in Slovakia. So I decided the best plan would be to go via Vienna, which would be nice for Philip and a change of route for me. We stopped over at my good friend's small hotel in Marktheidenfeld, Bavaria, for they knew me well by then, and from there proceeded on excellent roads through to Vienna.

At one point not far over the German-Austrian border we entered a rather attractive village by the River Danube and seeing a very nice hotel there I decided to stop overnight. We had quite an amazing experience because almost opposite the hotel there was a small road which led up to a kind of mountain. Philip wanted to go there and so we did. As we got to the top we came to another smaller village and there we stopped for some refreshments. But we then discovered that we had gone so high we were now sitting above the clouds! It was an eerie experience and as the clouds parted occasionally we could see our hotel far below. It was a very special experience indeed.

As we neared Vienna I looked out for signs to see if there was perhaps a ring road around Vienna, but I didn't see one. In any case, I thought it would be nice to see something of that great city. I was very pleased to see that the great palace of the Royal Hapsburgs was very close to the point at which we exited the road we had used and so we stopped to have a look at this very nice palatial building and wonderful gardens. When we had ended our small tour it was necessary to get on the road to Bratislava. So I proceeded in an easterly direction, but nowhere could I see any directions to that city. I knew it was but a short distance because in better times there was even a tram service which ran between Vienna and Bratislava. I stopped at one building, which proved to be some kind of sanatorium; unfortunately, I disturbed a small doctors' meeting being held there. They were very kind and tried to assist me and kindly gave me directions, but either I am an idiot or I misunderstood because after fifteen minutes or so we were once again hopelessly lost somewhere in Vienna and I did not have a clue where I was and where to go. And then I spotted a small taxi rank. So, in desperation now, I spoke to one driver and asked him if he would guide us to the road leading to Bratislava, for which I would gladly pay him, at which he replied, "Ah – Pressburg." At last the penny dropped – as is so usual in both the Austrian and Germanic border regions, they have different names on both sides of the border and the Austrian name for Bratislava was in fact Pressburg! So that is the reason why I didn't see any directions to Bratislava. As an experienced traveller I should have realised that it would be something like that. Anyway, the taxi drove ahead and I followed him until we reached the road. I paid him and gave him a good tip – I was so relieved. Shortly afterwards I saw a small hotel on this road and instead of going on to Bratislava I decided it would be good to stop there overnight, as we were both by now rather tired.

The next morning we made tracks towards the border. It was the usual kind of experience when crossing into a communist country, but not quite as bad as crossing from Germany into Czechoslovakia. We made very good time and in the late afternoon we duly arrived at Svit and to the Sos family with whom Philip was going to stay. We received a very nice greeting from Ladislav and Mila Sos, parents of the young girl Jarmila who stayed at our home in Surrey for a month some time before, and their children. I left Philip in their care whilst I went on to Kosice and then further to a smaller town called Trebisov, which was situated very close to the Soviet border. There in Trebisov was the Deva factory, which produced orange and lemon slices in drums for the English market. We shipped between 250 and 275 tons a year of this item and it was in fact my suggestion that part of the production should be switched to Deva – they were very grateful to me for doing so and could not do enough for me. When I had finished there I returned to Svit to find that Philip had had a very nice time. He had made pals with Tomas, one of the Sos' sons, and had even been invited to the school of Tomas. Apparently, everybody wanted to see what an English boy looked like and so Philip felt rather important there.

We then departed Svit and went back into Moravia via Olomouc, where we stayed overnight, then on to Prague and Marianske Lazne, which was our last port of call. There Philip had a great time too, because outside the town there was a large rubbish dump which was absolutely swarming with rats. My friend Slavek had a small calibre rifle and so one could stand at the top and look down and fire away at the rats below. Philip enjoyed this tremendously and became a very good shot. After M. Lazne it was time to go home. We had an uneventful trip back and everyone was glad to see us when we arrived at home again in Old Coulsdon.

At this point I would like to return to the subject of the Czech company for which I was responsible – Sugosa Ltd. I was beginning to feel somewhat dissatisfied for one reason or another. I loved my position and my work; it was a situation made in heaven for me and I had made many friends throughout the whole country from Kosice in the east of Slovakia to Marianske Lazne in the west of Bohemia. There is no doubt about it; I was very seriously and deeply attached to that country. I was even conquering the Czech language to a very reasonable degree. I never spoke perfectly and neither did I bother to spend too much time on correct grammar. My attitude was that as long as people understood me in conversation and understood what I was talking about, that's all I wanted to achieve, notwithstanding the errors. It is an exceedingly difficult language for us English people to understand and speak; personally, to speak Czech perfectly I believe one has to be born to it. Friends told me that, grammatically, I spoke Czech just as a child of maybe ten or eleven would speak and that I made similar mistakes as a child of that age, but that my accent, for an Englishman, was very good. That I spoke using poor grammar did not bother me at all and if I did make an error which caused laughter I joined in the laughter against myself. But I think my errors became fewer and fewer as time went on.

Before I began to motor to Czechoslovakia on my many visits, or better to say on those occasions when it was more suitable to go by air, I would often catch the train from Hlavni Nadrazi, the main rail station in Prague, to Marianske Lazne to join up with my friends there and I found that to be very interesting and a way to make my knowledge of the Czech language more natural. I would sit in the carriage and ask, "Prosim vas, ale jak dlhouho do Marianske Lazne?" which means very roughly, "If you please, how long does it take to Marianske Lazne?" Of course, I knew the answer, having made the trip many times before, but it was a way to begin a conversation, and because my question was not grammatically correct or word perfect, but understandable, the person would then ask me where I came from; I would reply, "England," then others might join in and say that they have never met an Englishman who spoke Czech before. So quite often nice discussions began, which I found very interesting and enjoyable and such occasions improved my Czech very considerably. I met quite a number of people that way.

During what we might call 'the bad old days' one such person I recall was a captain in the Czech Army, and during one particular journey from Prague to Marianske Lazne I got into conversation with him; we got along like a house on fire. I found him most likeable and he seemed to like me. We seemed to have struck up an affinity, which happens sometimes when people meet. He invited me to the restaurant car for a drink, which I gladly accepted, and when we returned to the carriage he said he would like to write to me and keep in contact. But then he thought it over and said that it would be too difficult for him and he asked me if I understood. I replied that I did, because he as an army officer would be in a very unenviable position if it were known that he was consorting with a chap from the West. But then a young lady sitting in our carriage overheard us and suggested we use her as a go-between. This seemed to be a good idea at the time and so we exchanged addresses.

After I returned home I wrote a letter to my new army friend through this young lady, but I never had any acknowledgement from her and I never received a reply from him. What went wrong I have no idea, but maybe he, or even she, reflected on the matter and decided not to take the risk. He would certainly have been in very deep trouble if it were discovered that he was communicating with someone from the West through a third party – my God, what suspicions our communist friends would have attached to that kind of liaison, completely innocent though it would have been. And as for the young lady, she may well have even been accused of some kind of conspiracy against the State if it were discovered she was being used as a means to convey such communications. As I have remarked, any such relationship would have been totally innocent, but how many times before had innocent behaviour, similar to this situation, been distorted completely by their Secret Police into something else and far more sinister? I wonder if the reader can understand how difficult, and how miserable it was too, to live under conditions like that. As a person who likes to be polite but also likes to speak his mind openly I do not think I would have lasted five minutes there if I were a Czech person. I loved Czechoslovakia and its people of the era too, and I felt very sorry for them indeed. But I was always glad to get home again and breathe the good and gracious clean air of freedom which in this country we take too much for granted and do not appreciate – simply because it has always been there. One further thought with regard to my army captain friend and the very nice young lady who offered to be a go-between: there is also the possibility that my letter was intercepted and never received.

But to return to my situation back home: the business was going well and as I have already related it was our supermarket programme by far which had developed to be the most important section of our trade. It was then that I suggested that the relationship between Eagle Confectionery Distributor Ltd and ourselves should be more contractual and legal so that everyone would be clear about where the responsibilities lay, how the profits would be calculated and how they would be shared. It worried me that we were involved in a very complicated commercial relationship with Eagle, which involved quite a lot of money. In the very nature of the business we transacted there were many forms of expenditure and there were forms of income. To eliminate risk elements on both sides I proposed that our two companies should work more in harmony and that we should enter into a proper and legally binding profit sharing arrangement. That nothing existed so far on paper was, in my view, quite wrong. I suggested, therefore, that a contract should be drawn up for a specific period of time, because time sometimes changes things on both sides, and that such a contract would set out every detail for anyone to follow. My proposal was received with some enthusiasm both by Sidney and Geoffrey Eagle and also our principals in Prague.

And so began a whole series of dreary legal meetings between the Eagles and their legal representative and us with ours, i.e. Mr Vowles. I am afraid the legal people pondered over, and saw danger in, every little word and any kind of description of goods, whilst we, on the commercial side, wanted to skip unimportant details and get on with the nitty-gritty of the Agreement. However, after innumerable and sometimes quite boring meetings we were eventually able to reach a clear understanding, or as near as we were ever going to get, and a draft Agreement was drawn up for both sides to study. Of course, the legal people continued to discover small points which they wished to clarify and I have to say that the Eagle's legal representative was the worst and most pernickety of the two. At last, however, despite the legal people and not because of them, we came to a finished document which covered a period of ten years and which, in my opinion, would be dealing with goods over that period of somewhere between £10 and £15 million – a substantial business by any standards, because we must remember we were talking and negotiating in 1966–7 or so and at that time the sums I have mentioned would have been regarded as huge. Today the equivalent amounts would be much larger due to the inevitable and seemingly unstoppable advance of inflation, of course.

I proposed that the signing of this ten-year contract should be celebrated with a special dinner, to which everyone agreed, and so I organised this in a lovely hall used as a temple for an old established City Masonic Guild. I then instructed a well-known firm of caterers, Ring and Brymer, to take care of the food and wine, but of course I had to guide them as to the courses and the wines. I discussed it all with Sydney and Geoffrey, because I did not want to commit any silly mistakes, bearing in mind that a number of Jewish people would be present. I think the act of signing that contract was the final important occasion in my time as Director of Sugosa, and I shall explain how that came about.

For me 1967 is to be remembered for two main events, both of which persuaded me that the best interests of my family and myself lay elsewhere and that I should consider resigning my position as Director of Sugosa and leave the Czech business, which I had started and developed from nothing, behind me. The first event occurred as a result of a Government edict on what they called the 'Second Pension' or Graduated Pension Scheme. Every company employing people in the UK was requested to seek the views of their employees and give them the choice of going along with the Government scheme, or, if they preferred, to have a company-run scheme. One way or the other we, our employees and the company, would all have to pay for this additional pension. I discussed this matter with our current MD, Antonin Vavra, and it was agreed that we must conduct such a poll amongst our staff. As it was well known that investments of money by the Government, any government, were less effective and would result in a smaller second pension – no government has ever had a good record in this respect – our company poll resulted in everybody, with one exception, voting resoundingly for the company scheme. Looking back, and to be frank, I am surprised that Antonin Vavra, good communist as he was, agreed to this somewhat capitalistic idea.

I duly began to work on this project, speaking with a number of insurance companies and pension providers until I came up with a scheme which, in my opinion, was a good one. It was a lot of work and took a good deal of my time. As I have already said, every stage reached was fully discussed with the MD. All the papers were ready to be signed when we had a sudden and quite unexpected visit from a director of Koospol, Prague, our principals. He was a certain Dr Hanus, who was head of our department in Prague. As soon as he heard of the company pension scheme he immediately ordered it to be cancelled – no discussion, no attempt to understand that this was according to the law of the land in Britain, the order was just to cancel the whole scheme.

Perhaps the most disappointing aspect of this situation was the refusal to even talk about the scheme. There was no willingness whatsoever to listen to anybody's view or to hear why the company Graduated Pension Scheme was being brought into effect – nothing at all. This was grossly unfair and totally unreasonable and not only I but also all my staff were very unhappy about this sudden and unexpected turn of events.

Of course, we were all bitterly disappointed and so we had no other choice but to inform the Government office dealing with pensions at that time that we must accept their scheme. We all had to endure deductions from our salaries whether it was for a Government scheme or a company scheme, and it is interesting that in my case, despite the additional contributions made over years, my own Graduated Pension now, in the year 2007, pays just £3.98 per month! Had the same money been invested privately, i.e. through the company but supervised by a pension provider or major insurance company, one could be positively certain that this extra pension would not be a derisive £3.98 per month but a considerably greater sum. For this we have to thank Dr Hanus.

I am sure the reader is wondering why this strange decision occurred. Well, it was simply communist policies interfering with a British company governed by British law. I was told afterwards that communist policy and ideology is quite firm that pensions are the responsibility of the state, not of private companies, and that had Dr Hanus approved the Sugosa pension scheme he would have almost certainly been very severely criticised back in Prague, or perhaps even worse. The same fate would have awaited Antonin Vavra almost certainly. This was unknown to me until afterwards and, to be fair, I cannot recall any other incident in all the years I associated with the Czechs where politics was allowed to interfere with company activity.

As to the second reason why I terminated my cooperation with the Czechs, this was connected to the continual and vexed question of being properly rewarded and reimbursed for one's position, responsibilities and achievements. 1967 was a record year in terms of turnover and profit for Sugosa Ltd, for which I was responsible. But between the three Czech companies in our UK group there was a Tax Subvention Agreement, arrived at with the Inland Revenue, which meant that the losses from any company or companies within the group could be set against profits made by any other company. As the other two companies in our group, Pilsner Urquell Co. Ltd and Inter-Allied Exports Ltd, suffered losses during 1967, so the profits attributable to Sugosa were utilized and were whittled down considerably. Nevertheless, by any reasonable standards we had shown excellent results. However, one would be better advised not to hold one's breath waiting for a word or two of praise or encouragement, for that would never be forthcoming! Good results seemed to be looked at as expected and one's duty – nothing more and nothing less. Just as in Prague, good achievements very often remained unnoticed and unrewarded.

During early December every year, when our final results were already well estimated, I always discussed with the Czech MD a review of the year and what our final anticipated results would be, and then I handed him a page showing the existing salaries of each employee, last year's bonus and what I recommended by way of bonus for the current year and whether each person's salary should be increased or left at the existing rate. I then discussed each person individually. This, as I have written earlier, I did as a mark of respect for the MD, whoever he happened to be, and because I realised that although I was, in effect, the Managing Director and therefore had the authority to make these decisions myself, it was not my money and I was always very conscious of that fact. I also admit that at the back of my mind was the fact that as in all dealings with money it is always better to have one's actions approved – one could not be too careful with our suspicious communist friends. Usually, the MD agreed with more or less everything I recommended or proposed and so these annual rituals were over within half an hour or so.

But this year, because of the excellent results, I did something I had never done before – I put my own name down on the list but without further comment except to mention my existing salary and my last year's bonus. I did this because although my system of salary reviews was effective as far as my staff was concerned, I was getting continually overlooked. It seemed to me that if I did not remember myself in this respect, nobody else would. And that is why, in 1967, for the very first time ever, I placed my name on the list, for had I not done so then my situation would have once again been passed by without change. Little did I realise that it would be even worse than that.

But our MD was now Mr Riha and somehow I suspected that the discussion this year on salaries and bonuses was not going to run smoothly; I don't know why; it was just a gut feeling I had. Anyway, we agreed everything on the list in respect of my staff, as usual, and then we came to my situation. First of all, Mr Riha stated quite coldly that he did not think my salary needed adjusting, and secondly he said that my annual bonus would have to be reduced by £100 because it was discovered that I had received £100 more the previous year than Mr Purdy, Director of our associate company Inter-Allied Exports. I took this on the chin rather calmly,

I thought, but not without making it clear to Mr Riha that to compare my efforts and the long hours I worked in a conscientious manner on behalf of Sugosa, not to mention the very good results I had delivered, with those of Mr Purdy, who rolled into his office at 10 a.m., went out to lunch at noon and didn't return until between 2 and 3 p.m. because he liked to listen to the political speeches down at Tower Hill, and who then left his office on most days at around 4.30 p.m., was not comparable and not at all fair to me. No, I found Mr Riha's reasoning and judgement to be very seriously at fault and I felt very personally much aggrieved.

However, I have always tried to take my disappointments and reserve judgement on what to do until I had fully considered what would be the best course of action, and, most importantly, to make sure I did it at a time most convenient to me. But after the Graduated Pension debacle this was yet a second blow and, as far as I was concerned, it was the straw that broke the camel's back. On my way home that evening I pondered over the situation and when I arrived home I discussed it with Lynne – as I always did. We had always tried to reach important decisions in our lives together, for we believed that is the correct way in any marriage.

4

I RESIGN AS DIRECTOR OF SUGOSA LTD

Lynne was as disappointed at this turn of events as I was and as we spoke about it one clear factor emerged, which was that despite the indisputable fact that although I had a good position which, when the company was running smoothly and without interference, was a wonderful and very enjoyable way to earn a living for me, the time had come to re-evaluate my future intentions because staying where I was would offer me very little opportunity to improve my financial position in the foreseeable future or to realise my eventual ambition to start my own company. However, inflation affected me as well as everybody else and so I believe I owed better prospects to my family as well as to myself. From the point of view of income it was impossible to accept a situation whereby my salary would remain frozen.

One of the great problems, always, was the fact that salaries in Czechoslovakia were very low indeed and by their standards I was, of course, very well paid; it was extremely difficult indeed to persuade those connected with my well-being that matters such as salary levels must be dealt with on the basis of conditions in the UK, not in Czechoslovakia. People that I knew in the City, with positions carrying far less responsibility than I had, were earning appreciably more – and they had fully paid company pension schemes as well as other 'perks'. And so, with very great reluctance and not a little sadness, we reached the decision that we had come to the end of the road as far as my cooperation with the Czechs was concerned and that I should resign my position as Director of Sugosa Ltd and move on. I duly wrote a letter to the MD, Mr Riha, and told him of my intentions.

I would like to remark that I had appreciated very much, and still do, the opportunity given to me by the Czechs to show what capabilities I possessed and I thoroughly enjoyed my experiences whilst representing them in the UK. It does not fall to every young chap to be given the chance of creating a new business and moulding it as I felt necessary. It was all wonderful experience and prepared me for the day when I would, as I was totally confident I would, start and develop my own business. They were good training days and stood me in good stead later on. Most of all it instilled in me a confidence level which perhaps I may have lacked somewhat before. Now, I thought, bring on whatever may lie before me and I will confidently work my fingers to the bone to ensure success for my family and myself.

In my letter I made an undertaking to stay at my post until the supermarket programme had been completed in terms of sales and organisation of shipments etc. I did this because I was not the kind of person who could walk away from my responsibilities in a flippant manner – that was not my style. I had the opportunity to join my new company as from March, but I asked my new MD if he would agree to a later date for my departure. He did and so I stayed until the end of August to complete the supermarket sales programme. It would have been exceedingly difficult, and caused a number of problems, for anybody else to have taken over in mid-stream.

In Czechoslovakia the political situation to many observers – including yours truly – had by now become alarming. In the beginning I was very pleased indeed for the people that matters were becoming better and better and, as I have remarked earlier, I shall never forget the atmosphere of great hope and enthusiasm that existed there during the Prague Spring of 1968 – it was truly wonderful. The light-heartedness and pure joy of the Czech people was there for all to see. But as I have also written earlier, Mr Brezhnev in Moscow and his hard line Politburo cronies were evidently determined to do something about a situation they just could not accept. They feared that if the other satellite countries saw what was being allowed in Czechoslovakia then they too would want the same and the whole communist edifice in Eastern Europe would come crashing down. And that situation they were determined to prevent. There were a number who felt the situation would not be allowed to continue – including myself – but not too many Czechs, who seemed to be in a state of denial. This was the situation, therefore, during which I was serving my period of notice.

Well, with my decision made and my resignation tendered I arranged a visit to Czechoslovakia by car later on to say as many goodbyes as I could to all the friends I had made over the years. A lot of them tried to persuade me to change my mind and withdraw my resignation, but they saw that my mind was made up and when I explained to them the reasons why I had come to this decision, they understood. There were some problems with regard to the supermarket programme that I had to attend to whilst there, but soon the time came for me to return to England. However, I had not said all my goodbyes – not by a long chalk. At the golf course in Marianske Lazne they invited me to take part in a tournament they were holding there very shortly, but I explained that I couldn't, as I had to return to England.

I made an uneventful journey back and duly came to my office. There I found a communication from the Czechoslovak Advertising Agency, Rapid, telling me that on my next visit to Prague there would be a sum of money waiting for me to collect, but the condition was that this money had to be spent in Czechoslovakia. This was a reward connected with a Food Fair they had held in Plzen some time earlier; it was, in fact, the only extra reward I ever received in all the years of my association with Czech business.

The situation was that they had sent a delegation to the UK to ask all those companies exporting items to Czechoslovakia to participate in this exhibition. I should mention that an additional part of my responsibilities as Director of Sugosa was to act as buyer of various confectionery lines, some food items and some brands of cigarettes on behalf of the Czechoslovak State Import Organisation for export to Czechoslovakia; so I had good relations with these companies. Instead of coming to me, Rapid decided to be independent and approach these people directly – they came away empty handed.

This delegation visited me a few days before returning to Prague and that was the first I had heard of the matter. I asked them if they would be prepared to leave the problem to me and that I would see what I could do. I did so and succeeded in getting every company to change their minds and participate in the Plzen Food Fair. Rapid was very pleased indeed with this turn of events and although I didn't attend the Food Fair myself, I heard that it was a great success; one of these successes involved Kellogg's Cornflakes, where I suggested that it would be good to introduce this easy form of breakfast and that they should hire a few girls locally to serve cornflakes to the public with some milk and sugar in small, plastic disposable dishes and plastic spoons. They did this and it proved to be very popular – the first proper introduction of cornflakes to the Czech public, I believe. And it was my idea! I am sure it is by now a very substantial business.

Anyway, when I heard about this sum of money I thought that it was a pity to let it go to waste and as I had not succeeded in saying all my goodbyes I decided to make a speedy return to Prague, do what I had to do, spend the money and take part in the golf tournament at Marianske Lazne. I still had holidays due to me and so I took a week, phoned the shipping company who carried our supermarket goods to England and asked them for a passage on one of their vessels for my car and me, which they were pleased to agree to, and so it was arranged. They offered me a passage on a vessel sailing from Felixstowe to Rotterdam and it was a very comfortable trip, for I found they had given me a wonderful cabin with a large bed, fruit in a bowl placed there for me and very nice furnishings. This was obviously a beautiful cabin, which they probably kept for directors of the company. At dinner in the restaurant I was allowed to choose any wine I wished and at the end, when I asked for the bill, I was told that there was no charge. The shipping company in question was aware I was leaving the company, were grateful for the business I had given them over the years and took this method of thanking me. I appreciated this gesture very much indeed.

I made a very rapid journey through Holland and Germany to the Czech border; it was so different to the years before and as I reached that part of Germany just before the Czech border, and as I have mentioned previously, I actually saw Czech cars – that is something I never saw before, because Czech people were not allowed to cross the border until Mr Dubcek allowed them to – it was very nice to see normality for a change. So I often waved to them and they cheerily waved back, probably wondering why that crazy Englishman was waving to them like a madman. The no-man's-land area was still there, but I didn't see armed guards on the conning towers or anything like that and the reception afforded by the Czech customs and immigration people was welcoming and smiling. They did not search my car, asked me no questions about currency and I was through in a jiffy – what a difference to previous visits! But this was the effect of Mr Dubcek's Prague Spring and his 'communism with a human face' policy. The atmosphere had completely changed and you could almost smell not only freedom but also a much lighter atmosphere in the air. Spirits among the people were very high indeed.

I proceeded immediately to Marianske Lazne where the golf tournament was being held and was just in time to enter my name and take part. But unfortunately, I didn't play very well and I was unplaced. Everywhere people were talking about their new freedom and discussing the situation and wondering whether there would be any interference from Moscow. I found the general attitude of Czech people to be quite naïve when I raised the issue of possible Soviet intervention; indeed, some of them became quite cross with me and insisted very strongly that henceforth only Czechoslovak people would decide what goes on in Czechoslovakia. I shook my head and doubted it. Even in Prague I found the same optimistic attitude; they regarded themselves as free now and free they would remain. To visitors the situation was very artificial; to the Czechs it seemed as though heaven itself had arrived and come to them.

I discussed the situation with all my friends but almost nowhere could I find what I would term a realistic opinion of the situation. I said that I could not see Mr Brezhnev and his hard-line cronies accepting these changes and what he called 'this drift towards capitalism', and I am afraid I adopted a pessimistic view, which did not endear me to some of those friends. As I said at the time, the Russian bear has a very large bite.

And so I attended to my last goodbyes and collected the money that Rapid had kindly awarded me; I can't recall how much it was now but it was quite a decent sum. I went shopping for a lot of things, because I was reminded again, and asked for a signed undertaking, that it was a condition of this monetary award that I had to spend it all in Czechoslovakia, i.e. I must not take any out of the country. I left on the Friday to return home – and what a good job I did because during the following Sunday night the Warsaw Pact nations collectively invaded the country, led, of course, mainly by the Soviet Union forces. The tanks rolled in from all sides and everything and almost everybody stopped working. Many people were trapped in the country and Shirley Black-Temple, as she styled herself then, and the famous footballer Stanley Mathews were among them. Had I not left on the Friday I would have been amongst them too – but I must confess that I would not have minded at all being trapped together with Shirley Temple, for as small boys we all loved her very much.

There were no trains and almost no form of transport at all. Russian tanks had bulldozed their way through Ruzyne (Prague) Airport and that was inoperative. To all intents and purposes, Czechoslovakia had totally closed down. Of course, the Czechs and Slovaks protested against this invasion; they threw stones at the tanks and generally showed their anger against the invading forces. The Soviet and other soldiers engaged in the invasion were very surprised at the reaction of the Czech public, for they had been told by their superiors that they would be welcomed with open arms for freeing the people from a fate worse than death. Therefore, they just could not understand why the crowds were so hostile towards them. Meanwhile, from Moscow they broadcast the reasons for the invasion, i.e. that there had been a resurgence of capitalism by the 'criminal' leaders of Czechoslovakia, that the USA was involved in a conspiracy and was behind everything, that caches of guns and armaments had been hidden in the countryside by the conspirators, that it was necessary to free the Czechoslovak people from this threat and to re-impose communism, because that is what the people really wanted. The entire free world regarded such reasons as total nonsense. But although many Czech people thought and believed that the world would come to their rescue, theirs was but a hope in vain. The free world decided to do nothing – much the same as when Hungary was invaded by the Soviets in 1956. I will never forget the tragic speech of the Hungarian Prime Minister, Mr Nagy, when he appealed for the world to come to their rescue and save Hungary back then. I could not understand one single word of what he said but his desperate message came through loud and clear in the tone of his voice. Sadly, the world was not listening. But then who was prepared to risk a nuclear war for the sake of Hungary? Mr Nagy, as I recall, was executed by the Soviets when the Hungarian revolution had been quelled.

Mr Dubcek and some of his colleagues were rounded up and arrested. They were flown to Moscow in handcuffs. There they were forced to agree to cancel all the 'capitalist nonsense' that had been allowed to ferment and with those undertakings, as well as guarantees that the situation in Czechoslovakia would be returned to its original communist basis with all that such guarantees entailed, they were allowed to return to Prague. So the Czechoslovak people had been given a taste of freedom but now it had all been snatched away from them. The country returned to an atmosphere of doom and gloom.

But the Soviets would not leave the matter there and they insisted on many changes at the top; more loyal and sincere Communists had to be put in place. Mr Dubcek was initially sent out of the country as Ambassador to Turkey, but that appointment didn't last more than a few months before he was brought back and banished in disgrace to his little cottage somewhere in the Slovak countryside outside Bratislava, for he was a Slovak. There he languished doing a simple clerical job and nobody heard of him very much until 1989 when finally the Communist yoke was cast off in Czechoslovakia and defeated. He did appear on the Museum balcony scene in 1989 in Prague, but his personal power, and much of his charisma, by that time had gone and although the people cheered and cheered him I do not think he was offered any major part in the new government of the country.

But let us return for a moment to the scene in Czechoslovakia and the aftermath of the invasion. First of all, the kind of spite and suspicion which is a necessary part of communism, and without which it could never survive, returned and reared its ugly head almost everywhere. Virtually every organisation throughout the country was politically examined and anybody who had said or done anything in favour of Mr Dubcek and his activities was kicked out.

No matter who they were or how important or vital their knowledge and experience, out they went. I remember one good friend of mine who worked in an institute concerned with studying cures for various diseases, including cancer, where they were making some good advances. I am not sure how many doctors or scientists worked at this establishment but a high percentage of them were thrown out of their jobs and because they were politically tarnished they were forced to take very ordinary and mundane jobs in order to live. It seems that political revenge was far more important to the Communists than finding a possible cure for cancer and other illnesses. And that kind of thing went on all over the country. Even at Koospol a number of my friends were obliged to leave their jobs. One friend was dismissed – not because of anything he did, but because he did not reject Mr Dubcek and his new theories; and he was a party member! It was madness and carnage mixed together and nobody cared two hoots for the obvious damage that was being done to the country. It was back to Communism, and maybe even worse than it was before, because now nothing was allowed to stand in the way of true idealistic Communist principles. The poor Czechoslovak people had to wait from 1968 to 1989, some twenty-one years, before they gained the freedom they had tasted for a brief period and so badly yearned for now.

At this point I would like to come back to my 'spy' friends Major Macek and Captain Vokac. As I explained in an earlier chapter, Captain Vokac replaced the Major and the usual contact was made when Captain Vokac phoned me to say that the Major had returned to Prague to con-tinue his duties there, that he didn't have the time to say all his goodbyes but he had left a bottle for me etc, etc. Well, I liked John Vokac and I welcomed the opportunity to meet him again. He too was a keen golfer and wanted to improve his abilities in that respect and so we played some games together.

This was during the Prague Spring when everything was appearing to be going so well. I got to know John quite closely and never once did I ever feel that he was exploiting my friendship with him to further any underhand work.

Suddenly, the situation completely changed, and shortly after the invasion of Czechoslovakia by the Warsaw Pact nations took place John was called back to Prague virtually at once, or as soon as the situation had calmed down somewhat. When he got to Prague he had to appear before a committee who asked him a lot of questions, especially about his attitude towards Mr Dubcek and his activities. They accused him of being a sympathiser, of being involved in this or that – all trumped-up charges in the typical Communist way. Poor John was dismissed from the army and forced to work as a common labourer for five years in order to 'cleanse himself'. Mostly he worked in the construction of the Prague underground rail service.

How did this come about? Well, it appears his former colleague, Major Macek, informed against him – a common occurrence and a useful tool to those who wished to remove anybody from their position. We know what happened to John, for I have related that story, but what happened to the Major? Well, for his excellent support of the Communist cause, and for informing against his colleagues, he was given the plum job as Military Attaché in Washington as a reward, and no doubt he was very pleased at this turn of events. But he had not been there very long when one day he stepped into the street, was knocked down by a car and killed. And so ended Major Macek. Would it be apt, I wonder, to describe this occurrence as 'just desserts'?

Another story of the aftermath of the invasion I have to tell. This concerned my hunting pal in Marianske Lazne, Slavek Svinger. Some days after the invasion, Slavek was in his office near to the forest when a Russian officer came in and demanded to know where the electric plug was. Slavek asked him why he wanted to know this. The officer replied that he wished to shave with his electric shaver. Slavek promptly showed him the door and told him to go and shave in Moscow. Well, the Russian officer reported the incident and Slavek was called before the usual committee.

He was questioned and told that his attitude was not satisfactory. He was barred from going to the forest; he lost his position, of course, and was made to work in a sawmill as a labourer for a year – this they did to an intelligent man who had a degree in forestry. But that was not all; Slavek had two daughters, Diana (after the goddess of hunting) and Inge. The two girls studied, of course, and reached the point where they could apply to go to university. They applied, but both were refused because of their father's earlier sins. Fortunately, Slavek was a resilient man and when his one year of labour ended he obtained a good position in an agricultural concern and after that began his own business, when it was allowed after 1989, importing used agricultural machinery from Germany.

I do not think this chapter would be quite complete without also mentioning Joseph Frolik, who came to the UK in the 1965 period as either Second or maybe Third Secretary. His appointed task was to liaise with the British Trade Unions. But at some point following his arrival he was 'turned' by British Intelligence, who managed to gain a great deal of valuable information from him, including the fact that no less than two British Members of Parliament were in the pay of the Czechoslovak Secret Service!

Now, I was very often at the Czechoslovak Embassy in those years right up to the latter part of 1968 when I resigned my position. I attended all the commercial Embassy receptions and met a large number of people there, as one does at these functions. So I knew almost all those people who worked at the Embassy and I must have known Frolik, if only by sight, or possibly I may have had the odd chat with him. Of course, I would have had no idea that he was working for British Intelligence.

Frolik gave much very useful information to the British, who, when they thought they had extracted everything of interest from him, then turned him over to the CIA, who proceeded to question him further and obtain information useful to them. But Frolik was recalled to Prague together with his family and at some point thereafter he must have felt that things were developing unfavourably for him – he was under suspicion. Eventually, when he noticed certain happenings in the background he came to the view that matters were getting too hot, and so he arranged to take a holiday in Bulgaria for himself and his family – informing the CIA of his intentions. This was quite OK and permitted because travel to and within any communist country was deemed acceptable. This gave an opportunity, therefore, that should not be missed and so the proposal of the CIA was to organise a speedboat to be sent from a Turkish coastal point to collect him and his family, virtually from the beach, and thus they were whisked away to freedom. He eventually ended up in the USA and it was there he eventually died.

But he wrote a book which he called *The Frolik Defection* and in that he certainly spilled the beans. He revealed a great deal, including the fact that the very man whom I regarded as being the caretaker at the Embassy (Commercial Section) and who helped me many times load my cases of beer into the boot of my car was the top KGB man in the building! All the intelligence people working for the various communist countries worked very closely together, especially with the KGB, and held positions in more than one intelligence organisation.

Frolik also told the story of a certain Minister of Trade, who previously was involved in food imports and exports. This gentleman said he had won a new car in a bet with a German buyer. Frolik states that no such bet took place – the car was nothing less than a bribe. Well, I actually travelled in that very car when the gentleman in question accompanied us on a visit to the former well-known factory of Lidka, situated in a town called Kutna Hora, which lies about 40 km to the east of Prague.

The months that followed my resignation were not easy for me. I had a number of possibilities that I could explore but my real ambition was to establish and run my own company. However, having been poorly paid considering the degree of responsibilities that my position as Director of Sugosa imposed upon me, and having a family to bring up and a mortgage to pay, I had never really had any opportunity to accumulate very much capital. Therefore, at that point it was not a time to be thinking of starting my own business. I decided to talk, wait and see what turned up over the coming weeks or months. I was sure that when the news got around that I had resigned my position with the Czechs I would receive some offers.

And then my good friend Alex Kraus told me that he had spoken to Dennis Patman, the MD of the Confectionery Buying Trust, Britain's largest wholesale confectionery buying group, about me and my situation with the Czechs and that Dennis would be interested to speak with me. I knew Dennis and had supplied his company with Czechoslovak confectionery products some years ago when I was with the former agent, Harold Frost, and I had found him to be a nice chap, quiet and inoffensive, someone I thought I could work with.

But the main attraction to me was the fact that if I were to be offered a position with Dennis Patman and the Buying Trust this would bring me into direct contact with the very leaders of the British confectionery industry. I would hope to make new friends and contacts in a different world to the one I knew as Director of Sugosa and this could only help me when I would be in a position to start my own business. But one or two other possibilities seemed to be developing and so I decided to think it over. Without doubt it seemed to be the best opportunity so far.

When I think back I feel that maybe I rejected the best opportunity of all, for although I never actually received a firm offer from him, one of my earlier customers threw out enough hints for me not to misunderstand him. His name was Eric W. Barker and he ran a firm which supplied imported confectionery items direct to retail shops. But he also had another business, which he ran simultaneously and which specialised in building commercial warehousing.

This building business was far more profitable to him than confectionery, but he had a soft spot for trading in confectionery for some reason. Eric Barker was Jewish and came from a well-established family in Prague which, before Communism, owned a big department store there. Eric himself left Czechoslovakia when Hitler began to make unpleasant noises against Jewish people, thank goodness, because I believe that the whole of his family he left behind perished in the gas chambers. I believe that when he went from Prague he managed to get a good proportion of the family wealth out of the country. This gave him the opportunity to become involved in business in the UK. Eric was a man of taste, whether in clothing, food, wine, cars or restaurants. He invited me to lunch with him on a number of occasions and it was he who introduced me to lunches at The Savoy hotel. He and his wife also invited Lynne and myself out on at least one evening and if I remember correctly it was to The Caprice. Eric knew all the best places to go to.

I got on very well with Eric Barker and I think he liked me too. I am almost certain that if I had asked him if he had a spot for me in his organisation he would have found one and welcomed me into the fold. He and his wife had no children and as far as I could gather neither of them had relations in the UK.

Eric died in the 1970s; he wasn't all that old and I am not sure then what the situation would have been or how it might have developed, but I believe I would have benefited in some way from his commercial holdings. But that is pure conjecture on my part. I had to look at things objectively and so eventually I decided that joining Dennis Patman and the Buying Trust would be my best bet as far as the development of my future plans was concerned.

So I duly made an appointment with Dennis and we reached an agreement. I left it at that for the moment because I first of all had to honour my obligations to Sugosa and, from Dennis's point of view, it did not matter when I joined him, as there was no great urgency. And so I had the choice to take up my new position at the CBT anytime after March; but I stayed at my post with Sugosa until August to carry out my responsibilities and obligations, as I had promised.

However, something happened at Sugosa in the meantime that deeply disturbed me and, I thought, might threaten my future plans. Later on I pondered again over these thoughts and now realise that I was panicking a little and over-exaggerating any relevance this matter had to me. The arrangements for the signing of cheques at Sugosa was that I would sign them first, because I was the only person who really knew on a day-to-day basis what was going on in the office in virtually every detail and whether any cheque was bona fide and justified or not. Our bookkeeper would then take the cheques to be countersigned by one of the two Czech directors, who were now housed in the office next to ours. This arrangement was made possible by me when I got to hear from the housekeeper that this additional office space would shortly become vacant. I asked him to reserve this office space for our associate company, Pilsner Beer Co. Ltd, and he did.

But I had previously warned both the Czech directors that if they signed any cheques that did not bear my signature first, I could accept no responsibility whatsoever for them. This was not grandeur on my part, it was simply that I was the only director who knew and was familiar with everyday expenses and I kept my eyes very sharply on such matters. I would never sign any cheque unless I knew why it was being drawn, and many times I had to order the bookkeeper not to just thrust a cheque under my nose for signature but to provide some information that would tell me that the cheque was fully justified. However, as I had resigned as from January 1st and was just hanging on for the completion of the supermarket programme, a kind of artificial situation existed in the office in the interim period. Everybody knew I would be going soon and so my normal authority was undermined somewhat.

Therefore, the bookkeeper, unknown to me, began to bypass me and go straight to one or other of the Czech directors and they, it seemed, were willing to sign anything the bookkeeper put before them without knowing if such cheques were alright and justified or not. How could they know? They had no day-to-day contact with office details within Sugosa. I had no knowledge that this was happening, because cunningly the bookkeeper did bring me bona fide cheques from time to time for signature which were perfectly alright and justified. But he didn't come to me for petty cash cheque signatures; it appears the bookkeeper was going to one Czech director and then the other and getting them to sign cheques for more and more petty cash. If he had come to me I would have known immediately that it amounted to far too much money and I would have questioned why so much petty cash was needed. The bookkeeper was well aware of this and obviously this is the reason he cunningly avoided me in this respect.

One day, as I learned only later, the bookkeeper was in the process of taking a blank cheque in to the office of the Czech directors to be signed when he bumped into one of them in the passage and asked for a signature. The director was taken aback somewhat and, thank goodness, said he could not sign it unless an amount was filled in; the bookkeeper returned to his office, filled in an amount but left everything else blank, and the director then signed it.

The bookkeeper went on holiday shortly after and one day the director who had signed the cheque came to me and asked if he could see the cash book for some reason or other. The company books were kept in a metal cabinet in the bookkeeper's office so we went there, but it could not be found. The director was quite disturbed as he remembered the blank cheque incident, which he then told me about, and so we both began to be rather worried. Closer examination later on showed that the bookkeeper had committed fraud, as he had purposely left a small space before the number of pounds in which he placed a three or a four, I cannot remember now which, and then completed the cheque by making it out to himself. It was a most stupid way to effect a dishonest transaction and its discovery before long would have been guaranteed.

But it just goes to show how untrustworthy people are caught, because if the cash book had been found when we first searched for it then the situation might not have been so immediately apparent. Neither would it have been deemed necessary to carry out the detailed examination that followed. As a matter of fact, that cash book was there all the time – it had slipped behind some other books and lay hidden behind them!

But it was indeed a very serious situation and I thought it might have reflected badly on me as the director in charge, at least in name, despite the fact I had resigned and despite the fact that I was completely blameless in the matter. Nevertheless, I was desperate to find a solution to this problem even if it was in no way my fault but the fault of the Czech directors who gave their signatures so willingly. I certainly did not want to leave Sugosa with any kind of a cloud over the office situation and especially one which concerned money.

My first objective was to find out where this bookkeeper had gone for his holiday and by a search of his desk I discovered a clue that he had quite possibly gone to Corfu. But where in Corfu? I looked in the phone book he used to record useful phone numbers and there I saw the name of a forwarding agent that we had used some little while ago but who also did travel agent's work. It was a long shot but I phoned these people who, although admitting that our bookkeeper had indeed made travel arrangements through them, were understandably reluctant to discuss another person's travel arrangements with me. However, I emphasised in no uncertain terms that it was imperative that I made personal contact with this bookkeeper and I eventually succeeded and they gave me the whole chapter and verse. I knew precisely where he was – now the task was to contact him. I phoned the holiday centre in Corfu and tried to speak with the man directly, but telephones were not fitted in the chalets so that was not possible. But one of the staff on reception, who was very helpful when I told him it was a very urgent matter, gave me the number of the bar which he apparently frequented each evening. I phoned the bar; he wasn't there. I left a message for him that he should urgently phone me either in my office or at my home, no matter what time.

To my surprise he did phone me – at home. I told him very shortly and sharply that everything had been discovered, we knew the whole picture and that he must return to London immediately so that we could sort this mess out. I said to him that I would try to help him if I could but he must return at once. At first he tried to bluster his way out of the problem, assuring me that all was OK and he could explain everything. At this point I lost my temper somewhat, shouted at him and told him not to be such a bloody fool, because he would make the situation even worse than it was, and that unless he returned to London at once I would wash my hands of the affair, let the police deal with it and not give him any help at all.

Fortunately, he took me at my word, promised to find out what flights were available and phoned me at the office the next morning to give me a flight arrival time at Heathrow for the following day. I was there waiting for him. He came out of the arrivals exit looking anxiously from left to right, for I think he suspected that the police would be waiting for him, and then he saw me. I took him to a lounge nearby where we sat down and I asked him where the petty cash book was, for that was missing, and which would hopefully tell us the final story.

He told me that it was at his parents' home, so I quickly told him that is where we must go. At first he refused because I think he wanted to avoid the shame of the matter being revealed in front of his parents. But I was not prepared to accept his refusal and insisted strongly, because that was the only way we could determine how much money had been stolen by him. And so we proceeded to his parents' home; I think he must have been in touch with his parents by phone beforehand because they did not seem to be surprised to see us.

I had the unpleasant task of explaining to the parents what the situation was and I repeated that if I could help him in any way I would endeavour to do so. They were embarrassed and quite ashamed of their son but left us to examine the petty cash book, which, plus the cheque that had been fraudulently altered, showed that the total value of the stolen money was something just over £2,500. In 1968 that was quite a lot of money.

So I had to think quickly to try and find a way out of this mess. It seemed to me that I needed to place the chap in a position to plead for help from his parents and his friends in the hope that the money might be refunded and that we could close the book on the matter. That was all I wanted to happen, then I would be able to leave the company in a good atmosphere. I was at my wits' end and unsure what to do. I consulted one or two friends, but I think the situation was just as puzzling to them as it was to me.

Obviously, it was necessary to start the ball rolling and I had £500 I had reserved to take my family somewhere on a short holiday before I started my new position at the CBT. Again I consulted one or two friends because my mind was in a complete turmoil and I was totally unsure if I should sacrifice my family's holiday money in this way. My friends were not, of course, able to help – that was a decision I had to make for myself. Together with Lynne we decided that the immediate future and reputation of the family's breadwinner was the most important subject at the moment. Therefore, I said to this bookkeeper, with the parents present in the room, that he needed a few friends willing to help him and that I would be the first by offering to lend him £500 on the condition that the balance of the money would be made up by other friends or family or both. The parents asked me if I could give them a little time to think the matter over and I had to agree to that request. Back in the office I informed the Financial Director of what I had done and he was pleased, because nobody was looking forward to a police investigation.

A few days later the father of our ex-bookkeeper phoned me to make an appointment and he came to my office to inform me that he appreciated very much my gesture and that he and his wife had decided to put up the balance themselves. This was eventually done and so we were able to put that problem to bed. But the father told me that his son was a perpetual liar, that all the stories he had told us in the office were not at all true, that he had in fact stolen before and had even previously served time in prison for a very similar criminal offence. He had, apparently, stolen from his previous employers.

He came to us with impeccable references, which may well have been forged, but I had no hand in employing him. The interviews for the vacancy for bookkeeper at Sugosa were carried out by the outgoing book-keeper, whom we were transferring to Eagle Confectionery Distributors Ltd, a new company started by Eagle Bros Ltd, to separate the confectionery business from their other business and our company accountant. I felt that was necessary, as in any case I was leaving the company and neither was I an expert on bookkeeping. I asked afterwards whether anyone had checked his references, but it seemed as though they were taken at face value and not followed up.

And so the Financial Director and I arranged to meet the bookkeeper and in his presence I handed over my £500 – money that I had intended to use to take my family on holiday before starting my new job. I wanted to have a witness that I had done so. The bookkeeper immediately handed the money to the director. A cheque for the balance was duly received from the parents and with that the whole sorry affair was brought to a close.

The bookkeeper thanked me very much and promised that he would repay the money to me and to his parents. I remember he said this in front of his parents and his father said very firmly that Mr Mitchell must be repaid first of all. As a matter of fact, I did receive a cheque from the bookkeeper a couple of months or so later for about £137, the proceeds of an insurance policy he had cashed in. His parents had insisted that money should go to me. But I never received anything after that, so I was £363 out of pocket at the end. So much for all his assurances that he would repay me. And yet he seemed so sincere in making such promises. I suppose that was just another feature of a good liar, for he was also a good actor. Needless to say, my family did not have their holiday.

But even so, I was very glad indeed to have cleared this matter up and now the time for my final departure from the office drew nigh. The day before my final day at the office the two Czech directors came to my office to say goodbye. To be frank, I did expect that as I had started this company from nothing and built it up by pure hard work over the years I would receive some financial award, even if it were only what I would normally expect as an annual bonus. I had thought that in recognition of the fact that I had stayed on to see the completion of practically all the supermarket sales programme I would have at least come away from that office with a bonus cheque. But my hopes were almost totally misplaced because the two Czech directors came to my office and presented me with a box in which there was a plated coffee pot, a tea pot, a milk jug and a sugar bowl. All those years and all that hard work and, yes, all that achievement for that? It is not that I was ungrateful but I was bitterly disappointed to say the very least. I think I was being naïve in expecting any financial reward in recognition of my years of service and what I had managed to achieve under very difficult conditions. Now I was sincerely beginning to wish I hadn't parted with that £500! To be sure, if I had known in advance about my 'end of service' treatment then I would not have dreamed of parting with my money. And may I say that if I hadn't taken an active part in solving this problem then both of the directors would have had a lot of explaining to do in Prague and I wonder what the consequences might have been. Evidently, they did not see it that way, but sometimes I do wonder what might have happened if I had not taken the decisive action I did.

And so the day came for my departure and as I left my office for the last time I reflected what a grand ride it had been over the past years. I had a last drink with my staff and left the office in a very sad mood. But as I drove home to Old Coulsdon I also thought a lot about the future, and when I thought about that I brightened up considerably. The future! I wondered what that would hold for me and whether I would succeed in beginning my own business somehow, sometime. Well, it would be up to me to make that dream come true and from that point of view the future could not come quickly enough for me.

5

1968-1972 - MY NEW POSITION AT THE CONFECTIONERY BUYING TRUST LTD

As explained earlier, I had decided to join Dennis Patman, who was Managing Director of the Confectionery Buying Trust and whose offices were in Albemarle Street, off Piccadilly. It was quite a change for me to work in the West End of London as opposed to the City; it was also a big change to go from being in complete charge to working and being told what to do, just like any other employee, except that I was recognised as being of managerial status. For example, I was given a key to the directors' toilet – what an honour! I believe I mentioned previously that I had known Dennis Patman from earlier days when the CBT used to import goods and were buyers of Czechoslovak confectionery products in the days when Harold Frost was the UK Czechoslovak agent (see Volume One). Therefore, I saw Dennis from time to time and visited him in his office, which in those days was in Bayswater.

The CBT was an organisation of wholesale confectioners which was formed some years ago in order to explore better buying terms with British manufacturers as a bloc, but also to negotiate and organise promotional activity on a national basis. Some 350 wholesalers, small, medium and large, belonged to the CBT and it functioned by negotiating a commission with the manufacturing members on all purchases by group wholesale members. Head Office retained these commissions and then shared them out amongst members at the end of each year according to each individual member's purchases, but after the deduction of Head Office expenses, of course.

Member wholesalers still placed their orders direct with manufacturers, and after delivery an invoice for such goods was rendered to HO, and then HO would debit the total amount bought each month by the member who, in turn, would settle with HO and thus the manufacturer's bills were settled. But it was recognised that the large and medium firms were entitled to somewhat better terms, for as individual wholesalers they would have the punch in many instances to negotiate their own buying advantages with manufacturers if they were acting as individuals and did not belong to a buying group. And so, in all fairness, members were divided into two classes, i.e. the medium and larger members were segregated into a group called Confex and the smaller members were concentrated into another group called Planit.

As one can imagine, quite a number of staff were required to administrate this complex and very large business. The whole country was divided into twelve areas and each area was led by one wholesaler, who was appointed to the Board of Directors in London. The rules stated that each area must hold a local meeting at least four times per annum and any member missing more than two consecutive meetings had to render an explanation in writing to the Board of Directors; failure to do that might result in expulsion and, therefore, omission from the annual share-out. The Main Board, therefore, comprised the twelve area directors plus Dennis Patman, and they met in London as and when necessary, but usually once per month.

It is clear that Dennis Patman could not properly and efficiently run and administrate such a business on his own and that was why he was seeking someone to join and assist him, hence my appointment to the group. My task as Sales Development Manager was to (1) encourage new suppliers to apply to be listed as a recommended manufacturer and negotiate terms with them etc. for submission to the Board of Directors for their approval; (2) attend as many area meetings as possible as HO representative; (3) negotiate beneficial national promotions with all supplier members and urge wholesaler members to participate to the fullest extent; and (4) begin and set up an import department for the company. In respect of (4), Dennis Patman was always very conscious of an undercurrent of discontent among members concerning the cost of running Head Office and the expensive offices off Piccadilly, plus large administrative staff numbers, plus entertainment expenses (most manufacturers coming to HO for any reason were entertained to lunch etc.), and there were members who voiced such discontent at meetings. So Dennis thought it would be a good idea to encourage and develop other forms of earnings by HO and we shall see later how his efforts in this respect led to disaster.

Although my motive for joining the CBT was ulterior, in the sense that I had no intention of staying ad infinitum, I nevertheless threw myself into my new duties with gusto. I went to many area meetings and revelled in meeting with members as well as manufacturers whom I, or the local Chairman, had invited to address the meeting. I am a reasonably friendly person and so it did not take long for me to begin making a number of new friends and contacts which would eventually be invaluable to me in my quest to start my own business. I also approached other manufacturers who although they were supplying our members independently, were not supplier members to the group. I invited them to HO, endeavoured to point out the advantages of being an official supplier to the group, explained how we worked and tried to extract from them an offer of terms which I considered to be satisfactory. These I discussed firstly with Dennis and if he approved I then presented the offer to the next Board Meeting for their approval. Finally, I sent out letters to many European manufacturers informing them of the formation of our new import section, which was named Intro, and I invited them to submit samples etc. These four duties kept me more than busy and I was here, there and everywhere until Dennis himself told me that whilst he liked people who worked hard I should not try to do so much as I may make myself ill. I was touched by his concern – at least in those early days he showed he had a heart. But I only ever knew one way to work and that was hard. I had a fierce, burning feeling inside that drove me on and on until I succeeded in what I had set out to do. Maybe it was pride, or maybe it had something to do with coming from my background and having a point to prove. I only know that I feared failure and defeat; I felt it personally and so always did my very best to avoid it.

I will not dwell too long on the affairs of the CBT and the less than four years I spent with them except to mention that I was appointed to the Main Board of Directors in 1970 – I had been with the company less than two years – and, furthermore, to explain how the CBT met its doom, because I believe most people will find it interesting. In fact, what happened to the CBT should be used as an object lesson in commercial studies, for it shows what can occur when one man has dictatorial control over a company. Dictatorship in any form is bad.

But I feel it is also important to mention that during the time I spent with the CBT, and no doubt partly because of the extent to which we were becoming known in Europe as a result of our new import activities, we were contacted by Interchoc, an international organisation formed from various wholesale confectionery groups from various European countries. They invited us to put forward two nominations for membership of this international and prestigious organisation. Of course, Dennis was immensely proud to be asked and he invited me to be the second nomination for the UK. This was because I was experienced in continental ways and also because I controlled the import section of our business, Intro. I have to admit that I too was proud to accept this additional duty and quite willing to do so because I knew it could only stand me in good stead for my eventual plans. This meant new European contacts and perhaps new friendships in other countries, and this again could do my future intentions no harm at all – on the contrary, it could, and did, do me a power of good.

Like the CBT in the UK, meetings of Interchoc were held several times a year and always in a different country. Thus we would meet in Aarhus, Denmark on one occasion and the next meeting might be in Munich and the next in Brussels, and so on.

I must say I liked this connection very much and I recall one occasion when Dennis Patman came into my office. He had, apparently, heard from Interchoc referring to an exhibition called IKOFA, which was to be held in Munich imminently. In the same period, they informed us, there would be a meeting of a group of German confectionery wholesalers, also in Munich, and we were invited to both observe the exhibition and to attend this meeting as a means of gaining experience of the group. Dennis didn't fancy the task himself and so he asked me to go. Of course, I was most enthusiastic and very quickly asked my secretary to rearrange my programme accordingly.

So off I went to Munich, but in true fashion Dennis had delayed informing me about IKOFA until the last minute and so I had no time even to arrange hotel accommodation. I believe I tried but our travel agents said there was a difficulty for some reason or another; however, they said that when I arrived at Munich Airport I should go straight to one of the several agents there or the Tourist Centre, which would certainly be glad to help me find accommodation, and they were sure that something would be found. On arrival I did just that, but when I enquired about accommodation they simply burst into laughter. They asked if I knew what was happening in Munich just then and didn't I know that the Munich Beer Festival was going on? They said that I would be very fortunate to find a spare bench in the public park, let alone a room at a hotel! With this alarming news I decided to make my way to the exhibition, meet some of the people from Interchoc and throw myself on their mercy, and that is precisely what I did.

I managed to get a taxi to the exhibition hall and went directly to the Interchoc stand. They gave me a splendid welcome, but as for obtaining any form of accommodation for me, all their efforts were in vain. They phoned and phoned everywhere, even well outside Munich, as much as 20–30 km, but completely without success. I had never realised before the enormous attraction of this beer festival, which brings hundreds of thousands of visitors to the city every October and they take over virtually all available accommodation. So what was I to do? Things were getting a little desperate now – until a young couple came to the Interchoc stand. I am not sure what they had to do with Interchoc; perhaps they were friends of friends, for he was still a late student and his partner was a dentist. They heard of my plight and they too made a few phone calls on my behalf, but once more without result. Then they spoke with each other and said that if I wished I could stay with them at their flat. I was, of course, most grateful and eagerly accepted their invitation, because by then I just did not know exactly what to do for the best. At least I would have somewhere to lay my weary head that night. I didn't realise that they had only a very small flat with no extra bedroom and that I would be obliged to sleep in the same room as they did! Had I known that I think I would have preferred the park bench – that is if I could have found a vacant one. By the time we reached their flat it was already too late to back out, but it wasn't as bad as I thought it might be.

I inspected the exhibition quite thoroughly and then, the following day, it was the occasion of the meeting of the German Wholesale Federation. To my pleasure the young man I was staying with offered to come along and translate for me. When we arrived, the quite large room was packed. But they found us two places at which to sit and so we listened to various speeches being made; my new found friend did indeed translate for me and it was clear that they were talking about more or less the same problems that we talked about at our meetings back home. However, I looked around me and if you had asked me to paint a picture of one of Hitler's Nazi meetings in the beer cellars of Munich I would have painted it just like that! Germans certainly appear to like meetings and speeches and each speaker was applauded loudly.

Towards the end the Chairman of the meeting spoke and looked in my direction, as did most of the many people in that large room. My friend then informed me that I was being invited to address the members. Me? Address the members? I swallowed hard and tried to think quickly.

How was I going to get out of this predicament? What on earth would I say? I didn't know enough yet to talk knowledgably about group activities to people who knew ten times more than I did. And so I asked my friend to respond by saying that whilst I appreciated very much the honour of being asked to address the meeting, I was there only as an observer and that I hoped to come back at some future date when I would be much more aware of group activities, and especially international group activities, and further, that I hoped the invitation might be repeated. I think that was about the best thing to say in the circumstances because I had been completely unprepared for such a turn of events.

As I have explained, the European delegates met quite frequently and when, in the course of time, it was decided that the next meeting was to be in London, Dennis put me in complete charge of all arrangements. Therefore, it was my task to organise everything connected with the visit of our European colleagues, i.e. hotel rooms for all attending members, arranging all lunches and dinners, deciding on the menus and which wines were to be served, plus organising a mini exhibition where I invited British manufacturers to exhibit their wares before these European wholesale buyers, terminating in a farewell banquet at which the British manufacturers sat down to dine with the European members of Interchoc. Taking everything into account, and I hope this does not sound like boasting, I worked very hard and the whole affair went down extremely well. I was proud of the job I had done even though it was an additional task to my many other duties. Other people had remarked on how well everything had been planned – but from Dennis, not a word.

At this point I must make a few remarks about Dennis Patman. When I knew him previously I regarded him as a nice, inoffensive and polite individual with whom it was a pleasure to do business. At that time he was just the Secretary of the CBT and the Board of Directors more or less told him what to do. But it was a failing organisation because interest in it by its members was falling. As a result of this deteriorating situation there was an upheaval which resulted in Dennis Patman becoming the Managing Director of the company, but in a totally revised form. It is possible that his new position of power went to his head somewhat because there is no doubt about it, in the process he had become a Jekyll and Hyde type of character. Nice one minute, not at all nice the next. Indeed, he was without doubt a very unpredictable man. It took me but a short time to realise this and to know that in his dark moods he was going to be a somewhat difficult man to work with on a continuous happy note. However, this did not worry me unduly because my intentions of joining the CBT were not long term

– just long enough to develop new contacts and, hopefully, make some friends in the British confectionery world. But meanwhile I carried out my duties and responsibilities to the best of my ability. In my long travels through life I now know there are a lot of people like Dennis Patman. To others they give an air of niceness, of politeness and consideration etc, but when you got to know them more intimately, i.e. after working side by side with them, you discovered their dark side, of which you previously had absolutely no idea.

The very nature of the CBT made it an organisation that could never go wrong – that is unless its financial structure and the risk element changed in any way. Head Office administrated the accounts with all members and manufacturers, received their cut, paid for running expenses and shared out the remainder amongst the members. What could go wrong with an organisation built on those principles? And yet it did and I shall explain why; it is an exercise on how not to run a business.

The beginning of the end started when one day the Managing Director of one of our manufacturers in the Midlands, a man called Leslie Oakes, called in to see Dennis Patman and have a chat with him. It appeared that the company in question, Parkes Classic Confectionery Ltd up near Birmingham, had got itself into some financial difficulties and Mr Oakes' meeting with Dennis was to discuss if there was any way the group could help him in his present predicament. Dennis sent him away without making any promises but the discussion set his mind ticking.

I have already described how Dennis Patman felt that the criticism by members of Head Office expenses was a personal issue and that he looked for ways to earn more money independently by HO activities to defray expenses – hence my having to start an import section, for example. What he would have loved to do would be to totally cover HO expenses by other activities, thus no member could then justifiably complain that HO was costing members too much and reducing their annual bonuses. In this instance Dennis came to a view that if the CBT could take over Parkes Classic Confectionery and make it work efficiently and profitably, this could earn Head Office an income which could only help him with his policies re extra activities and the covering of HO expenses from additional and external sources.

At first, Dennis kept his ideas strictly to himself with the exception of the Chairman of the CBT, David Jack, a wholesaler and cash and carry owner and a nice gentleman from Scotland. He didn't even share his thoughts about the matter with me or anyone else in the office. But of course, he couldn't do anything or take any action without letting other directors know and so he called a special meeting in London and requested that all directors be present. And now, before this meeting, he told me about his plans and it was clear that he thought that through the purchasing strength of the CBT it should be possible to turn Parkes around and make it into a profitable concern. I am bound to say that in my opinion too that should have been possible, but only if the whole affair had been dealt with differently and correctly.

At the next Board meeting Dennis outlined his plans and tried to build up enthusiasm among those present. He succeeded, with one or two exceptions, and these directors wanted to know much more about the proposition and the true state of Parkes before the company's money could be committed. There were many meetings and trips up to Parkes and then even more meetings. A confectionery manufacturing expert was brought in to give his view on existing machinery and potential production possibilities and eventually Dennis succeeded to get the Board fully on his side, but I think a little bit of bullying went on in order to achieve this. However, no director ever queried the most important factor, which was that to estimate the factory's production possibilities was one thing, but to sell it successfully and in sufficient quantities was quite another. They seemed to take that for granted. Furthermore, very little was done to fully inform members of what was going on; to have had their full support in the project could have made all the difference. This was, perhaps, the first error, but one can understand that for a time it was necessary to keep the matter behind closed doors. Anyway, to cut a long story short, the financial situation of Parkes having been supposedly fully examined by our accountants and a report having been rendered to each CBT director, the proposal was agreed between the whole board and an offer was therefore made to the Parkes Board of Directors, which they eagerly accepted – therewith the next error was made.

My own business instincts told me that if you are going to take over another company it is far better to freeze the situation at the point of takeover and, if necessary, form a new company, with the new company's financial responsibilities taking effect only from that point. I think this is a normal commercial precaution to take, if the sellers agree, because just to take over a business without being sure that every single obligation had been revealed places the buyer in a very risky situation. If the seller disagrees then one could have reasonable grounds for suspecting that perhaps everything had not been revealed. That is a matter of commonsense to any businessman and there is the rub – Dennis Patman was probably an excellent company secretary but he was no businessman and he didn't think like a businessman. Therefore, he tended to gloss over potential problems as if they were of no importance. Of course, I endeavoured in talking to Dennis to give him my thoughts and the benefit of my experience, but he was having none of it and dismissed what I was trying to say abruptly – it seemed as though every remark made when examining options he took as a personal affront, especially when such views did not accord with his own. I could smell danger here and when I felt that I might be overstepping the mark somewhat I gave up trying to convince or persuade him. As I have mentioned previously, I wanted to leave the company at a time of my choosing, not Dennis Patman's. And so having tried to put my point of view forward and failed, I kept my views quiet. I was not ready yet to form my own business. I estimated that at least another year was needed before I had made sufficient friends and contacts, but they were building all the time.

But by now the Parkes' project was out in the open; Dennis discussed it frequently and during one such conversation, when speaking about filling positions at Parkes, he seemed to be hinting frequently that he had me in mind to take over as Sales Director. This placed me in a predicament because I held firmly to the point of view that whoever took such a position would have to move up to the Midlands lock, stock and barrel, and furthermore, to be resident within a short distance from the factory and offices of Parkes because the job in hand would be a twenty-four hour a day task for someone. The sales problems were, in my view, very formidable and yet so vital to overcome if the operation were to succeed. Somebody was going to have to work long and hard to knock the Parkes' sales force into shape. And so I nipped that idea in the bud quite smartly because there was no way I would be prepared to move from Old Coulsdon in Surrey, where I was then living, especially bearing in mind my plans to start my own business. Therefore, I told Dennis of my opinion and said that for a number of reasons it would be out of the question for me to move, and apart from the matter of our children's education etc, I told him – and this was quite true – that we had bought a ladies' hairdressing business which needed constant and close attention by my dear wife Lynne and my daughter Jackie. Dennis did not react to this in any special way, although I could tell he was somewhat miffed, and the matter was left there. Somehow I think that any bond that may have existed between Dennis and me was broken then, for our relationship was never the same afterwards. I could understand his disappointment with me but there was no way

I could tell him the real reasons why I could not cooperate with him in the way it appeared he wanted me to.

But when he had finally made his decisions about who exactly was going to fit which positions he chose himself as Chairman, the confectionery expert as Managing Director, Harry Fallon, the CBT Marketing Director, as Sales Director, and myself as Export Director. However, apart from the MD, whose situation would be solely that, it meant that the other important Parkes' posts, the most important of which was Sales Director, would have to be held in addition to our normal responsibilities as CBT directors. In other words, we were part-time Parkes' employees only, and incidentally, for this extra work none of us received a single extra penny piece. These additional duties had been piled onto us; in my case that meant five separate types of duty, and it was quite clear to me that it was going to be impossible to carry out dual roles efficiently – either our CBT work or our Parkes work was going to suffer in the end. That, in my view, was the second major mistake and helped to make the recovery of Parkes a virtual impossibility.

The appointment of the confectionery expert was something of a disaster. He may have been quite proficient in gauging machinery and outputs but it takes far more than that to be an efficient MD who really had got to be a Jack-of-all-trades. But this gentleman, apparently, was not. However, Dennis liked to have people around him who agreed with his every whim and fancy and the new MD was certainly one such person. During that period we all spent hours motoring up to the Midlands for meeting after meeting, arriving back home on every occasion very late at night. These meetings produced a lot of waffle and a lot of brave words, but nothing of substance and certainly nothing that would cure the ills of Parkes Classic Confectionery Ltd. It had to be recognised, and as a matter of dire urgency, that the major part of Parkes' problems might be solved if only sales could be properly organized and substantially improved. Fallon had that responsibility and whilst he was quite good at organising sales gimmicks and promotional activities, some of which worked and some didn't, I do not think he was a good choice for the position of Sales Director. The results, which continued to be very disappointing, spoke for themselves. We were creating no improvement and that should have rung the alarm bells.

One might well have thought that the first point Fallon had to examine was the depth and efficiency of his sales force and ascertain where the main weaknesses lay. In this it surely needed much investment in time, and perhaps money too, and certainly some additional staff resources. I am sure that Fallon, to be fair to him, did not receive a great deal of sympathy, nor help or encouragement from Dennis Patman, who seemed to think that the role of Chairman involved only issuing broad and sometimes unfair and cruel criticism of those beneath him, none of which helped the situation at all. His remarks were never constructive and all he succeeded to do was make the victims of his criticism bristle. If I had been appointed Sales Director I would have made the sales force my very first task and, if necessary, I would have presented Dennis with an ultimatum – support me or I walk! Of course, that would probably have meant getting the sack – or he may have wilted. Who knows?

In my case, regarding exports, it was just a joke, for so much time was spent talking about home sales and factory matters that every time I raised the subject at meetings it was brushed away and I got precisely nowhere. Despite this unsatisfactory situation I continued to try and I managed to obtain quite some interest in our products. But our prices were far too high because they were loaded with domestic overheads, which should not apply to exports, and every time I endeavoured to explain that all factories having both domestic and export markets also have two levels of prices with export prices being stripped of domestic overheads. In desperation I even wrote a letter to Dennis in which I gave figures demonstrating why export prices should be lower than domestic prices, and I believe it put the case very clearly and showed how a healthy export programme could help Parkes a lot by reducing the overall production costs per ton. I even put forward an order for fifty tons of Brazil nut toffees at a lower price level than domestic but above the cost of production, only to be shouted down by Dennis who proclaimed that Parkes' problems were not going to be solved by selling goods at reduced prices. The man really had no idea. On the domestic market I agreed with him 100%, but a successful export programme, which is always useful for using up spare production capacity and thus keeping the machines and the employees busy and lowering overall production costs, needed special attention. I found it impossible to either obtain it or indeed give it. As Export Director I have to say I received absolutely no help or support whatsoever; exports were regarded as an unimportant sideline. I am not for one moment saying that exports could have solved Parkes' problems, but they certainly could have been a great help.

At this point I would like to break away from Parkes for a moment and tell of a small collection of incidents which, when put together, I found to be somewhat mysterious. In my search for new sources of supply for our new import section, called Intro, and possible markets for

Parkes' products I contacted the Bulgarian and Romanian Embassies requesting information on confectionery manufacturers in their respective countries. Soon after I was contacted by a certain Mr Walsh, who said he represented all Bulgarian confectionery interests in the UK and invited me to his offices, which were rather tatty, in NW London to have a look at various samples which he had there. So I went to his offices but I could see very little of interest; they were mainly samples of ordinary confectionery items which can be manufactured by British suppliers in their thousands of tons. But we had a chat over a cup of coffee and I told him about my earlier connection with Czechoslovakian confectionery products. He didn't say too much about this, as I recall, but I could tell from his reaction that this intrigued him.

I left his office and about two or three weeks later I received a call inviting me to have a drink with him at his private club situated in Pall Mall – and a very elite place it was in a rather old-fashioned sort of way; a typical well-to-do gents' club. We sat down to have a drink and after perhaps fifteen minutes another chap, purporting to be a friend, came by and Mr Walsh invited him to our table. Then followed a rather strange conversation and I had the feeling I was being interrogated. So many questions. There was no mistaking it and it wasn't my imagination – this was a very odd exchange and anybody experiencing it would have felt the same. When it was over I almost felt as though if not exactly brainwashed, my brain had been partly emptied by these two. But I had many other things to occupy my attention and soon forgot about it until I received yet another call from Mr Walsh. This time he invited me to come to his apartment for a drink and a chat. Remembering our last meeting I was rather intrigued and so accepted his invitation. I found his continued interest in me to be strange because he knew that he did not have a hope in hell of selling me anything. I asked him for the address, which he gave me as No. 1 Queensgate. As I wrote it down I began to think – surely Queensgate, as I know it, is a street of government offices and apartments. Anyway, I went there at the appointed time and was greeted by Mr Walsh, who showed me into a very large room, which was immaculate. Old fashioned, yes, but truly immaculate with elegant decorations and wonderful antique furniture. I am certainly no expert in furniture but even I could see that the pieces I saw in that room must be worth a fortune. There were also paintings on the walls and, well, the general décor and everything together gave an atmosphere of elegance and class. In some ways it reminded me of the apartment Lynne and I visited in Cadogan Square where the Czechoslovak Ambassador entertained his guests from time to time. I could not match either the elegant club in Pall Mall or this sumptuous apartment with Mr Walsh and his dingy office in NW London, which, by the way, gave one an impression that it was not at all busy. Once again, things did not quite add up; something, I thought, was not quite right here.

Anyway, Mr Walsh invited me to sit down, offered me a drink and the conversation started, right where we left it in that Pall Mall club, all about Czechoslovakia. But on this occasion I was not ready to be the punchbag all the time and so I began to ask him some questions. I wanted him to be on the receiving end for a change. And so I managed to extract from him the fact that he had been attached to the British Embassy in Prague some time before and spent two or three years there at least. He said he was in the department which issued visas to foreigners wishing to visit the UK. As we conversed it was surprising how many people from Czechoslovakia we both seemed to know.

We spoke about them and then the conversation changed somewhat when Mr Walsh began to speak of how it wasn't so bad in Czechoslovakia, that the people there had quite a good standard of living, that our press seemed to exaggerate matters in their papers, and so on. All of this was, of course, quite ridiculous and very irritating for me to listen to. What he was saying was utter rubbish, as anyone who had ever been to Czechoslovakia and knew the conditions there would know. This forced me to retaliate by arguing against him and I did so on almost every view he expressed. And then the penny dropped. I realised that he was simply drawing me out to get my real opinions and views about communist Czechoslovakia. Exactly who Mr Walsh really was and, more to the point, what he was I cannot say; I can only reflect that the whole sequence of events and every conversation and meeting I had with him was odd. Much later when I write about the 1970s I shall explain how this may possibly have had a connection with what happened then and my involvement with MI6.

And so, back to business: as time went by matters became worse and worse. Parkes was becoming a financial drag on its parent company the CBT. Sales were running but try as they may, were never increased to anything like the required level, not even to a break-even point. Facts had to be faced – Parkes was losing money. And that money could only be found from the parent company, which had very few assets of its own; all it had really was money that belonged either to the members who had paid their collective bills to Head Office or the manufacturers who required to be paid for goods delivered to such members. It does not take a mathematician to work out that as time went by payments to manufacturers inevitably became spasmodically slow and a number of manufacturers began to be a little concerned. Had they known something about the detail and the background story of why they were having to wait for settlement of their accounts they would have become very considerably alarmed. I too, with others, was also becoming alarmed. My own feelings about bankruptcy are that this becomes inevitable when you have stopped spending your own money and begin spending money belonging to somebody else. It was a dreadful situation to be in and it of course got worse and worse as time went on. But how much worse was known only to Dennis Patman – as far as I knew no other director or member of staff, including myself, who had nothing to do with the finances of the company, were made aware of the true financial situation.

Meanwhile, another blow hit the company, for it appeared that before the CBT took control of Parkes, contracts for new machinery, of which the new management were totally unaware, for they had not been revealed by the previous management, had been placed and now the people who had produced this machinery wanted to deliver and be paid. Parkes could not afford such machinery, but on the other hand, could not escape liability. As I stated earlier, if one is going to take over a company it must be made absolutely clear at the time exactly what responsibilities the new owner is undertaking – that, to me, is a matter of common business sense. As I have indicated previously, the best way to limit one's responsibilities is to terminate the old company or leave the old management to do what they wished with such a worthless title, and for the purchasers to take over the assets and start a new company; thus any overlapping contracts or commitments concerning financial transactions etc remain the obligations of the old company and are nothing to do with the new one. The accountants of the CBT should have known this and should have proffered such advice. But they didn't and so Parkes had to pay substantial penalties for not honouring the contracts for new machinery, otherwise they would have faced court proceedings and then the cat really would have been out of the bag. It was just another nail in the coffin of both the CBT and Parkes.

By now I felt I was at last ready to leave the CBT and start my own business. I didn't want to appear to be the rat that was deserting the sinking ship, but I had little choice. The timing could have been better, I agree, but I could not allow the situation with the CBT to interfere with my personal plans. I had now been with the CBT for a little over three and a half years and in that time I had built up very valuable connections, not only with British manufacturers but as a result of my activities in Europe as a delegate to Interchoc, a number of foreign manufacturers too. However, I was satisfied that I had more than earned my keep, so I tendered my resignation to Dennis Patman, who when he read it appeared unperturbed and acted almost as if he had expected it. I believe I gave one month's notice.

In the meantime, the CBT suffered yet another serious blow when as a result of faulty wiring in the old building in Albemarle Street, a fire occurred overnight. I was called early one Saturday morning by Dennis Patman and I of course immediately rushed up to London. When I arrived I observed that part of the offices was completely gutted and it was clear that many papers had been burned or ruined by water. As rumbles that all was not well with the CBT were already beginning to circulate within the trade and gathering strength, this was the last thing that the CBT wanted, and it all looked a very highly suspicious event indeed. There is little doubt that there were those who probably thought that this fire had been engineered. But I can truly say that this was far from the truth; it was an event that occurred quite naturally in an old building where the wiring must have been quite ancient. Nobody had anything to do with it; it just happened, but at an exceedingly awkward moment. The Albemarle Street premises were now quite uninhabitable and it was fortunate that the CBT had earlier taken a lease on premises just around the corner in Dover Street for earlier plans of expansion. So it meant that everything and everybody had to be shifted to Dover Street pending the substantial repairs that would have to be carried out on the Albemarle Street premises in order to make it habitable once more; it was quite an operation and would take some time. So, of course, we were obliged to move totally to the Dover Street premises where we were forced to work in very cramped and difficult conditions. Dennis Patman informed everybody that this was a temporary measure until the offices in Albemarle Street could be refurbished. Matters, however, conspired to ensure that this never happened.

Of course, despite the fact that the fire was a totally innocent affair that could happen in any old building, the manufacturers now began to smell a rat and as an inevitable consequence we were visited by a number of individuals representing various manufacturers whose accounts were rather overdue. Quite reasonably they wanted to be paid for the goods they had delivered to our members – but with what? Money was pouring out but very little was coming in. Furthermore, many of the members themselves were becoming very concerned and wanted to know what was going on. In those days, other directors, including Dennis himself, went into hiding somewhat, but that was not my way. Despite the fact that I had nothing to do with the financial affairs of the company I was the only director who had the courage and was willing to see and talk to these people. I refused to neglect my responsibilities, even though I was leaving the company.

I listened to their pleas and urgings and explained that I personally could do very little to help them but that I would bring the matter before Dennis Patman. Whilst it didn't help, and nor did it pacify, I did mention these visits to Dennis, but it was as if he were in a kind of daze and was just not listening.

Meanwhile, I think the death blow occurred when members, sensing that something was seriously wrong at Head Office, began to make their payments for goods received direct to the manufacturers. This virtually dried up any income and it was not really a surprise when I came into the office one day to find that the bank had appointed receivers – an inevitable development in view of the quite naïve and 'head in the sand' irresponsible attitude of our all-powerful Managing Director. Looking back it is clear that he was in complete denial of the serious situation in which the company found itself. However, to be fair, we cannot exclude the other directors, including myself, for allowing this position to worsen. If the majority of directors had recognized firstly the seriousness of the situation and secondly that Dennis Patman was not competent in his attitude of mind at that time to save the company from drowning, then they, collectively, had the power to remove him. In my own case I can only plead selfishness in that I wanted to leave at a time best suited to my future plans and I knew that any show of dissent or disloyalty on my part and I would have been shown the front door.

Of course, as a director of the company the receivers wanted to interview me also, but they realised quite quickly that I was concerned only with the sales development side of the business and knew nothing at all about the financial workings of the company; I had never been kept informed at any time of any details concerning finance. Perhaps as a director I should have asked, but I am sure that, knowing Dennis Patman, that too might have meant a short route to the front door. That was the province of Dennis Patman, the Company Secretary, and those members of staff dealing with the wholesale group members and manufacturers' accounts and payments, and I was never told about this part of the business or invited at any time to be involved in this section, and since it was not within the province of my responsibilities, I never asked. I explained to the receivers that I was in the process of working out my resignation period anyway and I requested to be permitted to terminate my employment with the company a little earlier, i.e. at the end of that week, to which they agreed. I did, of course, offer to be of any assistance I could, even though I was leaving the company, but they realised that there was little I could tell them.

With that I prepared my things at the end of the week, surrendered my car and left the office. I did subsequently receive a notice of a meeting of the creditors to be held in London. Of the twelve area directors, the chairman and the three executive directors, i.e. Patman, Fallon and myself, only two of us were brave enough to attend this meeting, and that was Dennis Patman and myself – we were the only ones with the guts to face the creditors. Of course, many questions were asked and although answers were given they were most unsatisfactory in a situation which in itself simply demonstrated exactly how a business should not be run.

On reflection, I think it was the grandeur and even arrogance of Dennis Patman plus his ignorance as a businessman and the way he ruled Head Office with an iron rod that produced the overall problem. If you crossed him you were out. If you were not for him you were against him. Sometimes he was a very reasonable man with whom you could talk frankly and openly, but the very next day he took on a different personality and woe betide the person who said something out of turn or anything which in any way could be regarded as personal criticism of himself. As one example only, and I shall never forget the occasion, a meeting of Planit area representatives was to be held in the afternoon. During the morning I asked to see Dennis and he listened very carefully as I detailed every point I proposed to make at the meeting. I then asked him what his opinion was and he stated his approval of everything I was going to put forward. Dennis chaired the meeting that afternoon, but when I was asked to say my piece he interrupted me half way through in a most unbecoming and furious manner, which was totally uncalled for, and was completely opposite to the attitude he had shown in his office in the morning. He made me look somewhat foolish, even humiliated, and I have to say that I believe that was his intention – just to show those present who was the 'boss' or perhaps to demonstrate his superior knowledge. How can one reason with a person like that? You never can tell where you are with individuals of that type.

I still believe that the basic idea to take over Parkes was not, in itself, a bad one; if any organisation was in a position to turn things around at Parkes it was the CBT with its enormous buying power – some 360 warehouses spread all over the country. But that strength needed to be harmonised and brought into play. As a kind of wholesale distributor myself later on I know how easy it would have been for all members to have given their backing to Parkes' products if only they could have been persuaded that taking over Parkes would lead to an improvement in their income. If their combined strength could have been harnessed and if the situation when taking over

Parkes had been explained properly to all members and their individual
help and cooperation requested, that could have been the saving of Parkes
and, by the way, the CBT too. The takeover should have been carried out
in a different way in every aspect, in my opinion; it was wrong for one
individual to have such power and control over everything, especially in a
situation whereby that person's word was law and must be obeyed without
debate or examination of other people's ideas and opinions, not to mention
experience. The power of that group had never been properly harnessed
and it was a tragedy because, as I have remarked elsewhere, there are
many ways that collections of people in whatever sphere can be utilised
for their benefit and those of the organiser. Today many supermarkets,
for example, carry out such policies, engaging themselves in every way
in which they can use the bulk and strength of their collective customers.
Well, I was recommending such collective and additional policies to the
CBT in the late 1960s, long before the supermarkets thought of involving
themselves in the many ways you can utilise collections of people. To
talk to Dennis Patman in such terms, however, was mostly like talking to
a brick wall and after listening to you for five minutes he would wave his
hand as if to dismiss the subject or tell you that that your ideas were too
advanced, they were for the future. Sometimes the future never arrives
unless you allow it to.

And so I left the CBT early in 1972 to begin new commercial
adventures which, hopefully, would lead to money in my pocket rather
than somebody else's. Dennis Patman, I heard, endured a period of unemployment and then took a position as Company Secretary to some dog
organisation. How the mighty have fallen, I thought, when I heard this.
I did keep in touch with him from time to time by phone, but it was always
me who phoned him; he never phoned me. I never met him in person
again but I know he was interested in the new company I had started. Not
very long afterwards the news reached me that one evening when going
home to Beaconsfield where he lived he ran to catch a train, collapsed on
the platform and died. And so ended Dennis Patman. He started off as a
nice man but allowed power to go to his head and lost his sense of reason,
fairness and consideration towards others somewhere along the way. He
became a dictator and dictators rarely, if ever, succeed.

As I related earlier, the CBT consisted of two groups, Confex for the
larger wholesaler and Planit for the rest. Planit died and was never brought
to life again, but Confex was started up again by one of the original directors, who although he did not come to the meeting of creditors evidently
did not want to see Confex disappear. It did not operate in the same way. It

had nothing to do with receiving payments from members and then paying the manufacturers; all that was done directly between the buyers and the sellers. And so really it became just a vehicle for organising promotional activities. I have no idea if Confex in its new format was a success or not, but it was a pygmy compared to the original concept.

Had Parkes not appeared in the picture, and assuming that Dennis Patman, a quite heavy smoker and moderate drinker, would have passed away suddenly as he did, then it is possible, and I put it no stronger than that, that I may have been offered the position of MD, i.e. assuming that I proposed to stay with the company. If that had come to pass I think I would have put my personal ambitions on ice for a while and would have tried to put some of my ideas into practice. For example, I proposed to Dennis Patman that we should consider the idea of a central warehouse; one to begin with and if successful others in different parts. If that were achieved it would mean that the CBT could collate orders from its members and act as direct buyers in bulk. In that strong buying position there would have been consequent advantages to both the manufacturers and the members. The members could choose between collecting goods by their own vehicles and receive a discount or, if they preferred, to have them delivered by CBT vehicles. I tested this idea out, verbally, with a couple of manufacturers and asked them if they would be prepared to negotiate more attractive prices for bulk deliveries of their goods into central warehouses as opposed to individual deliveries of smaller quantities all over the place and they were very enthusiastic, pointing out that with bulk orders they could plan and purchase materials more cheaply and some of that benefit could be passed on in lower prices. There would be an obvious saving in delivery costs on their part too. Dennis listened to me but once again dismissed the suggesting saying that I was talking ten years too soon. It was very disheartening to a chap like me who thrived on new ideas and loved working hard to put them into practice. In the same vein I later suggested to him that if he thought that a central warehouse scheme was too ambitious we could perhaps work out a way of centrally collecting orders for various items from our members and allow HO to negotiate deals with our manufacturers. For example, if we took an individual line of confectionery and collected orders for that item from 360 members, then instead of 360 smallish orders of let us say half a ton, HO would be in a position to negotiate a single order for 180 tons to the obvious advantage of everyone. With the advancement of central computerisation such a system could have been introduced to make our group a real, positive and big buyer and thus in a position to negotiate much better prices. But how can you persuade a man to consider such ideas when he is not even a businessman? I regret to say I could not find the way.

I also put forward my ideas of using the group members in many other ways too and suggested to Dennis that any group of people, or indeed wholesalers, can benefit from group activity in a number of ways. For example, why not have our own group insurance schemes, i.e. both business and personal? Any insurance company would have been happy to talk to us and offer preferable terms. And what about group saving and investment schemes, group holiday schemes and group purchases of commercial vehicles? If one thinks about it, we had a receptive market for many kinds of group activities, all of which could have helped HO to earn more money and distribute more to its members, and it needed badly to be exploited. Sadly, it never was because we had an MD whose vision was very limited. But later on, in years to come, other organisations did exactly what I was proposing, e.g. Tesco and other supermarkets are into every possible means of using their customers on a group basis.

6

I CREATE CONFECTIONERY MARKETING SERVICES LTD AND CANDYLUX; MI6 CONTACT ME AND I HELP THEM; AND MY TRIP TO USA, CANADA AND PUERTO RICO

When I left my office in Dover Street for the last time it was absolutely nothing like the great sadness and regret I felt when leaving my office in Mark Lane when I terminated my relations with Sugosa Ltd and with the Czechs. Now I felt a sense of exhilaration! I was free – free to put my own ideas into practice with nobody to ask permission if I could do this or that, that is except I had a duty and responsibility to the partner I had decided upon to help me in the formation of my new company, which I had decided to name Confectionery Marketing Services Limited.

My future partner's name was Charles Moody, whom I had known for quite a number of years when he was the assistant to the buyer of one of our clients when I worked for Harold Frost, the former agent for Czechoslovak confectionery products. I had always got on well with Charles; he, like me, came from a rather poor background. He was born and brought up in Bethnal Green. But he seemed to me to be a lively chap and quite energetic and, just as importantly, we got on quite well with each other. When I first approached the subject of joining me in a new venture he was employed in the printing profession, but he badly wanted to return to the confectionery industry.

So I offered Charles 49% of CMS shares if he would be prepared to join me. He baulked at this at first as, quite understandably, he would have preferred it to be a 50-50 arrangement. However, I pointed out to him that there would be occasions when positive decisions would need to be made and that, therefore, a 50-50 arrangement would be filled with dangers and possible stalemate. But I undertook to share everything with him down the middle, 50-50, and not to make any important decision without discussing the matter with him first. As I explained to him, we would be 50% partners in every sense but someone had to have the deciding vote in case of disagreement. I put it to him that as it was my company, my idea and my contacts which would make this business work, that deciding vote had to be mine. We finally reached agreement on my suggested basis. We had also agreed that our commencing capital would be £2,000, i.e. £1,000 each. However, Charles did not have that kind of money immediately to hand and so I had to put up the whole commencing capital myself until Charles was in a position to repay me.

Charles continued to work, therefore, whilst I did a lot of foraging. My first action was to seek an appointment with the manager at Barclays Bank in Coulsdon. I had been with Barclays for years and years and had always kept my nose clean and never taken the slightest liberty. My account had always been in credit and I was sure all this would help me in my discussions. I had already prepared a business plan in which I made estimates of running costs, estimates of turnover and profit levels etc, and I looked forward very much to my first meeting. I did not know this manager as previously I banked at the branch in Eastcheap in the City, where I was of course a tiddler, a nonentity in an area of financial giants. He seemed to be a little stiff and proper; people always worry me when they do not have a smile on their face when meeting someone new. I smiled – he didn't! So it was a hint that this was not going to be a cinch.

Never mind, I thought; when I tell him of my very considerable background, knowledge, experience and contacts in the British confectionery world and abroad I was sure that anyone would back me, and what I was asking for was an overdraft facility of £20,000, not so much to get us going but to be used only if our inward cash flow diminished unexpectedly and we needed resources to pay suppliers for goods delivered. Well, maybe anybody else might have been willing to back me, but not this manager. He looked at my plan, looked at me, gave it back to me and said that if we could put up £10,000 then the bank would grant me a £10,000 overdraft. But where was I to get £10,000 from? That was quite a lot of money to me back then and I had never had a position which paid so well that I could keep my family, pay the mortgage and save very much in addition. Yes,

I had some moderate savings, but not £5,000, for that was quite a lot of money in those days, and neither did Charles Moody.

So this was the first problem I had to overcome. But in the meantime I went searching for warehouse premises and succeeded in finding the upper floor of a 5,000 square foot warehouse in Sutton, Surrey. Not at all far from home for Charles, who lived in Morden, and not too bad for me from Old Coulsdon. The rent was £20 per week. That suited us fine, for I didn't want to begin with a white elephant or any huge debt around our necks. Charles and I agreed from the outset that bearing in mind our limited assets we must begin as a van sales organisation; that was not a major problem because Ford Transit vans only sold for about £800 back then and so it would be fairly easy to obtain hire purchase terms for say six such vehicles. But first of all we had to solve the overdraft problem somehow, because what we did not want to happen was to start purchasing goods for which we would be unable to pay in time. It was most important that we gained a good reputation for payment when it was due – not a penny less and not a day later. Therefore, in order to buy goods and keep adequate stocks in our warehouse we needed the backing of an overdraft arrangement. On the other hand, our plan was to try to organise our purchases and sales so that we would turn merchandise into cash as quickly as possible and pay our bills, thus trying not to touch our overdraft facility at all – if and when we obtained one, of course. I tried other overdraft avenues but as the people I was talking to didn't know me all that well, or perhaps not at all, I wasn't getting very far. What I thought would be a piece of cake and a mere formality was proving to be a much more difficult task than I had imagined.

And then a stroke of luck occurred, which we all need when we are faced with an obstacle that is seemingly impossible to overcome. It happened like this: the gentleman who had agreed to act as our accountant and auditor, knowing of our overdraft difficulties, made an appointment for me with the manager of Williams & Deacons Bank in Croydon. This bank doesn't exist any more as it was absorbed into NatWest. Well, I didn't know these people at all and didn't feel all that confident until I walked into the manager's office and lo and behold, it was a gentleman from Old Coulsdon to whom we had sold my daughter Jackie's horse about eighteen months before – she had grown too big for it. He recognised me immediately. I asked him how the horse was and to my great relief he said it was all going splendidly and that the horse we had sold him was lovely and docile, just what his own daughter needed and she was very happy indeed. So we talked about horses for about twenty minutes and then, eventually, we turned to business. So I made my little speech, passed over my business plan and within ten minutes it was all sewn up – I had our £20,000 overdraft, but with certain conditions, the main one being that he would expect us to put up our houses as collateral as we had no other assets. He apologised for having to ask this, but as he explained, he would need to justify the overdraft facility to Head Office. Of course, I said I would have to discuss such a possibility with my wife and my partner Charles and his wife, which the manager quite understood.

I was elated and had no worries about putting our house up as collateral because I knew in my bones that come what may I was going to succeed, even if it meant that I would have to work twenty-four hours a day and seven days a week. With Charles looking after the sales side and me looking after purchases and administration we should make a good team. And so, to cut a long story short, back at home I discussed the whole situation with my dear wife Lynne; I pointed out the possible dangers and so on, but she had a lot of confidence in me and, as ever, backed me 100%, as I knew she would. Charles had to have a similar discussion with his wife; I believe she baulked somewhat and was rather concerned to have to take this action, but Charles eventually managed to persuade her that all would be OK. So what it meant was that if we failed we might both lose our houses. It was therefore of tremendous importance for both of us to realise that we had to work our socks off and avoid failure.

Having now gained the overdraft we needed, as a protection barrier and only to be used in case of need, we could now get cracking. Our first task was to confirm the lease on our warehouse premises, contact suppliers to start the ball rolling, advertise for van salesmen and interview them, and so on. With manufacturers, most of whom I knew personally as a result of my time with the CBT, I had to negotiate special prices. In each case I told them that we would not be merely stocking their lines, as most normal wholesalers did, but we would go out hell for leather to sell them and ensure good distribution of their products in the south. That degree of sales attention does not come cheap, I argued, and called for a special price level so that we could do a good job. Fortunately, many suppliers agreed with that thinking – at least they were ready to give it a go. But with others I had to make some concessions – not so much on price, but in other ways. When I saw we had reached stalemate on price I asked the supplier firstly to make up the difference in free goods rather than cash reductions. I also offered to pay in fourteen days instead of the usual thirty. Finally, in some cases we were able to take lorry loads direct from the factory to our warehouse, thus reducing transport costs. In other words, to get my way on price it was a question of examining every which way we could cooperate with the suppliers and to be flexible in order to achieve the buying price levels which we required. In the vast majority of cases we got there in the end.

We began to interview van salesmen but we explained to them that most of their income would be completely dependent upon their own performances. I believed then, and even more today, that our staff policy was a good, fair policy which recognised success but penalised failure. Work hard, we told them, and you can earn a good income; work harder still and you can enjoy an excellent income – it was up to them. We didn't employ anyone; they all started on a self-employed basis, although we did guarantee them a minimum income whatever happened of £20 per week, not a lot but worth much more back then. We also paid for their vans and all their petrol expenses. That did change in time; they still received a basic assured wage but to that could be added a second level of income which was controlled by the total number of boxes they sold each day and then each week. So the more they sold the bigger their wage at the end of the week. Furthermore, profits were calculated at the end of the year and 33% went to the staff, 33% went to the shareholders, and 33% went to reserves.

It was a simple matter to calculate each person's contribution to the year's results as a percentage of the total achieved, and that percentage ruled (1) his share of distributable profits; (2) his share of pension allocation – every member of staff had a pension after two years' service, fully paid by the company, and each person's pension 'pot' annual award was determined by their contribution towards final results; and (3) a similar scheme which determined what each person received when going on holiday – we took the total pay earned by the individual and took an average from that figure, and that was what he received when going on holiday, which, by the way, was two weeks in the summer and two weeks over the Christmas period. All along the line we provided incentives to the salesmen to bump up their weekly earnings. In this way the salesman controlled his own income, his share of profits, his pension and his holiday pay – it was up to each individual to provide for himself.

It took a long time to work out this incentive scheme. If anyone came to me to ask for a wage increase I immediately got out my pocket ready-reckoner, asked them what increase they would like, made some rapid calculations and told them there and then what they had to do in order to reach their required income. The scheme was fully explained before anyone joined the company, and everyone was told quite clearly that we would be unable to carry anyone, and that whilst we would support them and give them any help needed, their income would be controlled totally by their own efforts and the hours put in. I always believed in people having incentives and receiving a fair share of whatever they produced; in our case it was sales that generated profit. Sales were also very important because the best buyer in the world is nothing without good salesmen behind him. Similarly, the best salesmen are nothing without a good buyer behind them – and I was a good buyer. We held staff meetings at intervals and the company scheme was always brought up and discussed. Everyone had the right to question or criticise their conditions of employment. If a point was brought to my attention and a suggestion made that was fair and reasonable, then we adopted it. Nobody ever lost a job with me because they spoke up.

One would think that such a basis would encourage people to work to their maximum effort, for I had high hopes that if you treat people decently and fairly, they would respond by doing a fair day's work. But I am afraid to say that they didn't. One salesman I know would never start before 9.30 a.m. each morning because he took his children to school. I recall he was also one of the first back at the warehouse each evening. The very same person had the cheek one day to tell me he couldn't manage on his income. I reminded him again of the terms upon which he joined the company and reminded him that any required increase in his income depended on his own efforts.

Also, when things went well I used to reward the lads with a nice meal somewhere or even a day out in France. I would take them all down by train to wherever the boat was leaving from, go over to Calais or Dieppe, or another coastal town, and give them a slap-up lunch. On the return journey I would invariably buy them a bottle of duty-free whisky plus 200 cigarettes. At Christmas when we broke up for the holiday we collected them by taxi, had a very nice Christmas meal and sent them all home by taxi with a large box filled with goodies for their families. Was it appreciated? In the beginning, yes, but then they got used to it and began to expect it as a matter of course, so the appreciation disappeared.

But I look back upon my company staff record very proudly. I believe I gave everybody the opportunity to work and earn a fair share of what their work produced, a pension which didn't cost them a penny, plus a share of profits as a bonus at the end of the year. I gave them full details of the company accounts for the year and invited any questions. That gave me the opportunity, after we had changed our system from van sales to a representative call and following delivery service, to point out to them the cost of deliveries and that some salesmen were coming back with small orders on which, after taking the cost of delivery into account, the company was not making very much profit if any. I pointed out to them that such practices only serve to reduce their own profit share at the end of the year and drummed home the necessity that we all have to bear such things in mind, for it affects all of us. That became a bit of a joke in the warehouse, probably because I repeated it again and again, and I will not apologise for that because it was true – every facet of selling affected the end result and, therefore, the income of every one of us. In a democratic company such as ours it was vital for every single person to be aware of and to show interest in all factors in the process from the taking of orders, to final delivery to the client and payment of accounts. It was, therefore, disappointing to me to observe that on too many occasions the salesmen let us down either by accepting small orders or not seeing that their clients' bills were paid on time, or even taking new orders when the customer already owed us money. There were other ways too when they failed to observe the company's best interests. All of these matters combined served only to lessen the income of us all.

At about this time I received a totally unexpected letter from the Ministry of Defence – MI6 no less. I cannot recall the exact wording of the letter but it read something like this:

> Dear Mr Mitchell,
> As a gentleman with a wide knowledge of Czechoslovakia and also knowing a lot of Czech people you have met in the course of your business dealings in that country it is very possible that you could be of considerable help to us. If you are willing to cooperate with us please be kind enough to phone the undersigned at the number given and we can then arrange a mutually convenient appointment.

The letter contained a few more words than that but I cannot recall them exactly. I do not have this letter now because the first thing that happens at any meeting with these people is that your interviewer requests you to hand it over to him. Later on he explained to me that there had been occasions in the past where some people they had contacted had taken their letter to the press, hoping to make something out of the story, and such occurrences only serve to cause embarrassment to MI6. As to my own response, as a proud Englishman I was willing to do whatever I could for my country, so I did not hesitate, and having telephoned the gentleman concerned he offered to come to my house, which of course was more convenient to me.

In the meantime I began to wonder how all this had come about. I am sure that working for the Czechs, as I once did, and travelling so often to Czechoslovakia, my name was probably well known to those in MI6, as would be the case with all employees of companies controlled by communist countries. Of course, they would have learned that in my case my dealings had nothing whatsoever to do with politics but purely a commercial cooperation. However, in thinking it over I became more and more certain that this had something to do with the mysterious Mr Walsh, of whom I wrote in the last chapter.

Anyway, the man from MI6 came at the appointed time. He was an older man, very well dressed and very well spoken – one of the old school, I do not doubt. We chatted for a while about Czechoslovakia and about some of my experiences in that country, and so on, when he reached for his briefcase and brought out a folder of photographs of people. One by one he showed these to me and I knew quite a number of them; he asked me to tell him about each individual and made notes of my remarks. To my great surprise, an inclusion was my dear friend Jiri Stepan, who was at that time Reception Manager of International Hotel, Prague. I quickly assured the MI6 man that Jiri was beyond reproach, for he was definitely anti-communist. In fact, I showed him a letter that Jiri had written to me quite recently and which he managed to get smuggled out via a friend who was going to West Germany, and which made clear some of his thoughts about the Communist regime. The man asked me if I would mind if he borrowed the letter and I allowed him to take it on the clear understanding that the letter would in no way be used to compromise my good friend. He promised that would be so and I therefore handed it to him.

Of course, our old friend Karel Jiracek was included in this parade of pictures and I was able to give a lot of information about him that they apparently didn't know. He had not yet been appointed to the position of Commercial Counsellor to the UK.

In about two weeks the gentleman contacted me once again and said he would like to see me once more, that he had a new batch of photos and he would like to invite me to lunch. Once again I knew a number of the people in the photos and was able to give him some details. We went to lunch, which was very enjoyable, and once again we chatted about Czechoslovakia the whole time.

After another two weeks he contacted me yet again and this time he invited me to the Ministry of Defence in Whitehall. Well, who wouldn't be curious in those circumstances? So I went up to London, entered the hallowed building and my friend came down to meet and greet me. He showed me all over the Ministry, explaining each function, what they do, how they do it etc., and it was jolly interesting. After that he took me to lunch in a pub-restaurant quite nearby, which was frequented by the Ministry people. As I sat there I wondered how many famous names had eaten in this very place. Philby? Burgess? McLean? And other spies? No doubt all of them had eaten or supped their drinks in that restaurant. It was again a very nice lunch with pleasant and interesting conversation and I ended by saying that if I could be of any further help at all please don't hesitate to contact me. With that I returned home and I never saw my interviewer or heard from him again. But afterwards I thought about all this and once again something did not quite add up. It seemed to me inconceivable that of the people I helped them with they were not already aware of the answers to many questions they put to me. Take Karel Jiracek, for example; I had known him since 1953, but I am sure they did too. It was not long afterwards that Jiracek was appointed Commercial Counsellor, second only to the Ambassador himself. I cannot bring myself to believe they were so ignorant of the background of people like him. Every member of all communist embassies was watched very carefully in that period when the Cold War was at its worst. Even after all these years I remain puzzled.

Returning to business matters, it is said that the average partnership lasts for five years – ours lasted for only four. I will explain how this came about. Firstly, let me explain that we operated under two headings: the company name was Confectionery Marketing Services Ltd, but the company also owned the trading name of Candylux. The company ran everything, of course, but the retail section now dealing with direct deliveries to well over 1000 shops in the Greater London area was carried out under the name of Candylux. I was kept quite busy dealing with the admin, the buying, talking and negotiating with new suppliers and using all my contacts and friends I made during my days at the CBT. I also kept my eyes open for any opportunity to use our buying connections to our advantage and pulled off some very useful deals. Sales via Candylux were the responsibility of my partner Charles; we had regular meetings and I kept him fully informed about any activities or whatever was going on with regard to CMS deals. I kept my word that whatever happened he would always get 50%, right down the middle.

But I began to get a little unhappy with the way things were going. As I have mentioned previously, the best buyer in the world is not effective without good salesmen to sell. So my first grumble was that sales via Candylux were not as good as I would have expected. In the meantime an incident occurred which rather disappointed me. On the CMS side, amongst the deals I was creating with distributors in other parts of the country, I had bought and sold five tons of confectionery which had to be delivered up north. I therefore ordered a freight car to be at the factory in Staines at 9 a.m. on the day and because I knew I would have no other help, except possibly the driver, to load the goods, I asked Charles if he could come over and give me a hand. He said he was unable to because he was taking his family down to the coast to some bay where they were going to stay for a week or two. I asked him if he could postpone taking them for a couple of hours and reminded him that drivers had been quite notorious and unreliable as far as helping to load up was concerned. I might be there loading five tons on my own. But he said he was unable to change his arrangements. As a matter of fact, I did get one of those uncooperative drivers who were not prepared to lift a finger to assist me and so there I was on my own having to load five tons. Had it not been for Freddy Tidman, the owner of the factory, seeing what was going on and organising a little help for me, I may well have done myself a mischief. I didn't like that occurrence too much. I think I made a profit of almost £600 on the deal, of which Charles would enjoy 50%, so in my view he should have been willing to make more of an effort. My conscience would never have allowed me to let him down like that.

The next thing that made me somewhat unhappy occurred when one of our customers phoned in to ask where our rep was, because they hadn't seen him for ages and they needed some of our goods rather urgently. By now we had changed from a van sales organisation to having reps call for the orders and a 24- or 48-hour delivery service. Anyway, I took an order over the phone from this customer and when I saw Charles next I asked him how he controlled the salesmen and did he have a checking system to see that they were calling on our customers on a regular basis? He told me he had no such system and that he had no idea of call frequency or indeed where the reps were going on any particular day. So I asked how, as Sales Director, he knew if our salesmen were functioning well if he had no check on them. He knew perfectly well that he was quite wrong about this and so we had a fierce bust-up. I told him flat that I did not feel he was pulling his weight and that the control over the salesmen and whether they were working well or not was his responsibility and that the key to any successful company was not only to buy goods at the right price but also to be able to sell them. So Charles then had the cheek to say that as we disagreed on how to run a company, we had better split up and that he would buy me out. I very quickly put him right on that one and told him if anyone was buying anyone out it was going to be me buying him out. We both agreed to consult our legal advisors and parted company.

Of course, we kept in touch by phone and spoke about the best way to approach the division of the company – after all, we were adults, not children. I suggested that we have the company accountant make a full evaluation of the assets, the stock, vehicles etc, less any monies outstanding and present us with a statement showing the correct total value of the business. I told Charles that legally I would be quite within my rights to pay him 49% of that valuation but that I would in fact pay him 50% and so keep my original promise. But I warned him that there would be no way that I could pay him everything immediately; that would have sapped the financial strength of the company. I continued that we would have to come to a satisfactory agreement on payments. He accepted that and so we reached agreement, and in that way we parted on good terms; I know from another person that Charles had said of me that I was a very fair and honest man. I would like to think that were true – I am very proud of my reputation.

And so, at last, I was now completely free from anybody else's views and opinions. I had nobody else to ask about anything and I could dictate my own policies without discussion. But in this difficult period I must say I was aided and abetted by Ray Annis, my son-in-law. He was married to my eldest daughter and had studied at Loughborough University for his degree in chemical engineering. But he did not find it easy to obtain a position and so I asked him if he would fancy coming to work with Charles and me. At first, Ray did deliveries, which he didn't mind as he liked driving very much and it also introduced him to a wide selection of our customers and gave him the opportunity to learn something about our business. Later on Ray became Warehouse Manager and to assist his authority in the warehouse I appointed him a director of the company. When I thought he knew enough about the business I gave him the responsibility to do the everyday buying; this bolstered his confidence and I thought he spoke to people much better after that. I was very appreciative of Ray's loyalty and support and I am not sure how I would have coped without him.

My first thoughts were how we could expand our business. Simply put, the problems related firstly to buying the right goods at the right price, which we already were to an extent, making sure we had adequate stocks and negotiating with potential new suppliers both at home and abroad.

Thinking about this I always remembered the words of my old friend Sydney Eagle when he said to me: "David, always remember that there is money to be made from goods that other people do not want."

Being now part of the EU I imagined there would be a lot of small and medium manufacturers in EU countries who would want to explore the British market, the largest consumers of chocolate and confectionery per capita in Europe. That brought forth some degree of interest but not as much as I had hoped. After a while I thought again about Sydney's wise words and sent a further 'round robin' letter to all European manufacturers that I knew, suggesting to them that if at any time they may be in the position of having surplus production capacity or any stocks on hand which, for marketing purposes, they did not wish to dispose of on their home market, then I would be an interested buyer.

I awaited reactions and before too long things started to happen. The very first call I received was from Ed Fenimore, President of The Philadelphia Chewing Gum Corporation, USA, who told me that he had a twenty-ton container of a bubble gum product lying in Copenhagen that he would prefer not to ship back to the USA – would I be interested? I told him I would and requested he send me a sample box by air. I received the sample box in very reasonable time; I found that it was a small plastic container filled with tiny coated bubble gum pieces called Disco Shake, and it looked to me to be an attractive item. The idea was, of course, that the kids could shake the container whilst dancing, create a rhythm of their own and then eat the contents afterwards. I made a judgement on the price I could pay, phoned Ed Fenimore in Philadelphia, who accepted my offer, and the deal was done. The container was eventually delivered into our warehouse and sales began. Suddenly, the whole world seemed to be calling us – we had a real winner on our hands and it went like absolute wildfire. On reflection, I think this was probably the best-selling line I had ever handled in my life. The price I paid ensured it could be sold to the public at 5p – a high level for kids in those days, who mostly wanted 1p and 2p items – but if the line was good enough it would still sell well; it was and it did. Shops were placing such ridiculous orders we had to ration deliveries to five boxes per shop; and even our competitors were ringing us to see if we could supply the line to them. We made a very good profit on that item and as stocks began to dwindle I called Ed Fenimore for further supplies, which he was willing to send but not at the same price level as before. We did bring in further shipments, but the much higher retail price meant that the line was not the same best seller any more. However, we did buy other items from Philadelphia and I was able to ship around ten tons, i.e. half a container, now and then; and so a nice, friendly new contact had been made.

And further offers began to flow in. I found that I could not handle all such offers through Candylux alone and so I contacted other distributors in various parts of the country and began to supply them. What pleased me was that we were being recognised as big buyers and that could only be good for us in every direction. We were even approached by British manufacturers when they had stock problems and we dealt with them all.

I would like to mention that during this period I made a number of attempts to develop some other business possibilities with Czechoslovakia. During 1975 or so our old friend Karel Jiracek had returned to London as Commercial Counsellor, second only in hierarchy to the Ambassador. As such he had to dress in morning suit and top hat to go to Buckingham Palace when the new Ambassador presented his credentials to the Queen. When I knew he was in London I phoned him and he invited me to visit him in his office. I did so on a few occasions. He had stopped smoking by now but he certainly had not stopped drinking and each time I visited him he instructed his secretary to bring whisky, for that was his favourite tipple. Karel greeted me in a very friendly way when we met again. In his present position as Commercial Counsellor there is no doubt whatsoever that he could, had he so wished, have been very influential in arranging some business activity between myself and some Czech organisation or another. On a personal note, although I have always suspected that there was something rather sinister behind Karel Jiracek and wondered sometimes who he really was, I have to admit my admiration for him. To imagine that as a young lad he used to sweep the floors of the Orion Confectionery Factory near to Prague and was now Commercial Counsellor to Great Britain, and second only to the Ambassador himself, was a real achievement and I willingly take my hat off to him and people like him.

He made a lot of friendly noises in respect of helping me and made a number of promises to find something of interest for me in Czech business. But he never did, and I do not believe he ever tried. I knew of old that Jiracek's promises were not worth a lot. However, Jiracek or no Jiracek, I tried and tried again. I even went to Brno in Moravia where great commercial fairs are held. I walked around the various exhibitors' stands, spoke to a lot of people and saw people there I knew quite well from earlier days. But I have to say that I had not a flicker of a commercial opportunity or possibility with any one of them. Again, a lot of talking but nothing of real substance. It seemed to me as if someone had erected a brick wall before me which prevented taking interesting discussions at the fair any further.

On one occasion I thought I maybe had the answer. I purchased a whole lot of items in English shops, which were simple and very useful lines but not seen in Czech shops or the supermarkets which had recently started up there. I took these to Prague and spent a lot of time showing them and discussing them with a variety of my friends there. I wanted to find one item on which I could concentrate and in this I had the backing of Jiri Vencovsky, who was the former Managing Director in London of Vitrea, the Czech glass people – the company also owned Horseferry Wharf about which I have written previously. Anyway, after his return to Prague, and with an evidently clean copybook as far as his activities in England were concerned, he was given the job as director of a new concern designed to promote business between Czechoslovakia and other countries. As a State Department, items recommended by this concern were treated with special consideration and in a great many instances business developed. So with Mr Vencovsky supporting me I thought that to find an item in obvious demand would be the first step on the way ahead when hopefully I would find the way towards resuming a commercial relationship with some organisation(s) in the Czech Republic. Of all the items I had the opportunity of showing it transpired that without doubt Brillo Pads was the item that caused most interest and which most housewives would like to see in the shops and would most certainly buy. I asked Jarka, the wife of my good friend Jiri Stepan, how she cleaned her pans in the kitchen and she showed me a small yellow cloth, which, I was quite certain, could not clean dirty pots and pans efficiently. Indeed, I asked her if it was efficient and she answered in the negative. I then asked her if that was all she could buy and she said, "Oh no, I can also get it in green!"

On my return to London I therefore contacted the company in Slough that produced Brillo Pads and between us we arranged for a case of samples to be sent by airfreight to Prague to be forwarded to the company importing such items on behalf of the State. With the cooperation of the manufacturers I even arranged for each box to be labelled in Czech, describing the usages of the pads. Also, in my prices I had reserved a special 5% commission for Mr Vencovsky's organisation for helping us with the business and I really thought I had gone about this the right way; I had crossed my t's and dotted my i's. I truly did not know what more I could have done, but what I did know from my investigations is that Brillo Pads would be welcomed by the Czech housewives and that they would sell, of that I had no doubt; I had researched my product well and thoroughly.

I waited patiently for a response from Prague, which eventually came – it simply said: "We already make a similar article in Czechoslovakia and so we must reject it." This was rubbish and quite untrue and when I told my Czech friends that Brillo Pads had been rejected they could hardly believe it and were all very disappointed indeed.

From that point I gave up. There was no point in hitting my head against that invisible brick wall and I began to think that perhaps as I had been a past employee indirectly of the Czechs they did not want to do business through me for some reason or another. I could not afford to waste more time on such unsatisfactory attempts to do business in Czechoslovakia. It had involved me in a lot of time and a lot of work – I could use both in a much more profitable manner. In business, time is money. And so I forgot that possibility.

On the domestic front, 1977 will be remembered as the Silver Jubilee of our Queen Elizabeth. It was still an occasion for celebration and most streets held a street party. Caterham Drive, Old Coulsdon, where I lived, was a very long road (almost a mile, they say) and so for easier management it had to be broken up somewhat. In our particular area the kids had the usual beanfeast, but we had already been warned that the weather was not going to be so good. So, with the weather warning and knowing that the adults would like the opportunity of enjoying themselves too, Lynne and I offered to use our lounge, which was quite large and could fit in 100 or so people – if they were friendly. The neighbours helped us to move our furniture out into the garage so there would be ample room in which to dance the night away. Yours truly provided the live music for some of the evening; I had an electronic organ at that time and we relied upon records for the remainder of the evening.

Anyway, we had a jolly good time and I think everybody enjoyed the occasion. On the following Sunday morning, as part of the Jubilee celebrations, we had arranged a darts match between those who lived on the northern side of Caterham Drive and those who lived on the southern side. I was captain of the South whilst my good friend and neighbour John Rowe was captain of the North. With eight a side we agreed to play eight single matches, four double matches, two foursomes and a final match consisting of all players. We had already organized a barrel of beer and it was agreed that the losing team would pay for the beer, as is the age-old custom. Lynne very kindly supplied various trays of food items, which were well received by all. This was so successful and enjoyable that everybody voted that it should become an annual affair – the darts match that is. And it did.

But I would like to describe the very last darts match which took place in my garage, which fortunately was a very large garage. Once again we divided the matches up in the same manner. My team, the South, did very poorly in the singles, badly at the doubles and terribly at the foursomes, and so it was absolutely necessary for us to win the vital team match when all players took part. In that case our points would be just about the greater and we would be the winners. The North had rather belatedly changed the rules meanwhile, because instead of going straight off, i.e. not having to start with a double, they wanted in fact to begin all matches with a double. That was the start of our woes on the South side because try as we may we just could not manage a start whilst the North did, quite easily, and so galloped ahead. Things were looking pretty black for us because the North was almost in a position now to finish the match, which, of course, must end with a double. And then we finally managed to score a double and so our scoring could begin. Meanwhile, the North was trying to finish but now the tables had turned – they were the ones who could not get the right double to end the game. Slowly we grew gradually closer and closer and then it was my turn. At this point in the game I had been left sixty-six to score and so I thought it best to keep on the left hand side of the board where the sixteens and eights are placed; then if I misdirected my shots I would at least leave my following player a double shot on which to finish. I took careful aim, threw my dart and it landed on the sixteen. That left me with a terrible dilemma. What on earth should I do for the best? If I went for the bullseye and missed I could leave my following player with a difficult finish and so spoil our chances of coming up on the outside to win as it were. I quickly decided that I should throw caution to the wind and go for it. No backing down now. The atmosphere in the garage was absolutely electric with everybody's attention centred on me. I took careful aim, threw the dart and it landed smack in the middle of the bullseye! There was a deathly silence, despite the number of chaps in the garage, but when our team realised that I, the captain, had won the match – and a barrel of beer – with what might have been, and indeed was, the last throw of the match – they went berserk. They cheered me to the heavens and I felt very proud at that moment. It was truly a fantastic match, the very best I had ever played, and I used to play for one or two pubs in my time. I was so pleased that we had won and that it had ended in that dramatic and memorable way.

Around 1980 I decided that it would be interesting to go to the USA to talk to importers and distributors just like ourselves to see if I could learn anything from them, and in return maybe I could teach them a trick or two. But on the Monday of the week I was destined to fly to the USA I was called by Alain Baumard, who was then acting as Export Manager for General Foods (France) whose HQ was in a suburb of Paris. They produced a wide range of confectionery, including Hollywood Chewing Gum, which I tried hard to sell in the UK, but against the power and publicity of Wrigley's it was not possible to reach worthwhile sales unless a great deal of resources were poured into such a project. Anyway, on this occasion Alain told me he had some forty-five tons of sugar confectionery in stock which he would like to sell abroad in order not to disturb his home market; would I be interested? Well, forty-five tons would be the largest single purchase of one item I had made to date, but that didn't deter me – I was more concerned about the fact that I had much to do before leaving for the USA. On the other hand, I was not going to reject such an opportunity, so I told Alain that providing he bought me a very nice lunch in Paris I would fly over the next day, have a look at the samples, give him a price and hopefully do the deal. Alain agreed to that proposition and so I did exactly that.

I took the earliest plane I could get from Gatwick, but a funny thing happened to me there. The customs or immigration officer checking the queue of people waiting to go through to the departure lounge looked at my passport and then asked me to step to one side. Another officer then plied me with many questions concerning my reasons for travelling to Paris, what amount of currency I had – there were restrictions in force at that time – and lots of other questions. Unfortunately, in my haste I had forgotten that I had quite a lot of sterling notes on me; over the limit I was told. He kept me there for quite a long time and I thought I was in danger of losing my flight. Anyway, this officer made me take all my money to an exchange office outside in the reception hall and change it into francs, for it was the export of sterling that was not allowed beyond the permitted amount. I protested that I was returning that same afternoon, but it was of no use. Rules were rules and had to be obeyed. I had no idea why I received this treatment but my passport was choc-a-bloc in those days with details of many trips behind the Iron Curtain and maybe I was therefore regarded as a suspicious character! After changing my money I then had to get back in the same queue and go through the same inspection procedure as before.

Anyway, I was just in time to catch my plane and Alain Baumard was there waiting for me at the Charles de Gaulle Airport. We went quickly from there to where we could inspect the goods I had come to buy. We argued and argued about what was a fair value for the forty-five tons in question but I was as tough as nails and he finally accepted my price, grumbling all the time that I was cutting out his heart. I had little sympathy for him. As a ruthless buyer I had no option to grant sympathy to those who sold to me – but I always inflicted punishment with a smile on my face! Just like my dentist! A good buyer cannot allow himself the luxury of feeling sorry for his 'victims'. Alain then took me to a restaurant on the Bois de Boulogne, which I was told was the favourite Paris restaurant of Barbra Streisand. Unfortunately, she wasn't there at the time and I recall it was the period when there was a great deal of trouble between France and England regarding the importation of British lamb. So cheeky me ordered lamb – British if it were possible, please! The waiter appreciated the joke, winked at me and smiled. After a wonderful lunch and a splendid bottle of wine Alain drove me back to the airport – and I was home in time for tea. That, I reflected, is the way to do business.

As for my trip to the USA, in those days when you bought a single ticket to the US this entitled you to purchase a further run-around ticket within the country at a very reasonable price indeed – but you were obliged to keep strictly to your originally stated programme. So I took advantage of this possibility. Before going I tried to make some arrangements to meet distributors but I was assured that once there I would experience no difficulties in meeting people – they would all be happy to meet me. However, I did make one arrangement to meet a Dutch friend of my Dutch friend Anton van Zeyl at my first port of call, which was Miami.

And so I duly took off from Heathrow by National Airlines, an airline no longer in existence, I think. Frankly, I expected a higher standard from an American airline – I was not impressed. The airline stewardesses were not very smartly dressed – even somewhat slovenly – and the cleanliness of the aircraft was not of a high standard. I was very surprised, for I had always thought that everything American was of a better class; I was wrong! Anyhow, as I have related, my first stop was Miami, Florida, and after some long hours we were there. It was a bit of an ordeal getting through immigration and customs, who both wanted to make sure I was not trying to commit the extremely serious crime of trying to smuggle through an apple or maybe an orange or, God forbid, even a banana! I collected my baggage and went to obtain a taxi when I was accosted by a Mormon who was really quite a nuisance with his religious preachings. I had only just arrived in a strange country and I did not wish to be rude to anybody. He then asked me if I would make a contribution towards something or other and without thinking I gave him $20 or some amount, which was not insignificant; I just wanted to get rid of him. He looked at me as if to say, "Is that all you can afford?"

and then gave me a religious book in return, which I tried to refuse but he wouldn't allow me to.

Once I managed to rid myself of him I then took a taxi to my hotel. It was a Holiday Inn, but just a small one and nowhere near to the centre of the town. However, it was nice and clean there and right by the sea. When I arrived the receptionist said, "Mr Mitchell?" I said that I was and he reached down below and brought up a big basket filled with the most lovely flowers. I was totally astonished. Who could possibly have sent me flowers? And why? Just at that moment the Dutch friend arrived and when seeing me with the large basket of flowers said to me, "Ah, David, I see you have the flowers," and it became clear that they were from him and that he had only sent them because he thought I would be accompanied by my wife! I am not quite sure what the receptionist thought of all this! Anyway, this Dutch fellow, who was there because he had married an American girl from Florida, told me that he had arranged a meeting for me with a wholesale confectionery distributor for the following day. In the meantime my new Dutch friend invited me to have dinner with him. I accepted his very kind invitation, but I paid! Why does that always happen to me?

The next day I duly called a taxi to take me to this confectionery distributor, which was about twenty-five miles or more away. They seem to think nothing of distances in the USA. But I recall the taxi fare cost quite a lot of money – but not as much as I thought it would be. When I arrived I entered the warehouse complex and was immediately introduced to the boss, who invited me into his office. He was a Jewish man with a Jewish name, which I cannot now remember, but that was fine, for I had always got on rather well with Jewish friends. He asked me why I was there in the USA and the purpose of my visit. But he was one of those busy-busy people who cannot sit still or concentrate on one thing at a time. His mind was partially listening to me but he was thinking mostly of matters concerning his business and so he was continually interrupt-ing our discussion by calling his secretary in and asking her for this file or that one. Quite frankly, after twenty minutes of this, or even less, I could see I was completely wasting my time. He wasn't really listening with any interest to anything I was saying, but when I wanted to compare profit margins with him his ears pricked up immediately and he said with typical Jewish suspicion, "What, do you want to set up in opposition against me?" So with that I muttered something along the lines of that I could see he was very busy and so I took my leave. He shook my hand and whilst doing so immediately called to his secretary for some other file that he needed! What a total, utter waste of time! He did ask a girl to call a taxi for me but I walked outside to wait; it was very hot and I was most uncomfortable standing there in the sun until the taxi arrived. I would just like to say that during the half an hour or so I was with this man he never once offered me a cup of coffee or a cool drink – nothing. So much for American hospitality, I thought.

If this had happened in England and I had been asked to meet an American distributor who wanted to compare notes with me I would, if necessary, have sent a car for him, he would then be taken to my home where he could wash and brush up if he wished to, he would have been offered refreshments and then taken to lunch. Politeness alone would have obliged me to concentrate on his every question, and I would have asked some in return. I would have done my best to make it an interesting discussion. Afterwards we would have taken him to his hotel – that is British hospitality! I have since been convinced that I was unlucky to meet that particular person on that trip, and subsequent visits to the USA proved to me that that was the case.

During the rest of my tour of the USA, quite opposite to the advice I had been given in England, I did not find it at all easy to meet people from the confectionery trade. Everybody seemed too busy, or away, or pre-occupied on other important matters, or perhaps totally disinterested to have a chat with someone from England in the same line of business as them; and so from that point of view I cannot say my trip was successful, and it surprised me immensely, for before my trip I had a totally different opinion of the USA and American businessmen. From the point of view of exchanging and comparing our methods of operation here and there I began to wish I hadn't come.

I changed my mind totally when I eventually got to Canada, but I will tell of my experiences there later on. Meanwhile, I went from Miami to New Orleans – a city I wanted to visit but which I did not like at all. Again I stayed at a Holiday Inn and I think I can truly say it was the worst Holiday Inn I had ever stayed at – anywhere! It was dirty; for example, I had to ring down to reception to have them change the bedspread, which was stained – there was no way I was going to sleep with that on my bed. But I managed to see all the sights of New Orleans and walked down the famous jazz street. Towards the end of the street I saw a film in the process of being shot; it was a warm day and so I took my jacket off and placed it over my arm while I stood there to watch the group of jazz players begin their parade. The director gave a command to begin, they put their instruments to their lips and started to move, but not a sound was heard. Apparently, this was being filmed only – the music would be filled in later!

However, when the parade had fully passed a man tapped me on the shoulder, pointed to the gutter and asked, "Is that yours?" There in the gutter was lying my wallet with over $1,000 in it, air tickets, credit cards – just about everything. If I had lost that I am not sure what I would have done; it seems my wallet had fallen from the inside pocket of my coat as I folded it over my arm. Oh Boy! Was I lucky that day or what? The bad thing, I found, about New Orleans was the number of black men who were continually stopping people, begging for a dollar. You cannot possibly give a dollar to everybody who asks and if you refused sometimes these people would get a little ugly. I regret very much to say that I was glad to leave New Orleans behind me.

From New Orleans I flew to Las Vegas. I was passing over it so why not stop off and call in to see this famous place; this was purely for pleasure, as I knew I would almost certainly not meet any confectionery distributors there. On the plane I sat next to a jolly, fat lady who was going there to gamble – just for the hell of it. She told me she goes every year with her husband's permission, always loses and often has to send for more money to get home! I suppose one could say she was a gambling addict, but she spoke about it all in such a jolly manner that I think she thought it all a bit of a lark. And then just a couple of seats back there seemed to be a bit of a commotion. We all turned round and saw that a lady sitting by her husband was in considerable distress. Her husband, who was sitting by her side drinking a glass of whisky, had collapsed. She thought at first he was sleeping but sadly it proved that he had passed away. The stewardesses were extremely good and laid him out on the aisle. Then they proceeded to give him resuscitation treatment. They tried and tried for perhaps fifteen minutes, but it was of no use. The captain asked if there was a doctor on board; there wasn't but it would have been of no use, for the poor man was beyond help; he was dead and there was nothing anyone could do except comfort the poor widow. When the plane landed we all had to remain in our seats whilst they removed the man from the plane. There was no customs or immigration searching for apples or whatever – this was an internal flight now.

As I have already written, I knew I would accomplish nothing in Las Vegas except the satisfaction of going there, although it does not matter where you go – if you are meeting people you never know who you might meet and who one day might be useful to you. As a matter of fact, I met a few interesting and nice people, but nobody from the confectionery world. Whilst sunbathing one time I sat next to a Jewish couple from New York who were very interesting to speak to, for, as I have remarked, I get along very well with Jewish people. He was a clothing manufacturer and asked me if I had seen any shows whilst in Vegas. I said I hadn't and he recommended me to do so, advising me that the young lady in the small kiosk just inside the hotel could arrange things for me. So I went to her and mentioned the magic show the Jewish gentleman had recommended. She asked if I would like dinner and show or just drinks and show. Well, perhaps it was stupid of me, but I didn't fancy sitting at a table filled with people I didn't know, eating dinner and so on. Why I suddenly adopted such a silly attitude I really cannot say; I have no explanation. I can only say that if those circumstances were presented to me today I wouldn't hesitate for a moment and would gladly sit at a table of strangers for dinner – a situation that I would relish. So I chose just the show and drinks, for which the young lady charged me just $8, less than a fiver.

When I got to the hotel where this show was I was shown to a small table, suitable for just one or two people only, and two glasses of whisky and a bottle of ginger ale were plonked in front of me. There I sat, quite alone. I looked around me and down, and there below were a lot of tables sitting from four to about twelve, I think, and all enjoying dinner. They were all laughing and joking with each other during the meal and making toasts etc, and so I thought maybe I hadn't made the wrong decision after all. How would a total stranger fit into that picture? On the other hand, maybe I would. Who knows? Anyway, there I was with just two glasses of whisky to keep me company, and then the show began. And all I can say is that although I had seen many magic shows in my life this one was out of this world. I will not bore you, dear reader, with a description of what occurred; just take it from me that what I saw was totally impossible.

In that day and age Las Vegas was a resort with quite amazingly low levels of cost. Almost every place offered cheap food or drink in order to attract you in to gamble. I visited almost every hotel and/or gambling joint there was – even Caesar's Palace where Adrienne Posta, the actress, was being paged as I sunbathed by the large pool. I wasn't staying there – I was at the Holiday Inn as usual – and I have no idea if I was allowed to use the facilities or not. But nobody asked me who I was; it seemed then that you could wander in and out of any establishment and nobody cared if you were staying there. I gather it is rather different these days.

After Vegas I went to San Francisco. This enabled me to fly over the Rockies and Grand Canyon etc, and I took a number of photographs. Again, I had booked at the Holiday Inn and was quite pleased with this one. It is sometimes not known that the wide differences in the quality of Holiday Inn hotels are because it is a franchise organisation and much depends on the franchisee. Some are good, some are just OK, but some are terrible. I didn't know this and chose Holiday Inns for my trip, because those I had known in Britain and Europe were very good – I thought it would be the same in the USA, but it wasn't, and that both surprised and disappointed me.

Anyway, this one was OK and so I marched towards reception; just before me was a couple enquiring if they could have a double room. When my turn came they could not find my booking, despite the fact that it had been made and confirmed by the Holiday Inn central booking office in London. They looked and looked but could find nothing. I showed them paperwork confirming my booking – I had even made a deposit in London as requested when the booking was made – and it seemed everyone was perplexed. So I asked them what I should do now, as it seemed they had no further vacant rooms at all. But at the last moment they said they could offer me a small room, but it was by the lift. Well, I had no choice; I had to take it or leave. So I took it. But I can only advise: never, ever accept a room next to a lift, because not a lot of sleep will come your way if you do. I was silly and should have kicked up a fuss and demanded to see the manager, but I was tired and wasn't in the mood for a fight.

I found San Francisco to be very interesting. I had a very nice Chinese meal in the famous Chinatown there, but I had to drink Chinese tea – no wine was served. I also had one of only two memorable meals that I had in the USA at Fisherman's Wharf, and I found a jewellery shop with a sale on and so I bought my dear wife a pearl ring, as it was going to be our Pearl Wedding Anniversary soon. Although I tried I didn't meet anyone from the confectionery world and I realised that I should have paid much more attention to making these arrangements to meet other distributors before undertaking this trip. I had been wrongly advised, and by an American confectionery businessman at that. Furthermore, just allowing two nights at each destination was a poor plan and gave me so little time; but it was a question of doing that or cutting out a couple of cities from my tour. A few people expressed interest and were willing to meet with me, but not at such short notice. I have always prided myself to be quite good at planning – on this occasion I rather let myself down.

From San Francisco I went on to Los Angeles. Once again I had booked in at a Holiday Inn and when they had asked me at the travel agent's back home in Coulsdon which one I would prefer, and mentioned several, I chose the one that was in Sunset Boulevard; I thought that was bound to be in the centre of things. But nobody told me that Sunset Boulevard was about thirty miles long and that my hotel was nearly at the other end of it!

The taxi took ages to get there in the traffic, which was the worst I have seen anywhere in the world. Finally, we arrived and I went immediately to reception to book in and as I left to go to the lift a man spoke to me, obviously English, and said, "Hello, just arrived?" I said I had and asked him what the hotel was like; we had a short chat whereupon he invited me to have a drink with him up in the bar situated high in the heavens somewhere. Well, after my journey I really did fancy a nice cooling drink and so I agreed to meet him upstairs after I had unpacked and refreshed myself. I entered the bar and saw my new friend sitting there with another man.

He introduced him to me as a taxi driver who takes him everywhere and generally looks after him. The taxi driver told me some horror stories of his experiences of being a taxi driver in LA and showed me the gun with which, he said, it was necessary to protect himself. After some minutes the taxi driver had to go and so left the two of us together. I casually asked him why he was in LA and he told me he was a film producer and was there to raise financial backing for a new film he wanted to make. I then told him why I was there and that I wasn't having a great deal of success from the commercial point of view, but I was finding everything interesting nevertheless. I asked him where he lived and when he told me I nearly fell from my chair. He came from Old Coulsdon where I also lived! In fact his house was in the same road as our village library. Earlier in my first volume I already described how I met a man from Coulsdon in the wilds of the Tatra Mountains, and here again the same thing had happened, but now I was about 6,000 miles from home, so what were the chances of that happening? Anyway, the chap was going home the next day having been successful in his mission and he asked me for my home phone number and promised to call Lynne to tell her that he had met me, that I was fine, and said he would invite her to a film premiere. He kept his word and did in fact phone Lynne and he did invite her to a premiere, but she decided not to accept the invitation. She said she didn't want to go without me. It's very nice to be loved!

On my return to my room I decided to look at the telephone directory to see how many Mitchells there were in Los Angeles and try to make contact with any relative of the film actor Thomas Mitchell (of *Gone with the Wind*, *It's a Wonderful Life*, *Stagecoach*, and so many other films), as it was alleged he was part of our family line and at that time I had no reason to believe that it wasn't true. This arose after my immediate family had left Prestage Street in the East End of London following the condemnation of our house at No. 2. However, my sister Elsie continued to occupy No. 1, and one day a man knocked upon her door saying his name was Mitchell, that he was from Liverpool, and having seen that No. 2 was derelict, did she know where the Mitchell family lived? Elsie invited him in and offered him a cup of tea, which he happily accepted. During the conversation that followed, Elsie had explained that she too was originally a Mitchell before her marriage, and so he asked my sister if Thomas Mitchell had been to see her or any Mitchells in London. Elsie was unaware of any family connection with this film actor and replied that he had not. Whereupon the man said that he, Thomas Mitchell, had been up to Liverpool to visit his relations there. So this story or rumour of a family connection had existed for quite a number of years and so I thought that as I was there, very near to Hollywood, I would try to make contact, for if I found just one relative of Thomas Mitchell the likelihood would be that I would find all the others. I realised afterwards that my idea was rather naïve because Los Angeles is a huge place and the directory I was looking at was just one of a number which covered the whole of the city. Nevertheless, I made a lot of calls and had some interesting chats with various people until one lady told me that her husband was indeed related to Thomas Mitchell. I was elated that I had at last made a connection and I therefore arranged to call back later on when her husband would be home from work; I did so only to be told by him that he had no family connection with Thomas Mitchell whatsoever and that he could not understand why his wife should say what she did. So I was rather led up the garden path there, just when I thought I had succeeded. Then I gave up the search. Subsequently, I accepted that I was trying to look for a needle in a haystack – until then I really had no idea how common the name Mitchell was.

I thought it better to see the sights of Hollywood by going on an organised tour, as I was only there for a short time. This was quickly arranged for the following day. The coach duly picked me up at the hotel quite early, but as I boarded I could see that it was quite full – I must have been the last pick up. We went to Universal Film Studios, which was quite interesting, after which we called in to the farmers' market. I had a quick look around there and saw a wine bar. I thought a nice cool glass of Californian wine would be very welcome during that warm day and so I entered, sat down and was served with my order. At the next table was a rather old gentleman with whom I got into conversation. I bought him a glass of wine too, as I saw his glass was almost empty. I have no idea of course if what he told me was entirely true, but he claimed to have been an old vaudeville performer way back when and actually knew Al Jolson, Eddie Cantor and other famous theatrical people personally. He told me some stories of his vaudeville days and all I can say is that either he was a wonderful liar or he was a very interesting gentleman to talk to. I wished I had more time to talk to this old fellow, for he was certainly a character, but I had to go back to my coach before it left without me.

Towards the end of this tour the coach took us through famous streets of Hollywood and announcements were made as to which houses belonged to which film stars, and then the driver came to a Spanish-type villa, which he pronounced was the villa of the late Thomas Mitchell. I quickly took a picture of it and blurted out, "That's a relative of mine!" without even knowing if that were true. A lady in front then turned and said that a daughter of Thomas Mitchell was a headmistress of a school and she mentioned the town, which was over in the east but the name has unfortunately vanished from my memory. Many years later on, having acquired a computer and become involved quite a lot in family history, I did explore this alleged relationship with Thomas Mitchell. I found that he was the son of Irish immigrants in the nineteenth century and apart from knowing that my paternal great grandfather, David, also came from Ireland, I was unable to discover, or rather to prove, that there was any connection whatsoever.

And so I left LA and flew from there to Seattle. At Seattle Airport I found I had a couple of hours or so to burn before my next connection to Vancouver Island, so I decided to have lunch there and entered the restaurant, which was very appealing to me because it was of a high standard. By this time of my life I had become well accustomed to all the best places to eat, whether at home in the UK or abroad, and this restaurant was of a high class. It was not at all busy and so when the waiter took my order we began to converse. Having been by myself for so long I was by now hungry for conversation, for I am a chatterbox, and we had a chat about British restaurants and those I knew in Holland, Belgium and, of course Czechoslovakia. We also spoke about wine and the fact that there is at least one red wine that is better served slightly chilled – Beaujolais. He was quite unaware of that; indeed I found a lot of people in the USA did not know the first thing about wine, at least those that I spoke to. But that was a pleasant break and I enjoyed the conversation with the waiter.

The journey between Seattle and Vancouver Island is very short and no sooner have you strapped yourself in your seat than you are there. Of course, I had no chance to see anything of the island because I was immediately transferred, after going through customs and immigration, of course, to a plane which took me to the mainland. There I went by taxi to my hotel and had the opportunity to have a look at Vancouver. I would like to say that arriving in Canada after my lengthy tour through the USA was really quite another experience. As soon as I set foot on Canadian soil I somehow felt more happy and contented and a little 'more at home' than I had felt in the USA. I reflected on the last couple of weeks and must honestly say that I did not care too much about the USA; but that may have just been bad luck in not coming into contact with the right kind of people. However, I loved every moment in Canada where I found it cleaner, the people far more polite and yes, even more friendly. I took the ferryboat and went back over to Vancouver Island to explore a bit later and found it to be very oldie-worldie – a throwback almost to Victorian times. I also toured around Vancouver city itself; I was interested because had our earlier plans (see Volume One), when we were young, come to fruition this was the city I would have tried to reach when working my way across the country – unless, of course, I had found somewhere very nice in the middle of that vast nation.

And so I left Vancouver, after having been very impressed with Canada already, and flew to Winnipeg where I was to stay with old Czech friends that I knew in Prague – the Adamec family. The daughters of this family were well known to us as they had travelled to London from time to time and one of them served as an au pair. When in Prague I often went to their apartment and it was such a nice change for me to be out of a hotel atmosphere and in a family atmosphere. Gabriel and Blaza were the parents and I got on with them very well. Zoli Ferenzsci, the boyfriend of one of the daughters, Dagmar, was often there at the Adamec flat in Prague, as was his brother Lacy, both of whom also left Czechoslovakia in 1968 and came to Canada – but although Zoli settled in the eastern part of the country, Lacy chose to settle in the west. Then there was the second daughter, Gabriela. They were all jolly good company and the parents were glad to see me from time to time in Prague to repay me for the hospitality that Lynne and I had shown to their girls when they were in London. I recall my very first contact with Gabriel and Blaza; I was in Prague and they had invited me to dinner. They knew that one of my favourite dishes was Spanielsky ptacky or, in English, 'Spanish birds'. This is a meat dish with a very thin piece of steak rolled out, then a frankfurter and some ham, and a gherkin is placed on top and the whole thing is rolled into a longish shape. It is then cooked in the oven – and, by the way, it is delicious. Well, on this particular trip to Prague I was so busy and various arrangements were being made for me by the people at Koospol with the result that two evenings running I was unable to turn up at their apartment. Of course, they were advised of this by phone. On the third occasion I managed to make it and Blaza said to me that she was very glad I was able to come at last because they were all fed up with eating Spanish birds!

Anyway, to explain further my relations with the Adamec family, 1968 will be remembered because that was the year that the Warsaw Pact nations, led by the Soviet Union, invaded Czechoslovakia and for a while it was turmoil in that country. The BBC asked for volunteers to take in some of the many Czechs and Slovaks who had become trapped in the UK and after Lynne and I discussed it we agreed to put our name forward. Easier said than done. Apparently, the number of volunteers willing to take in Czech or Slovak people were swamping the phone lines and I felt proud of the British public for the way they had responded and offered their help. I did succeed in making contact with the BBC after a couple of days and the lady told me: "We will do our best to help you but the response has been so great that we have run out of refugees wanting help!" I left my contact details but didn't hear anything more, which was just as well for after a further day or two we received a telegram from Gabriel Adamec in Prague to say that his eldest daughter Dagmar was arriving at Heathrow Airport the following day and would we meet her. Well, of course we met her and took her home with us. Later, Gabriela also came to London; we couldn't accommodate both of them but we managed to find a family in Purley who took her in. And then after another couple of weeks or so I was coming back from shopping somewhere when I turned into Waddington Avenue, which led down to Caterham Drive in Old Coulsdon, and saw people in a car with Czech number plates asking someone for directions. I got out of my car, walked to the Czech car and to my great surprise there were Gabriel and Blaza! After the invasion there was a period when order was non-existent and the borders were wide open; anybody could leave or enter the country without any control. Of course, that situation eventually changed and it was back to the dark days and personal restrictions of communism. So the Adamec parents had taken advantage of this situation and left when they could. First they went to Switzerland and then made the long car journey to England. They left with almost nothing except their immediate belongings and a painting that was hung in their Prague apartment, which someone told Gabriel was worth a lot of money – it was sold eventually in an art gallery in New York but I believe Gabriel was very disappointed with the price he received; it wasn't as valuable as he had been led to believe.

But here they were in England, tired, hungry and thirsty. So I led them to our house where Lynne gave them something to eat and drink and then we recommended them to take a rest in our bedroom and said that we would contact Dagmar, who, in the meanwhile, we had helped find a job in London and it was more convenient for her to live somewhere nearer to her work. I believe she became romantically involved with her boss who organised accommodation for her in a property he owned together with another Czech girl. So I phoned Dagmar, who came at once, and after something more to eat and drink she took them to her place.

Eventually, they decided to go on to Canada where the authorities were offering generous assistance to incoming Czech refugees to get them on their feet, and as Gabriel knew some Czech people who resided in Winnipeg that is where they headed. Gabriel could hardly speak English when he went there and they arrived with nothing – except the 'precious' painting. They were found a small apartment and were then further assisted with a few sticks of furniture – a very difficult beginning of a new life in a strange country. Gabriel succeeded in getting a job as a bookkeeper and Blaza was quite skilled in making men's toupees. Eventually, the department responsible for helping refugees paid attention to Gabriel's repeated wish to be involved in business and they assisted him further by paying his expenses for a trip to China to explore possibilities. Whilst there he found that there was a plentiful supply of rice in China and a shortage in the Philippines, or perhaps it was vice versa, but anyway, he bought 1,000 tons of rice, sold it and made a nice commission. So that was the start of a business, which he built up, and one can only admire people like that. It only goes to show what commercial talent lay underneath the society in Czechoslovakia under communist rule which was never given the chance to blossom.

Anyway, Gabriel met me at Winnipeg Airport and I was pleased to see him again. Back at his home I also received a nice welcome from Blaza, who made me feel at home immediately. I enjoyed some days with them and of course met up with Dagmar and her husband John, a doctor who specialised in diabetes. We also visited Gabriela and met her husband Kas – also Czech – and her two sons, who, I remember, marvelled at the magic tricks I showed them. They took me all round Winnipeg, and once again I must say I was impressed with everything I saw. So I began to think about the possibility of emigrating there once more. Certainly, it appeared my family would enjoy a much better standard of living and lifestyle in Canada. And so I began to think of commercial possibilities there. In this respect I was told of a motel on the US-Canadian border just above North Dakota. I was told that the prospects there were very good as many young Americans come over the border to have a good time, as at home they were not allowed to drink until they were twenty-one.

Then I met a confectionery manufacturer there who would have been willing to sell me a share of his business, or even the whole of his business, in order to expand. And then finally I was invited by Dagmar and her husband to spend a couple of days on an island in a lake which John's family owned; well, it was yet another new experience and I gladly accepted. With us we took Dagmar's son Jason from her first marriage, for he and I had became pals; there was a rowing boat and we explored the whole lake. Their cabin on the island was quite nice; I enjoyed the weekend there and yet another commercial possibility opened up. The complex consisted of a small petrol service station near to the house in which they lived, a small supermarket with a bar and large hall attached where meetings, parties and weddings could be held, and five log cabins for holiday letting purposes. I spoke with the owner and he said he wanted to sell up and retire. I asked him to give me some idea of price, which was not out of this world for me. So I thought very deeply about these possibilities; however, I of course had to discuss all of this at home first.

But a further experience I had in Winnipeg was very interesting. It was now Sunday morning and Gabriel and Blaza told me they were going to the Czech-Canadian Friendship Club that afternoon to see a pre-war film which was being presented by a well-known but old Czech film star, Adina Mandlova, and wondered if I cared to accompany them. I readily agreed because I had heard the name of this lady before and someone told me, in Prague probably, that she was the girlfriend of Hermann Goering, who was second only to Hitler at one time in the Nazi hierarchy. So we went near to the centre of Winnipeg where this friendship club was held. Chairs had already been set out and most were occupied, so we found a place where three chairs were vacant and sat down. As I did so I noticed this rather old lady in the row behind. I smiled at her and she returned the smile. Then they turned the lights on and they showed an old black and white film. It was a comedy but all in Czech; my Czech, however, was not good enough to follow all that was going on; I could understand some, but not all. Nevertheless, it was interesting to watch, especially the beautiful blonde girl who took the lead. Yes, you are quite right. This was the old lady sitting behind me! This was the famous Adina Mandlova herself.

But just a few words about her. She was very famous in Czech and German films in the period before and during the war. She was a great friend of Lydia Baarova, also a very beautiful Czech film actress with whom Josef Goebbels, the notorious Nazi Minister for Propaganda, fell deeply in love. So much was he in love that it was his intention to divorce his wife and marry her. But Hitler, hearing about this, forbade Goebbels to carry out his plans because he felt that it would be very bad publicity for the Nazi Party.

Both Lydia and Adina travelled to Germany very often to make films, for there was a strong relationship between the Barandov Film Studios just outside Prague and the largest studio in Germany, which was just outside Berlin. Goebbels was fascinated by the film-making industry and was often to be seen in the Berlin studio and very probably the Barandov studio too. Both girls were invited to many parties attended by all the leading Nazi hierarchy, including Hitler himself, who had an eye for pretty girls. But he only looked – he never touched! So this was the brief story of Adina. I should add that both Lydia Baarova and Adina were arrested at the end of the war charged with collaboration with the Germans and helping their cause by appearing in propaganda films made in both Czechoslovakia and Germany whilst the war was on. I know that Adina was sentenced to one year in prison and I think that Lydia received the same sentence, but I am not certain.

After the film had ended Adina asked the audience to bring their chairs forward and come to a small table situated before the screen where she sat. So everyone gathered round her and she asked if anyone would like to ask questions – and people did, but it was all too rapid for me to understand. I could tell, however, that this lady was some comedienne, for even though I could not understand what she was saying, I too was laughing. After about forty-five minutes or so Adina brought everything to a close, at which point Gabriel told me that one of the Czechs there had organised a private party at their home in honour of Adina and that we were invited too.

So we went in Gabriel's car to the party venue. It was a very nice house indeed and like nearly all Canadians they lived in underground rooms to a large extent, as when the temperature falls well below zero, and often as low as -30 °Celsius, or in a bad winter even lower than that, these basement rooms retain the heat more. Our hosts had prepared a table filled with snacks of various kinds. At first most of the guests clamoured around Adina. Being an extrovert only when in the role of a businessman, I sat by myself quietly because I have known a number of famous people in my life and I know that they do not like to be harassed like that. But after a while, maybe because Adina had tired of being bombarded with so many questions and by so many people, I noticed that she had retired from the fray and was sitting quietly opposite just like me. I left her alone for some minutes and then went over to sit on the chair next to her. At first she thought I was Czech too, but I explained that I was English and just here on a visit to my friends. "Ah,

London," she said. "I have been there many times – I liked London." And so we began to chat away. Her English was very good and she had an attractive accent.

After a little while, when we seemed to be getting on so well, I tempted fate and said to her, "Adina, would you be angry with me if I asked you a very personal question?" She replied that she would not and that I could ask her anything I liked. So I put my question to her very bluntly and said, "Adina, is it true that you were once the girlfriend of Herman Goering?" She looked just a little surprised at the question, hesitated for some seconds as if she were thinking over how to reply, smiled a funny smile and said, "No, that is not true. I knew all the top Nazis from Hitler, to whom I spoke many times at parties. They gave quite a lot of parties. And of course I met those under him as well. They liked to have pretty girls at their parties. But I was never the girlfriend of Goering." I then asked her, "What was your opinion of Hitler?" and she replied, "Well, I must say I found Adolph Hitler to be a very charming man. He was certainly charming to us ladies. Sorry, but I have to speak as I found him." So there you have it – straight from the horse's mouth, if Adina will excuse the expression. But was it true? I really cannot say. I have searched and searched and asked so many older people who remember the period before and during the war and nobody could confirm whether her relationship with Goering was a romantic one or not. But I did discover, or rather my friend in Holland, Anton van Zeyl, discovered, that it was almost certain that she had a liaison with Hermann Frank, the Reichprotektor of Bohemia and Moravia after Heydrich was assassinated. Frank was also arrested at the end of the war and hung. Do I believe Adina? As a gentleman I have to say I do believe her. But … I cannot forget that funny smile she gave me before answering! What did it mean? Is it possible that …? No, I must not allow my imagination to run away with me.

Well, the time came to leave Winnipeg and from there I flew to Toronto to see two things really. Firstly, I had been successful in arranging a meeting with a confectionery manufacturer there and so I called upon them. I was very pleasantly surprised to find that some of the staff there were English and so we had a few very pleasant chats together, for they were very keen to speak with someone who had just arrived from England, as it were, and to ask about the old country. I looked completely through their range of products and there were a few items of interest to me. But I doubted if I could fill a twenty-ton container with what I would risk buying of those few lines. On top of that their prices were quite high and to these would have to be added to the cost of transportation, so the eventual consumer prices of these items in England, once they reached the shops, I think would have been prohibitive. Estimating what those levels would be I could see that nice people though they were and despite the fact that they would like to see their products sold on the British market, it was very doubtful, even impossible, to contemplate placing orders at those price levels. I explained my point of view, which they completely understood, and so we parted on that note and I returned to my hotel.

The second thing I wanted to see was the famous Niagara Falls. From Toronto that is quite an easy journey. I think I took a coach there and back. The Falls were truly magnificent. I dressed up in the seaman's outfit and great big wellie boots in order not to get drenched. So I did the whole thing, but the experience is one among many that you need to share and I wished, not for the first time, that my dear Lynne was with me, as I did often during that whole trip of solitude. But at least I had seen one of the Seven Wonders of the World.

From Toronto I flew to Montreal. There I was met by my old friend Zoli Ferenzci. The reader may recall he was formerly the boyfriend of Dagmar, daughter of my good friends Gabriel and Blaza Adamec, whom I had left behind in Winnipeg. Zoli lived in a small place called Sherbrooke, which from memory I suppose is about sixty miles from Montreal, and it was jolly nice of him to come all that way to the airport to meet me and pick me up. Zoli had invited me to stay with him and his charming family for a few days. He had studied medicine in Prague, but when he, like so many others, left Czechoslovakia following the Warsaw Pact invasion, he found the medical qualifications he had attained so far were not recognised in Canada. So he had to complete his medical studies in Canada all over again.

It should be said that in 1968 a number of countries stated their willingness to assist any refugees, or those who had decided to leave the country, after the invasion. At that time I think the whole world felt very sorry for Czechoslovakia and the people there and wanted to help. I think that a proportion of people had some options but certain countries became very popular and Canada was amongst them. Anyway, Zoli completed his studies, passed his final examinations and qualified as a Doctor of Medicine.

Quite a number of years had passed and he was a well-known doctor in the Sherbrooke area, enjoying a standard of living of which he could only dream back in Prague. He married a charming girl named Josie and settled down to start a family – they had three girls. But I knew Zoli when he was a student in Prague and he managed to obtain permission sometimes to come to England when matters improved somewhat in Czechoslovakia. On such occasions we were always glad to see him and welcome him to our home because he was a very nice chap.

At the airport I didn't recognise Zoli at first because I had not seen him for quite a while, plus he had grown a beard. Anyway, he was pleased to see me and I was pleased to see him too, and although it was quite a distance to Sherbrooke it did not seem long before we were there and we chatted the whole time. Zoli's house was large and we were welcomed at the door by his wife Josie. Zoli took me on a tour of the whole house and, as is normal in Canada, a number of the rooms were below ground level. These included a sports room with a table tennis table. I challenged Zoli to a game but first of all he asked me how the English game of darts was played. He had a nice dartboard on the wall and I explained the game to him. We promptly played a game – and he beat me! I was thoroughly ashamed of myself – I shall never live that down. A complete novice beating an old darts hand like me!

Later in the evening we played table tennis. He was a good player, and in my day I wasn't bad either. He beat me 5–4 with the last game going to 21–19, I think. I said immediately that the game was so close that I deserved a return match and we agreed to play one the following day. Meanwhile, there were other things to do, such as seeing what Sherbrooke was like and fishing (for I had heard great things about fishing in Canada). I caught nothing but Zoli caught quite a large inedible fish weighing about one pound, perhaps.

The day before I was due to leave after a very pleasant stay with Zoli I reminded him of our agreement to allow me a return table tennis match and so we played it that morning. I think I won the first game but during the second I came over decidedly poorly. I was quite dizzy and a feeling of nausea came over me. Well, I had chosen the right place in which to be unwell – a doctor's house. We of course stopped playing and Zoli gave me a quick once over, after which he said he would take me to his hospital for some tests. As a matter of interest as to how the medical world works in other countries, Zoli explained to me that in Canada when one of his patients goes into hospital he continues to look after and care for that patient by paying daily visits and he confers with the consultants and specialists to agree the form of treatment to be given. This is, of course, quite unlike the British system where if you are taken into hospital you do not see your own doctor again until you are discharged. As Zoli explained, theirs is a much better system, as the patient feels more comfortable seeing a familiar face involved in his/her treatment.

Anyway, to return to my predicament, they gave me blood tests, which were fed into an analytical machine. The machine apparently measures certain enzymes in the blood which indicate whether or not a heart attack is imminent. Well, Zoli told me that my test showed normal results. But, he said, something had caused that minor happening and suggested it might be just tiredness after quite a spell of travelling with just two nights here and two nights there etc. He suggested that I change my plan and forget about New York and Washington, both of which were in my planned schedule. My last port of call, as it were, was San Juan on the island of Puerto Rico. I was going to end up there for a short rest and then fly home. I took Zoli's advice and changed my plan accordingly; I found it was a relatively simple thing to arrange, even though such a change was against the rules of my 'further travel in the USA' ticket.

I was sorry to say goodbye to Josie, Zoli and their girls, but all good things come to an end. Zoli again drove me to the airport at Montreal, which was very kind of him, and from there I flew to New York – not to stay there, just in transit. I landed at the Kennedy Airport and took off from there to San Juan, where I arrived just as it was beginning to get a little dark. I had to get a taxi, but in the melee I was forced to leave my baggage for a few minutes lying by a wall whilst I went to find the taxi rank. Afterwards I was told that I was very lucky that it was not stolen, as many things like that happen at San Juan Airport.

Soon I arrived at my hotel, another Holiday Inn, which looked absolutely wonderful in the brochure pictures I was shown. But the reality did not match the brochure and although it was quite a large hotel with three swimming pools it was also like a youngsters' fairground establishment with gambling machines all over the place and lots of young people milling around. It was noisy and as soon as I entered the place I knew it was not for me. But I found my room – I had to struggle with my luggage myself – entered it and, as one does, I inspected the bathroom only to find some monstrous insect lying in the bath. I have no idea what it was – I had never seen anything like it in my life. I called down to reception to ask if they had another room for me, but they hadn't, but at least they sent somebody to remove that monster from the bath. Further inspection of the room showed that the flimsy sliding doors leading to the small balcony were very rickety and looked as though they might have been forced open at some point – quite possible, for it would not be too difficult to go from one balcony to the next if one had such an intention. No, this place was fine for younger people but it was certainly not my cup of tea. I made up my mind to seek alternative accommodation, for there was no way I was going to stay there for the next week or so.

In the evening I went out to eat and found a very charming restaurant, which inside was decorated like a gigantic oyster shell. In the ceiling of the 'shell' were lights shaped like pearls. It was a class restaurant and I enjoyed the ambience very much. I cannot recall the meal so I suppose it must have been OK, but maybe not memorable. But I did get talking to the waiter there, who was quite a nice fellow, and spoke to him of my predicament. He recommended I cross the bridge where I would find a Hilton hotel. He said he was sure I would be comfortable there. So the next morning I wandered round to the Hilton and sure enough they had a nice room for me. This was 110% better than my present hotel so I booked the room, crossed back over the bridge and had a word with reception. I told them the honest truth – that I needed a bit of peace and quiet and that it would be better for me to go to the Hilton. They quite understood and even refunded the deposit I had placed back in England when organising my trip. With that I departed for the Hilton and enjoyed a good rest there for the next few days until it was time to go home. But I did manage to see a lot of San Juan and it was a special thrill to me to stand by an opening in a wall of a seaside fort there through which guns were fired at Sir Francis Drake and other British marauders sailing in the Caribbean hundreds of years ago, because, of course, Puerto Rico was Spanish in those days.

Well, soon I found myself back on the mainland to catch my plane from Miami back to Heathrow. On the plane, which was packed to capacity, I had the misfortune to sit next to a gay young man who told me he was travelling via London to Amsterdam to meet his lover there. If he told me that once he told me half a dozen times. He chattered away to me during the whole trip and on at least one occasion I looked behind me to see that those sitting there were chuckling away. I quickly made signs to make it clear that he was nothing to do with me. When the plane landed I made a very speedy exit, making sure that our gay young friend wasn't following me. But of course we had to wait for our baggage to be offloaded and made available; however, I kept my eyes closely peeled to make sure I didn't cross his path again. I did see him waiting for his baggage, but moved to a spot further away from him. It is not that I have anything special against gay people but this fellow was a nuisance and his chatter was incessant – he just didn't stop; in any case, I really didn't want to know about his lover in Amsterdam. After about eight or more hours of that my poor ears were suffering!

After clearing customs I went through the exit to see Lynne and daughter Jackie waiting for me, and it was really good to see them both. Soon we were at home again and my lovely dog, Sheba, went potty when she saw me. I expect she had missed our regular morning expeditions into the surrounding countryside. But we soon got back to normal again.

7

DEVELOPMENTS IN THE LATE 1970S AND EARLY 1980S

Back home again after being absent for almost a month I plunged myself into CMS and Candylux work once more and tried to get back to normal just as soon as possible. I was still not very happy about Candylux sales figures. Of course, with salesmen there are inevitable changes in personnel for one reason or another, but I tried my best to avoid such changes as far as possible. I was convinced that I had worked out a scheme full of incentives but some of the salesmen were achieving sales figures which only just provided them with an acceptable level of income and I tried to point out to them that they had the opportunity to really increase their income substantially, for the incentives after a certain level began to increase quite a lot for them – they were earning their bread and butter but no jam.

And so when going over to the warehouse at 4.30 to 5 p.m. on occasions it was disappointing to me to find the office filled with salesmen, all drinking cups of tea, smoking and laughing and joking with each other as if they had experienced a terrific day and had achieved lots of sales and that all was well. But when I asked one or two of them how they had got on, in so many cases I heard the same thing: "Bad day today, I'm afraid." Well, if it was so bad what were they doing back in the warehouse so early? If it were me in that position I simply could not do that. I would have to stick with it until I had succeeded in obtaining a reasonable number of orders. I am writing this book in my study in the period 2006–7 and I am very lucky in that my study window looks out over the village. I can see the village shop and post office just before me, and every day I see salesmen and van salesmen making deliveries or maybe canvassing orders up to 6 p.m. and beyond. Now, with all that I offered to my staff, why couldn't I find people willing to work for me like that, I wondered?

There is no question about it – if anyone felt they were not earning enough money working for me then they should look in the mirror firstly and ask themselves some serious questions, including, "Do I have what it takes to be a good salesman and work hard?" If the answer to that was no, then it seemed to me that it would be better to go and find another job somewhere else, for they were of no use to me or themselves. However, from a commercial point of view it is bad to continually have changes in representation – customers get used to one man and they do not like it if you keep changing their rep. Somewhere, somehow, one has to find an acceptable balance.

There were times when I considered giving up the retail distribution section completely, for very big changes had overcome the retail sector. The main change concerned the way we transacted our business. When we first started it was cash on the nail when the van salesmen called and that worked well. But then we had a large influx of Asian people, especially after Idi Amin threw them all out of his country, Uganda. Many of them came here to Britain as they, as members of the British Commonwealth, were allowed to do. Quite a number of them took over retail businesses – they seemed especially to prefer those with a post office attached – and so the pattern of our clientele changed. There was no problem about that, for many of these Asian people were very nice, but their ways were different from ours and our reps kept coming back with lovely orders but on the condition that we allow them two weeks' credit. The orders were only valid if a credit period of two weeks applied.

The pressure grew in this respect and in order not to dishearten the reps I reluctantly agreed to commence offering credit to some customers, but only when they insisted upon it. Looking back, I think that was a big mistake on my part to give way on this question because firstly, we then had a big task that we didn't have before, i.e. that of keeping detailed records of sales and payments of every individual customer and that was a big administrative task which was ably carried out by my dear wife Lynne. Secondly, it is all very well making rules and regulations about how credit facilities should be handled, but in actual practice it doesn't work in the way that one hopes for. Soon, when it became known that we were granting credit to some, everyone wanted it, but not everybody kept to the rules, including our reps, because there were late payments, bad cheques and fresh orders were taken from people the reps knew still owed us money. The problems kept coming one after the other, and instead of being an easily run business it became a continual worry to us.

So I had to decide: should I retain Candylux or eliminate it and concentrate on the much more profitable CMS business? I thought about it over and over but came to the conclusion that I really needed Candylux behind me as a form of insurance, because its very existence gave me a powerful outlet in case I ever made a buying mistake via CMS. So we carried on putting up with all the aggravation of retail distribution, people not paying, cheques that bounced etc, plus trying to extract an honest day's work and a more conscientious attitude on the part of our employees.

Meanwhile, CMS activities were going well. I had by this time already purchased the freehold of our warehouse plus an adjoining property, which took almost all of my and Lynne's savings; but I always knew that would be a good investment, and it was. The purchase also included a three-bedroom semi-detached house right next to the warehouse, but an old lady lived in it, a Mrs Worker, and she paid me £1 per week rent (council rates were at least £5 to £6 per week, which I paid). I didn't have the heart to terminate this arrangement and kick her out and so Mrs Worker continued her occupancy and we made a loss. You do not encounter such attitudes from truly wealthy people, because not being like that is how they become so wealthy! But I made a mistake there. We should have done what the people who eventually bought the warehouse from me did – they bought a new flat for Mrs Worker, with all modern conveniences, and let her live there, rent free if necessary, for the rest of her days. That would have given us vacant possession of the house, which could then have been sold later at a very good price; and the flat would have reverted to us in due course, almost certainly showing a handsome profit. However, I thought Mrs Worker was so attached to her semi-detached house and that it held so many memories for her that I was reluctant to even suggest that she move away from the district and her friends.

Then a small catastrophe occurred when Cliff, who was married to my youngest daughter and who worked for me, announced he would be leaving the company to work in plumbing in his father's business down in Somerset. I never once tried to stop any of my staff, especially my family, if they had an opportunity to obtain a better position, better prospects or better pay than with me. I didn't even discuss the matter – I accepted the decisions they made and wished them well. But it was a blow; the family firm, it seemed, was beginning to break up and this was the first instance of that occurring.

One day I was talking with Bob Walker, a chap who I admired because he too came from nothing just like me. The story as I know it was that his mother had a small sweetshop in London and one day she found she had a little too much stock, so Bob had the idea of mixing and putting these various sweets in half pound bags and offering them to the public. They went like a bomb so Bob bought more and they sold too. Then he began supplying other shops and before long he had a warehouse and was dealing in all kinds of confectionery and foods too.

Well, on this day in January he was telling me that he had bought over 1000 hampers with various contents after the Christmas holidays. He said that he would get his staff to unpack them and sort out the food items, but he had a bit of a problem with the wine contents as he did not have a licence to deal in wines and spirits. Each hamper had two bottles and so he had just over 1000 bottles of a quite nice French sparkling wine and just under 1000 bottles of a red wine, of burgundy style and named Arc de Triomphe. So I made him an offer of £1 per bottle and bought the lot!

As I bought them at that price my idea was to use them as promotional material, i.e. give one bottle free with every eight or maybe ten boxes of certain lines where my buying price allowed it. Of course, some of this wine naturally ended up in my wine cellar and the red wine especially had a rather unusual taste. Not unpleasant, but unusual. And as a matter of fact we were drinking this Arc de Triomphe for quite some time and so we became very accustomed to it; in fact it was an easy wine to recognise because of its unusual flavour and bouquet. About two months later I went to a confectionery exhibition at the Excelsior Hotel by Heathrow Airport – the same hotel where later the IRA used the car park to fire rockets at the airport. I was by myself and wandered around talking to many of our existing Candylux suppliers and also those with whom we were not currently doing business. At around 1 p.m. I thought it would be nice to have a spot of lunch and after making enquiries it was a choice between a quite nice cafeteria or the more upgrade restaurant, so I thought it would be better for me to be seen in the restaurant, which is where I went. There I was shown to a table and sure enough I was surrounded by all the sales directors of the various companies exhibiting.

The maître d' came to me with a menu, I made a choice and he said he would send the wine waiter to me. When he came to my table I asked him if they served half bottles, as I was on my own and would not want to drink a whole bottle. He replied that unfortunately they did not but they did a house wine which he could recommend and which I could order by the glass. I asked him what kind of wine it was and he suggested that he should bring a small glass and I could taste it for myself.

He duly arrived with the taster; I held it up, sipped it and immediately recognised the unusual flavour of the wine I had been drinking for the past weeks at home and so I turned to him and said, "Arc de Triomphe?" The wine waiter was quite astonished and said, "My God, sir, are you a connoisseur? We have clients who can tell the type of wine and sometimes even the district from where the wine has come, but never have we had a client who could actually name the wine!" And so I looked at him with a knowing smile, winked at him and said nothing, but my goodness, how I had impressed him.

Almost a year had passed since my visit to the USA and Canada and after speaking to Gabriel by phone I decided to make a further trip in order to explore commercial opportunities in Canada, about which I had been thinking for some time, but also to take the opportunity to come back via Philadelphia so that I could meet the Fenimores of The Philadelphia Chewing Gum Corporation, as the business we had started with them was going quite well. I wanted to look at their whole range to see if there were other items we could purchase from them and so increase the volume of our shipments in to the UK.

So off I set, but this time I flew directly to Winnipeg where once again Gabriel kindly picked me up at the airport and took me to his home. I will not dwell on this part of my trip because it would be a little repetitive. I finally decided, after discussing it with the family back home, that it was the motel on the Canadian and North Dakota border that interested me mostly. It sounded like something we could introduce some new ideas to and a business in which all the family could work. Furthermore, the price was within my reach. But I wanted to check out the position concerning employment in Canada, for I had heard that there were severe restrictions.

At the immigration office in Canada, which had been so helpful to Gabriel when he arrived there in 1968, I first of all met a man with a Dutch name who spoke with an accent. He was quite encouraging but he was not an expert in labour regulations, so he referred me to a Chinese lady who was. This lady coolly informed me that if I were buy this motel with the object of employing my family to run it I would first of all have to advertise each position in the press for a period of six months and only then, if I was able to prove to their satisfaction that no Canadian was available who could fill such positions, would they permit my family to come to Canada to work for me.

I politely told this lady that such restrictions would be impossible to follow, for if I could not come with my family and have their support in expanding this motel, which did involve some extra land too for possible development, then I would not be able to come at all. I would not be willing to buy the motel under such restrictive circumstances.

Gabriel was quite amazed about this when I told him and could not understand how it was possible that he and his family, who had arrived in Canada with nothing, had received so much help himself, while so little support was being shown to me, an Englishman who would be bringing money and assets into the country. In this respect we have to go back in history somewhat, but I believe it is true to say that the British influence in Canada had been waning for some time. They have had such an influx of immigrants from countries all over the world and now it really is a multi-national and multi-cultural country. Thus our influence there, once so strong, is now of much less importance. In 1950–1, when we wanted to emigrate there, we were welcomed with open arms by the immigration office in London, even though our plans were to arrive there with nothing; now we would be arriving with money and assets to develop and improve an existing business, but they made it impossible by imposing such restrictions. It is very difficult to understand such policies, for Canada is a large country with considerable development possibilities and one would think, therefore, that they would encourage suitable immigrants, especially those with assets who could pay their own way, instead of placing such severe restrictions in their path.

So I am afraid that we had to forget about any plans for emigration to Canada. Pity, because for the sake of our children, their wives or husbands and our grandchildren, I think they would all have had grand opportunities in Canada and a much higher standard of living, of that there is no doubt.

After Canada I then flew directly to Philadelphia and was delighted to see one of the Fenimore sons had come to the airport to meet me. He drove me to my hotel, which, unfortunately, was undergoing some kind of renovation. I wish I had been told this when booking, as it would have given me the opportunity to have chosen somewhere else. On reflection, I am not sure if the Fenimores didn't book it on my behalf. Never mind, I was only there for two nights. On what remained of that day Ed Fenimore, the President of The Philadelphia Chewing Gum Corporation, drove me around to see the sights of the city. I had not realised what a historical place Philadelphia was. Ed demonstrated his in-car phone system, which, he told me, most people had as a form of security, for there was a high degree of crime and muggings. I saw the Liberty Bell and other places of historical interest; it was indeed a short but very educational tour.

In the later afternoon we went to Ed Fenimore's private club – a splendid establishment which served excellent food and wine. I noted that in my limited experience of contact with Americans they, unlike us in England, rarely invite you to their home. It is almost always out to a restaurant or club. But never mind, the club we went to was absolutely first class and I thoroughly enjoyed my visit there.

After that Ed took me to the famous stadium of The Phillies, the baseball team. There we were shown to the private box of his bank. He had apparently made this arrangement earlier with his bank manager. We were offered any kind of drink we wished for, served by attractive waitresses. I resolved to let my bank manager back in England know about this, for it would be nice to have similar facilities where we too could, by arrangement, entertain our clients back home in this manner with the help of our bank. I looked around this famous stadium and saw it was packed to the rafters. I do not know exactly, but I would estimate that at least 80,000 people were there that evening. Suddenly, an announcement was made over the loudspeakers which said: "Tonight we welcome among us Mr David Mitchell, President of Candylux, from Coulsdon, London, England, and we sure hope he will enjoy our American game." Ed looked at me and I was totally aghast. It was certainly nice to be called 'President' for the first and last time in my life! I didn't understand too much of what was going on down below on the pitch. It seemed to me that the crowd became unusually excited, with lots of very loud 'oohs' and 'aahs' and people jumping to their feet at what I thought were very ordinary occurrences. What a wonderful thing it would be, I thought, if this crowd were to become accustomed to seeing first class and exciting football matches, and what a wonderful atmosphere it would be because if they could get so excited at this, how then would they behave at some of the wonderful soccer matches I have seen? I am sure one day it will happen in the USA.

I left Philadelphia the next morning to return to England and never went to the USA again, but unlike my visit one year earlier, I enjoyed this trip rather more. Pity about our plans for a new life and challenge in Canada, though.

At home once more it was back to business with CMS and Candylux and in the early 1980s two more happenings occurred which gave Lynne and I food for thought. First of all, our second son-in-law, Ray, who was married to my eldest daughter Jackie, announced that he too wanted to leave the family business. He believed he would be able to earn more money and make better progress in this life with another company. His earnings with the company were also controlled by Candylux sales and profits, for as I said so often, these factors affected all of us. Once again, I never attempted to ask him to change his mind. We had noticed something of a change in Ray over the past months and knew he was not happy. As I had entrusted him with complete charge of the warehouse operation, buying and stock control etc there was no question but that this development was a severe blow to our small company; but there was no point in fretting over it. Both Lynne and I recognised that we must both knuckle down and look after the warehouse operation ourselves, which we did. However, this did have the effect of reducing my CMS activities and so the volume of good offers and deals became somewhat fewer for the simple reason that my contact with various suppliers – especially the overseas ones – was not as frequent. But in taking over the running of our warehouse we recognised that another event had occurred which also affected our own enthusiasm in retaining Candylux and developing it into a real family business. Now only Lynne and myself plus our son Philip continued in the firm, together with our other employees, of course.

I also took into account a failed new development, which led to my buying six brand new Mercedes vans, having them fitted out with wooden shelving and appointing new and additional salesmen. My plan was to have these new van salesmen co-ordinating with the representative of each area. I had this idea of two people working in harmony with each other, and making teams in each area to ensure that all possibilities within that area were fully covered; this would be a good strategy – if we could get it to work.

So we advertised for van salesmen and conducted a lot of interviews. We chose what we thought were the best, but they were, almost without exception, dismal failures. One chap, for example, was in a desperate position because his father's printing business had failed; he had a family and he was unemployed. If I said it once I said it ten times that he must not expect miracles when coming into a new business and that he must have patience to build up his round of clients and get to know them. He lasted just one day, brought his van back to the warehouse and said he could not carry on – the job was not for him! Another one took over £1,000 of stock, which he had collected from the warehouse, and after a week he too left his van outside the warehouse, virtually empty, with a note saying that he could not carry out the job any longer. He never paid us for those goods; we pursued him via solicitors but the matter was dealt with on a rather inefficient basis and so he got away with it.

What was wrong, I wondered? Were we so totally inadequate when choosing people to work for us? Well, it was either that or we had been so very unlucky, but it is a fact that we failed in the main to find good, hard-working people who were able to take advantage of the generous opportunities that we offered. As a young man fighting for a chance to test my abilities I would have given my right arm for an opportunity such as we were offering. But it was a system that was not good for the shirkers, only rewarding for hard workers. I have often pondered upon this subject over the years and I still am unable to explain our staff experiences. I could not understand it then and I cannot understand it now. We offered a deal which I maintained then, and maintain now, was attractive and gave them earning possibilities, controlled by their individual performances: a pension fully paid for by the company, a guaranteed share of the profits, four weeks' paid holiday, plus there were social occasions from time to time, also paid for by the company. I do not think there are many firms who could have bettered our staff policy. What we required in exchange were people with a genuine interest in the job they were doing and a high determination level and work rate. Somehow, we were unable to find such characters.

In the meantime, Ray had now left the company and so we had to learn to cope without him. But now a further incident occurred which had a deep effect upon us. It came to my notice that one of our customers in South London, an Asian man, who drove around in a Rolls Royce and was rumoured to own a castle or mansion somewhere in Kent, had run up quite a bill with us.

The rep concerned should never have allowed this to happen, but he gaily continued to take more orders, knowing that money was outstanding and overdue; he was simply mesmerised by the very nice orders this man was placing, forgetting that it is not at all difficult to obtain orders from people who do not pay. This individual apparently took great delight in issuing cheques which he knew perfectly well would bounce, but he did this only with smaller and less important suppliers like ourselves. It seemed to be a hobby of his. He didn't dare treat his larger, more important suppliers in this way. Well, this had happened on a couple of occasions and when I heard about it I decided to step in on this one myself.

First of all I tried to telephone the man, but he wouldn't speak to me. Therefore, I told his secretary to tell her boss that I was sending a rep to see him and that unless he returned with a cheque in full settlement of the sum outstanding I would be forced to take the matter further. The rep in question duly returned with a cheque, but I had a feeling in my bones that this one would bounce too – and it did. That, for me, was the last straw.

I tried to speak with the owner once again, but once more he refused to take my calls.

So I decided to take the bull by the horns and went to this man's place of business, because if you are going to issue a summons it is absolutely necessary to get every detail correct, otherwise your application would be thrown out by the court. I needed to have the correct address of the firm's registered office, which is often not the same as the address from which they operate commercially, but I was unable to obtain it by normal means. So I liaised with Lynne by phone and she called them pretending to be somebody else and managed to confirm the address of their registered office. After I had all the information I needed I then went immediately to the nearest court and requested papers to take out a summons. I am usually not very good at filling out forms but I managed to complete this one to everybody's satisfaction and on our claim against this man I put on it absolutely everything – every expense I could possibly think of which was connected with this customer's refusal to pay. I claimed for the amount owed, an amount in lieu of interest on overdue payments, bank expenses incurred as a result of worthless cheques, the rep's time and petrol in having to go there on a number of occasions, phone calls and other items which I cannot now recall in detail. Thank goodness I had taken so much information with me. And so I paid the summons fee, which also formed part of my claim, and left either for home or most likely the warehouse.

After two days had passed I received a phone call from this man. He was in a furious rage; he shouted at me, he demanded to know why I had lodged this summons, that didn't I know who he was, and that he would never do business with me again, and so on and so forth. I let him rant on for a couple of minutes and then it was my turn. I am normally not an aggressive person but that man had truly annoyed me and I told him that he was a disgrace to his race, that we do not do business like that in this country, and that he must pay his bills like any other honest merchant and furthermore, that it was an offence to issue cheques knowing they will not be honoured – in fact I gave him a good telling off.

He was a big buyer who owned a supermarket and other businesses. He was not at all accustomed to being spoken to like that – also I think he was probably aware that if this summons came to court it would be published and there would be a black mark against his credit rating. His major suppliers would almost certainly get to hear of it. Being branded in that way would be very harmful to his reputation. So he demanded in a very angry voice that I withdraw the summons immediately or I would not see a penny. Equally as angry I told him that I would not withdraw until

I saw a bank certified cheque on my desk for the full amount of my claim. He tried to bluster and negotiate some items forming part of my claim but I was having none of it – I wanted the full amount, otherwise I would see him in court, I told him. Would you believe that the very next day there on my desk was a certified cheque for the full amount!

8

WE DECIDE TO QUIT THE RAT RACE AND CONSIDER RETIRING TO SPAIN

To be honest, although we had won the day neither I nor Lynne had enjoyed the experience. It was stressful and very annoying. Neither did I like shouting the odds or to be unpleasant with anybody; it is not my way. In any case, although it was the largest, it was by no means the only instance where customers took liberties with their credit accounts with us. It was all a continuous headache. So that evening Lynne and I sat down with the intention of discussing the matter and to redefine our immediate future, especially in view of recent happenings. It is true that via CMS we were doing nice deals and earning money and I believe that if we had reached the decision to carry on and found a good energetic young man to take charge of the Candylux operation for me we had a great future ahead of us. My name as a substantial buyer who pays his bills on time was by now well known and this could only augur well for us.

But we discussed what we considered to be most important – what was it that we really wanted at this stage of our lives? A good and enjoyable life? Even more money? We came down very heavily in favour of enjoying a good and happy life and, if possible, without a lot of stress and worry. That, in our joint opinion, was more important than anything else – much more important than more money that in any case we would probably never spend. We had had a lot of court cases over the past two or three years or so and in some cases we lost our money, not because our cases were flawed but simply, even though we secured judgement in our favour, the customer had negligible assets and was unable to pay us. In such instances we were awarded derisory monthly payments and even those were often not made or kept up. This made it necessary to reopen the case in each instance of default and that involved us in more work and more stress. It was so annoying to us because we ran our business in an honest and forthright manner and we had hoped our customers would treat us likewise. Unfortunately, a number of them didn't.

In the period in which he died I was not in a position to help my parents very much, because in the first place although I had a wonderful position with the Czechs I had not yet begun to earn a high level of income; also I had a family to bring up and a mortgage to pay. I certainly didn't want to follow in his footsteps in regard to retirement; I considered I had worked hard and well all my life and that Lynne and I deserved a decent life after we had retired. So we roughly evaluated our assets, for the purpose of our discussion, and we decided that we had sufficient to keep us in comfort both then and through our old age. Therefore, the choice was before us – to carry on, in which case we would almost certainly end up as millionaires (this was assured in property assets alone), or go for the good life. There was no contest and so there and then we reached the decision to sell up and go for early retirement.

Apart from business worries there was also running through my mind the fact that I did not come from a long-living family. My father died at sixty-nine, my older brother at sixty-eight, my other brother Lenny at only forty-nine and my sister at fifty-four. My poor old dad never enjoyed one single day of retirement in his life.

My next task was to see if I could sell the business lock, stock and barrel, so I placed it in the hands of a business agent; but it was not the kind of business that one could easily sell. One or two people showed interest but they came to the conclusion, wrongly in my view, that the greatest part of the earning power was in CMS activities, in which they were correct, but that such activities depended very much on my personal relationship with our suppliers at home and abroad which had been developed over a period of years. In response I offered all kinds of incentives, i.e. that I was prepared to continue as a non-executive director of the company if so wished, and undertook to return to the warehouse or office from wherever I might be for any meeting if required and to maintain an interest in the company. I even offered a peppercorn rental arrangement as far as the warehouse was concerned. But it was of no use; either people did not believe my promises and undertakings or they felt such an arrangement would not work. And so the weeks and months went by without anything happening.

Meanwhile, one day I had to go up to London to the Institute of Directors, of which I was a member. They had very nice premises in those days at Belgrave Square, which was more like a gentlemen's club with elegant, restful lounges and bars with waiters at one's beck and call, and a quite decent restaurant too. It was a valuable connection for me, for as a member I could meet my business contacts there and entertain them in quite impressive surroundings. One felt very comfortable meeting people in the atmosphere of those wonderful rooms.

Well, I held my meeting and returned to Purley railway station, as I had decided to go by train, and had parked my car nearby. Coming downhill from the station there was an estate agent situated on the corner of the main road. In the window I saw a magnificent villa which caught my eye. I stopped to look at it and although I was a little suspicious of the wording 'Prices from...' I went in to ask about these villas. They were, of course, in Spain. And right there a germ of an idea came to me – I wondered if Lynne would like to live in Spain and enjoy a long period of relaxation in a sun, sea and sand locale for a time.

So when I arrived home I spoke with her about it and to my great pleasure she said that the idea was attractive to her. It was simply a coincidence that our local paper had an advertisement of an exhibition of Spanish property that was being held that very weekend at the Airport Hotel, Croydon. Well, we thought, no harm in going along to have a look, and so we did.

As we entered the large room where the exhibition was being held we were approached by a middle-aged man and a younger lady. She was representing the London, or better to say Surrey agents. His name was Michael Ratcliffe and he actually lived in Spain, in Teulada, actually, which was quite near to a larger coastal town in Alicante called Calpe. We spoke with this couple and told them that we would like to know more about living in Spain; they answered us fully, but when our questions became a little more technical they advised us to speak with the Spanish representative, a man called Manolo. So we plied Manolo with more questions and, for example, told him we had heard that the best weather occurred further south in the Malaga region. Manola said that if we wanted to be burnt to a crisp, or made to feel uncomfortable by the excessive heat, or did not want to see greener surroundings, then Malaga is indeed a nice place. But, he pointed out, the climate in the more northerly areas, such as Alicante, was much more reasonable, more enjoyable and everything is more green. He said the best way to judge would be to go to Calpe for a few days and he offered us a trip, including hotel accommodation, at quite a low figure. Well, we thought, why not? And so we accepted this offer and details were arranged by the Surrey office and the young lady to whom we had spoken earlier.

So on the appointed day we went to Gatwick Airport and from there we flew directly to Alicante, where we found Michael waiting for us; we were impressed by this service. Our flight was late in the afternoon and so by now it was getting dusk. However, he did not take us to Calpe but to a small hotel in Moraira, a fishing village along the coast. The hotel was situated in the main street of Moraira and as we arrived a small group of Spanish children were sitting on some steps singing delightful Spanish songs. This was a charming scene and was Spain just as we had imagined it. The only point was that this hotel was closed for normal business, as it was out of season, and so we were told that we would not be able to get breakfast there. Neither was it a particularly good hotel; we were to learn later that Michael was a bit of a skinflint as far as hotel accommodation for prospective clients was concerned. We spoke of this to the young lady in the Surrey office at a later date and she was both surprised and a little angry to hear it – I believe she was the niece of Michael. Anyway, we did not have cause to complain again – we were upgraded thereafter.

As far as breakfast was concerned, Michael offered to show us a small restaurant just around the corner where we could get breakfast; we enjoyed a glass of wine there with him and agreed that he would pick us up at our hotel the next morning and go to Manolo's office, which was in a small town not far from Calpe called Benisa. There we saw Manolo again, who welcomed us to Spain. We had a short discussion and learned that Manolo was not only acting for the organisation selling plots of land, but he was also Sales Director for the builders. This arose from the fact that the landowners and developers were really the same family company as the builders. Of course, you could select your own builder if you wanted to, but Michael Ratcliffe praised the company that Manolo worked for very highly; therefore, we thought this arrangement simplified things, and in any case we seemed to get on well with Manolo.

Anyway, Manolo accompanied us and our first stop was way up in the hills. We left the main road at Calpe and took a side road that went up and up until we reached an urbanisation named La Empedrola. This urbanisation was not at all fully developed and there were then many plots offered for sale. So our first task was to select a plot and start talking prices, because by now we had both been bitten by the Spanish bug and we both thought we could be happy here in this carefree, balmy atmosphere. Now we had to evaluate it all and see what it would cost to buy a plot and build our villa in the way we wanted it. Manolo said he would show us the very best first, and I think he did. It was plot No. L15 and although Empedrola itself was quite high anyway, this plot was situated higher still.

No chance of any flooding here, we thought, which was a good point. Well, we examined this plot from this angle and from that angle and we decided we liked it very much. It overlooked the town below and beyond that was the blue Mediterranean. To our right were the beautiful mountains in the Sierra Bernia range, and behind us even more mountains. Lynne and I looked at each other; we didn't say a lot but I knew that both she and I thought this was a plot on which we could visualise our villa being built. From there we were shown other plots and even more plots until it was all becoming quite bewildering. I think we were glad when the day came to an end and we were able to have dinner at the same restaurant where we enjoyed breakfast in the morning. They had quite a lengthy and interesting menu and we enjoyed our food there – and the wine too.

By now it was Saturday morning and it was obvious that Michael was not going to leave us alone – all these agents are the same and they think that just because you are out of their sight you are going to meet some other agent and give your business to him. So they keep very close tabs on those likely buyers whom they have invited on these cheap inspection trips. But in the meantime Lynne and I had been talking in earnest when we were on our own. We liked it in Spain and we had to decide if we wanted to spend our retirement somewhere in England or did we prefer somewhere a lot more exciting, like Spain? We both came down heavily in favour of Spain. So now we had to make some decisions and we both agreed that of all the plots we had seen, L15 at Empedrola was by far the best. It was offered to us at £15,000 and I did not hesitate or haggle – I thought it was a snip and we had better buy it before somebody else did.

So when we saw Michael a bit later on he asked us if we had any thoughts or questions on the plots we had seen. I answered him by saying, "Yes, where do we sign for L15?" He was quite taken aback and muttered something about the fact that we sure kept our cards close to our chest. I don't think we did at all; without going overboard, I believe we showed just the right level of enthusiasm. So we went to Manolo's office, signed the papers and I undertook to forward the equivalent of £15,000 to him in pesetas as soon as I returned to England. So there we were – we had bought our plot and now we had to consider what kind of a villa we wanted. Manolo gave us some brochures with designs of certain types of villas to look at and we took them away, promising him we would study them and get in touch with the young lady at the Surrey office.

After our arrival home we informed the family what we had decided. Our main problem was Lynne's mother, who lived in Banstead. But then Jackie and Ray, who lived in Purley, just a couple of miles from her flat, promised they would keep an eye on her, as indeed did Philip, our son. What we were completely unaware of was that some months after our departure for Spain, Jackie and Ray would be moving down to Tedburn St Mary, a village near to Exeter, Devon, since he had been given a transfer in his job with Superdrug down that way. Had we known at the time we made our decision that Lynne's mother would be very much on her own I just wonder if it might have affected our intentions. Looking back, I believe it would have made us have second thoughts, because to leave her there like that, with nobody nearby to keep a watchful eye on her, is an action I don't think our consciences would have allowed us to take. The point was that we were quite unaware when coming to our decision that this change in circumstances was due to occur. Maybe, if we had known, we might have tried to persuade her to come with us – not to live with us but to live independently in her own flat somewhere nearby; they were very inexpensive at that time. However, we had made it clear to the whole family that we were going to build a family holiday home and that we would equip it with everything possible to ensure a nice and enjoyable holiday or break for everyone. All would be welcome at any time and no matter for how long, and we told the same thing to Lynne's mother; she could come to us any time she wanted, as indeed they all could. As I have said, what we would have done had we known about this change in the situation and if she had refused to join us I am unsure. But Lynne and I have discussed this a number of times since and I think we came to the conclusion that it would have been very difficult indeed, and even heartless, for us to go off to Spain and leave her like that.

And so, unaware as we were of what was to come, we planned accordingly. We studied the various designs of villas and one, called Lantana, seemed to us to be something like what we wanted, but we needed some alterations and additions to be made to make it more suitable for our requirements. So I made a rough design and spoke to the young lady in the Surrey office, who advised me to get in direct touch with Manolo in Benisa. But it was difficult to deal with such matters by post, and as we were now talking about a further investment the young lady offered us a further trip, also at an attractive price. This time we had to go to Valencia Airport, but Michael, once again, was kind enough to meet us there and drive us to our hotel together with his Spanish wife Maria, a plump and very jolly lady.

On one of the days we were there we stopped at a place which was reminiscent of a ranch. But it was laid out with benches and tables, for it was in fact a barbecued chicken open-air restaurant which was quite well known for its delicious, heavily garlic-flavoured cooked chicken. I hesitate to use the word restaurant because it wasn't a restaurant. I am not quite sure what to call it, but I know this: I had never tasted such delicious chicken in my life and Lynne thought the same. Wonderful! They took us to our hotel – a much better one this time – and it was what the Spaniards call an hotel-apart. In other words, the building consists of apartments which are owned by various people but which are let out when not in use to visitors like us. Our apartment was excellent and we had our own private verandah on which it was very pleasant to sit in the evenings sipping a cooling gin and tonic – but also absorbing the absolutely wonderful balmy night air, which had an amazing mixture of floral and pine fragrance.

We met again with Manolo, who showed us new plans of our proposed villa based upon his Lantana design but altered to include the changes we wanted. We did make last minute adjustments to that final plan but nothing really serious. Basically, what we wanted was a three-bedroom villa with a nice porch, a big lounge with a recess, which I wanted for my desk and for writing etc, a downstairs toilet and washbasin, a nice adequate kitchen with marble worktops and plenty of cupboard space, a utility room where we could house our dishwasher, a large freezer (although we had a fridge/freezer in the kitchen too) and washing machine, and plenty of space where I fitted shelving, making a terrific kind of walk-in larder. We also managed to fit a small library area in this room for the number of books we intended to take with us. And so the day for our return to England came and once more Michael drove us to the airport and we flew to Gatwick quite happy in the thought we had tied everything up.

But not quite, for I had to go again to Calpe/Benisa twice, on my own, in order to choose internal and external lighting fitments and floor and wall tiles etc. On one of these short visits I experienced yet another one of those strange occurrences that keep happening to me. I had hired a car and it was a Sunday. With nothing to do on that day I decided to take a run over to Moraira and see what was happening there along the coast. I parked my car and began to stroll here and there. By now it was a hot, sultry Sunday afternoon and I suppose that most people were either taking lunch or maybe having a siesta. But anyway, there were remarkably few people around. I sauntered into the narrow main road running through Moraira and at one end was me and at the other end two people who were walking towards me, stopping occasionally to peer into the shop windows.

We were the only ones in that street.

As we advanced towards each other I thought there was something familiar about this couple and as we got closer I could see that it was Peter and June Ash, who had sold us a small ladies' hairdressing salon, called Sarah Louise, in Old Coulsdon, which Lynne and my daughter Jackie ran! Of course, they were as surprised to see me as I was them. I remembered back to the strange coincidental meeting with the gentleman from Coulsdon in the High Tatra Mountains, as well as the film producer in Los Angeles who came from Old Coulsdon, and it seemed to me that this was almost as remarkable – but they do say that events happen in threes. We stood there chatting for a few minutes and then I asked them if they had already had lunch; they said they hadn't, so I invited them to lunch with me.

We found quite a nice restaurant nearby serving Balkan or Slovenian food, which was very enjoyable for a change. During the lunch we remarked how strange it was that only three people were in the main road of Moraira on that hot afternoon and how amazing that we all knew each other. I also told them all about our plans and our villa and suggested that when we had finished I would run them up to Empedrola to have a look at it, for it was already quite well advanced. They were very keen to do so for they too nursed ideas to do much the same as we were doing. So off we went along the lovely, winding coast road back to Calpe and from there I took them up to La Empedrola where we viewed our villa now in its final stages of construction. They were very impressed indeed and June especially was tickled pink that we were building such a nice place in which to enjoy at least a part of our retirement if not all, and looked forward to the day when they would do the same. Tragically, serious illness suffered by June forced them to cancel all their plans. She developed a form of leukaemia from which she subsequently passed away.

Back home the business agent into whose hands we had placed the sale of our business still wasn't really having any degree of success. Those so-called 'interested clients' he introduced were a waste of time. So I was becoming more and more resigned to the fact that we would have to simply liquidate the assets of the company and close it down. However, before we had taken any action in this respect I received a phone call from a man purporting to speak on behalf of a group of van salesmen who worked for the main competitor of Candylux, a firm called Wisepenny. He said that he had heard our company was up for sale and that he, together with a few of his colleagues, would like to have a discussion with me about it. We arranged a time for them to come to the warehouse one evening and I think four or maybe five of them turned up.

They explained to me that they were dissatisfied with their existing arrangements with Wisepenny, their existing employers, and would like very much to act on their own. I replied that I could not think of a better arrangement, because to marry their clientele with those of Candylux, plus the blending of the two sales forces would, in my view, present a powerful coverage of the Greater London area and would give the amalgamated firm an excellent position of strength. So having agreed that the blending of these people, totalling seven or eight van salesmen, I believe, with our own was an excellent idea. I explained the conditions under which I would be ready to pass over control of CMS and Candylux, but when the subject of money came up, as it most inevitably must, I detected an air of discomfort from them.

The fact was that between them they did not have a lot of capital. I knew the feeling, but for my part I obviously needed some kind of financial settlement from them. They asked how I got started and I told them, i.e. that I succeeded in obtaining an overdraft arrangement with the bank by putting my house up as collateral. They looked at each other and went away promising to think the matter over and come back to me.

They did so after a few days, but not with good news. I think only one of them said his wife was agreeable, but it was clear that most of them were having problems getting their wives to agree with the only way open to them to raise capital. I thought about it quite quickly and made an awful lot of concessions to them, for I would have liked very much to find a way for the business which I had started and developed to carry on. In fact, I bent over backwards in an attempt to place before them an offer they could not possibly refuse, including a peppercorn rent for the warehouse and, if they wished, my continued connection with the company to facilitate a smooth transfer of my relationships with various suppliers from me to them and to advise them on the general running of the company. But, as I explained, there was no way I could hand everything over to them without a satisfactory financial settlement; they would have to find the way to raise capital.

They went away once again to talk to their wives. However, it was all to no avail – they just did not have wives like mine. And so this commercial marriage of two very similar firms – an arrangement which was made in heaven – was rendered impossible due to lack of capital and their reluctance to take risks in order to obtain the necessary backing. This was more of a pity for them than me – I could still liquidate, and that is exactly what we did. However, they would now be forced to carry on being dissatisfied, working for somebody else as before.

But in the subsequent disposal of our assets what a difference in values I found when you are selling as opposed to buying. Our assets, i.e. fixtures, fittings, vehicles, plus warehouse and office equipment, all went for peanuts, and it was quite heartbreaking when I thought back to the prices we had paid for them. Overall though, I don't think we did all that badly. The final sale was that of the warehouse and the adjoining house. We had two people who wanted it. One dithered and messed me about and so after a final warning I sold to the other. But after I had given my word the first people came along, realising they had made a mistake, and offered me a higher price. I refused – I had given my word and as a man of honour that, as far as I was concerned, was that.

On the last day there I sat and reflected on the past thirteen years. I recalled how it all began, remembered the difficulties we had to over-come when we started from nothing and then proceeded to good times. I remembered too the disappointments, how in spite of setbacks we succeeded in the end – and now it was all over. There was also the issue of outstanding amounts still owed to us by various customers; individu-ally they were not terribly large sums, but collectively they came to a considerable amount. But chasing each of these was a task beyond me and I decided that the work and effort involved in chasing this number of small amounts was just not worth it. It irked me that these people had got away with our money, but I think it was probably the best decision. Locking the doors to the warehouse for the very last time was a sad action for me because this is where my true independence all began to take shape some thirteen years previously. Never mind, I thought, even better times lay ahead, and without the worry and the headaches. And so, as I walked away, I braced myself and began to look forward not backward.

The last task we had was to sell our house in Old Coulsdon. Fortunately for us that did not take long, for we had spent quite a bit of money improving the property by making extensions, thus it now had a wine cellar attached to the side of the house, a luxury second bathroom and a larger kitchen. It was really a nice house and I never did think we would have a lot of trouble selling it, even though the property market was going through a rough patch at that time.

And so the big day came when two large lorries appeared outside our home; everything was packed by them into boxes with great care, with our clothes going into strong cardboard wardrobes, and finally, when everything had been loaded, off the lorries went, leaving us there in an empty home. What a strange and eerie feeling that was and our minds went back to the many happy times we had enjoyed there since 1967. With just a touch of sadness mingled with excitement in anticipation of the great adventure now before us, we drove away from Caterham Drive having already said our goodbyes to those members of our family who lived in the vicinity, and, of course, to our neighbours.

We told the family yet again that they must visit as often as possible, and off we drove to Taunton in Somerset to say goodbye to our youngest daughter Debbie. From there we set forth, leaving a weepy Debbie behind, for Weymouth and from there we sailed to Cherbourg. From Cherbourg we intended to motor down the peninsula, through Brittany and stop at La Rochelle, very famous for its seafood, so I had heard. In the next chapter I shall describe our journey, what happened to us en route, our arrival in Spain and something of our lives there.

9

1985 – OUR JOURNEY TO SPAIN
AND OUR EARLY YEARS THERE

After landing at Cherbourg we made our way south following the route that takes one down towards Rennes, but we had not travelled many miles when we were interrupted by a series of diversions of a rather complicated type so that we had completely lost our sense of orientation. But when I saw, as we were going along, that the sea was visible to our left I realised at once that we must be going in the wrong direction – it should have been on our right! So at a suitable point we turned around and drove off in the opposite direction.

But quite soon we felt it necessary to begin looking for somewhere to stay overnight. Before we had travelled any distance at all we thought we were extremely fortunate indeed to find a very nice house with a sign indicating that they had rooms to let. So we went there, rang the bell and a charming lady greeted us who spoke some English. The house was immaculate and very clean and we would have loved to stay there if only overnight. I explained that we would like a room just for the one night but she shook her head and said that unfortunately she did not have a room to spare – all were taken. But she advised us of a place, almost on the beach and not too far away, where we might well obtain a room. So we followed her instructions and found the hotel she had described to us.

It was down by the beach but wasn't such a terrific place; frankly, I was disappointed. Young men dressed in only swimming trunks and with bare feet were running around all over the hotel and making quite a lot of noise. I was a little unhappy because I wanted this trip down through France and into Spain to be nice and enjoyable for Lynne and myself. This was the beginning of our retirement and I hoped that we would have a trip to be remembered and that we would be staying in better places than this. But then, we thought, it is only for one night and tomorrow, for sure, we will find a better hotel. So we wandered down to the restaurant below to have dinner and were pleasantly surprised. As we have found in so many small French hotels, the quality of the restaurant is far higher than the quality of the actual rooms. So we had a nice meal there and then retired.

The next morning we left quite early after breakfast and made our way following our planned route in the direction of Rennes and thereafter to Nantes and down the coast road to La Rochelle. We wanted to go to La Rochelle, for we had been told that fabulous seafood is served there, so we looked forward to a gastronomic treat. However, after we arrived there we drove around the town for a spell but found the traffic very busy indeed. First of all we wanted to find a nice place to eat, but because we were all loaded up it had to be a place where we could keep an eye on our car. I am sure that to leave our car in any public place with our goods and chattels on display in France, or anywhere these days, would have been a foolhardy act. Of course, it is always difficult when you are driving in a strange place on the 'wrong' side of the road in busy traffic conditions. You want to go slowly in order to see and find what you are looking for, but the others want to go fast because they know where they are going. After seemingly going round in circles we tired of this merry-go-round, for we just could not find a suitable place to park or a suitable place to eat. So we reluctantly decided not to stay in La Rochelle after all but to proceed a little farther – we would be sure to find something, we thought.

And so we did, in the small town further south made world famous for its cheese – Roquefort. There we spotted a hotel which stood in its own grounds and had a car park too in which there was plenty of space, because having decided not to stay at La Rochelle we were reasonably early. So I parked the car, went inside and to our joy they had a room to offer us. Of course, it meant that we had to carry all our visible belongings to the room with us; we didn't bother with those things in the boot of the car because although it was full, that of course was lockable and out of sight. Later on we wandered down to the restaurant and were shown to a table for two, which was just in front of a glass tank containing various sea creatures, i.e. lobsters, crabs etc. Whilst we were waiting for the menu to come the proprietor came with a bucket of lobsters, which he promptly put on the wooden area just behind Lynne's head. He was evidently going to do something to these lobsters and I think perhaps it was to place elastic bands on their claws to prevent them from nipping. But one lobster crawled towards the back of Lynne's head; she, of course, could not see it, but I could. I was laughing away with Lynne wondering what on earth I was laughing for – if she had known what was happening I am not sure what might have happened. But the man was very observant and in control of the situation and caught hold of the wandering lobster, and the crisis was over. Afterwards I told Lynne why I was laughing and if I remember correctly she was a little angry with me for not telling her. But she knows that I would never have allowed anything unpleasant to happen to her. Anyway, we had a nice meal and a good bottle of wine there and all was well.

We went down for breakfast in the morning feeling quite refreshed and while Lynne was sitting at the table I popped out to get something from the car. The car park had filled completely and some guests had to leave their cars parked on the streets nearby. I went to the boot and tried to open it but I couldn't. Looking more closely I could see why; the lock had been tampered with. Someone had tried to force the lock and in doing so had smashed the cylinder. Whether they had succeeded or not I couldn't tell because there was no way I could open the boot. So I returned inside and informed the proprietor, who came outside with me, examined my boot lock and saw for himself that it was quite badly damaged. We then examined other cars and all were the same. An attempt had been made to force entry on every car in that car park. But we could not tell if the thieves had been successful.

The proprietor called the gendarmerie and a mechanic. The mechanic succeeded in opening my boot by hitting the lock with a hammer or a spanner, but in the process of this very violent means he destroyed the lock completely. We were very relieved indeed to find all our goods and chattels there untouched. Meanwhile, the gendarme in charge said we must report to the gendarmerie before leaving to make a statement. It did not appear that we had lost anything but the gendarme's report would be needed if I was to make a claim against insurance for the damage done. Meanwhile, although the mechanic had managed to open our boot, we found that once we closed it again we could not reopen it; the lock was completely useless. We had a problem to which we just had to find an answer, as most of our belongings were in the car boot and somehow we needed to gain access as and when necessary.

After reporting to the gendarmerie we went on our way, and then we experienced another stroke of luck – this time it was good luck. After travelling for about twenty miles or so we saw an exit from the main road.

I had absolutely no idea if it led to a town or a village or what but somehow I had to find a garage to try to get my boot lock repaired and, laugh if you will, but my intuition told me that we would find help in this small place. About 150 yards down this road I saw three men standing by a gate, so I stopped and in my very poor French explained we had a problem and tried to ask if there was a garage here. They saw that my car was a VW and gesticulated very excitedly to the road ahead, mentioning figures – I think they were telling me how many metres away this garage was.

Anyway, I drove down and there, in front of our very eyes, was a large VW depot and repair shop! What terrific luck, or was it my intuition, to have turned into this place! It was only a small town, or it might even have been a large village, but it contained a VW depot. A mechanic came out to examine the damage and after he'd looked at it in a flash he said, "Bon. All ees OK." I understood from him that we should go to a restaurant just along the road, have lunch and my car would be ready by the time I came back. You can't imagine how happy and relieved we were to hear that. So we went to the restaurant, which was an ordinary but very nice place, had lunch, which I recall was remarkably cheap and extremely good, and sure enough when we returned to the workshop my car was ready. The bill came to only an equivalent of about £15 – I think in England fitting a new lock would have been more expensive, and I am not sure I would have been able to obtain such a speedy service.

So off we set again on our journey south heading in the direction of Bordeaux. It didn't seem to take all that long to get there but soon we found ourselves in the midst of quite heavy traffic. It is not a pleasant situation to be in heavy traffic when you are trying to find your way and quite naturally going rather more slowly in order not to miss a traffic sign. Others seem to have no patience or understanding of your plight and make their objections to your driving activity well known. The French, I found, are very impatient.

And then we had another problem; poor Lynne was trying to follow the signs in order to guide me but these were situated up high and with the blinding setting sun just above them. It was impossible to read them and so it was inevitable that we got completely lost. We wandered around a little, trying all the time not to get mixed up in that impatient mass of traffic again, but then we saw a sign to Toulouse. Well, at this point there were two options – either carry straight on and hope it would lead us beyond Bordeaux and onward to the north western Spanish border and go to Calpe via Pamplona and Zaragoza, or we could take the Toulouse road, in a southerly direction, and go over the mountains, or maybe through the tunnel, via Carcassonne, Perpignan, and then over the Spanish border and down to Barcelona, Valencia and eventually Calpe. We had to make a very quick decision because of the traffic, which was building up again, and so we decided the Toulouse and the mountain route would be more enjoyable and that is the one we took.

But now it was getting dark again and so once more we needed to look for a place to stay. However, we were now in deep, wild countryside and we could see nothing ahead for miles and miles until at some point well before we got to Toulouse, and in the middle of nowhere, we saw a sign on the roadway indicating that there was a hotel along the side road. We decided to investigate, went along the side road and came to a very nice wooden mountain or chalet-type hotel. It looked not only quite new but also quite interesting. We stopped and I went to reception and we were very pleased when they told me that they had a room they could offer to us. Lynne had had quite enough of motoring and map reading for one day.

This hotel was a really first class place. It had a few lakes in its grounds and it became clear that fishing was a speciality there. Also it was in an area where wildlife abounded and I could hear that strange but very similar cry which all birds of prey seem to have (something between a whistle, a squawk and a scream) and we actually also saw eagles fly-ing above later on. After settling in we went down for dinner and the restaurant was equal to the class of the hotel. I recall we had an excellent meal and it was most enjoyable to be in a standard of hotel that appealed to us. All too quickly our time there passed; we had breakfast and it was time to go. I gulped a little when paying the bill, but never mind; it was worth it, every franc.

And so we set off on the road to Toulouse. I seem to remember that there were no ring roads around this city so we passed right through it, but without any problems that I can remember. As we went further we were presented with the necessity to make another decision on our route because we came to a point in the road where we had to make up our minds whether to negotiate the mountains via the tunnel that runs right through them or go over the top by normal roads. As the traffic was get-ting somewhat heavier, especially with lorries, we decided that it would be easier to overtake any trundling lorries when on a road rather than in a tunnel, so we decided to keep to our original plan and chose the road over the mountains; in any case, we had plenty of time and the road route would certainly be more enjoyable compared to a fume-ridden tunnel. It was – we saw some lovely scenery. We also saw a mountain café and with visions of some delicious hot sausages with bread and mustard and a nice cooling glass of beer we stopped there for 'elevenses', even though it was barely 10 a.m. But unfortunately the choice of what they had to eat was somewhat meagre and disappointing; we were surprised at that and so just had a small snack and a drink and then carried on.

We passed by the famous walled city of Carcassonne, which is very picturesque, and before we knew it we had arrived at the French-Spanish border. Crossing was not difficult and we had no problems with customs there. Very shortly after we arrived in Spain we saw a most delightful restaurant. It was a trifle early for lunch, but we had had only a snack since our early breakfast and so decided to take lunch there. We thought that with a little bit of luck and perseverance that would last us through until we arrived at our final destination and future home – Calpe on the Costa Blanca. Surprisingly, the restaurant was virtually empty, probably because it was a little early. We had a nice and very enjoyable lunch and Lynne and I both agreed that this was a very encouraging start to our new lives in Spain. We were also able to keep watch from our windowside table over our loaded car, which was a very important factor too.

After lunch we resumed our journey and found ourselves approaching Barcelona, but thank goodness there was a ring road so we did not have go through the city. After that we were on our way to Valencia, but here there were no bypasses or ring roads, at least there weren't in those days, and so we had no choice but to go right through the centre.

It is all so different now, for with billions of Euros granted to Spain by the EU in later years they were able to build many roads and bypasses etc. But this was the situation in 1985 and, horror of horrors, there seemed to be a fiesta going on. It was approaching dusk now and people were milling all over the place, many of them rather drunk and crossing the road everywhere and anywhere without having a care in the world. Therefore we had to go rather gingerly to avoid knocking somebody down. But we didn't get lost there, as I recall, and then we found ourselves on that clear stretch of road from Valencia in the direction of Alicante.

However, before we reached Alicante we knew we had to leave the main road when we saw the road sign for Calpe – our final destination. As we neared the point when we broke away from the main road we saw the Penon de Ifach, the sea mountain at Calpe, which they call the 'Gibraltar' of the Costa Blanca and which, incidentally, I was destined to climb no less than six times. The views from the top are quite fantastic – on a clear day you can see all the way to the Balearics. In future trips on our way back home from one of our England journeys this came to be a welcoming beacon for us, as when we saw the Penon we knew that we were only a few miles from our villa. Very soon we arrived at the Hotel-Apart Galetamar, which we had booked in advance and where I had stayed before when I had visited on my own to select tiles and lights etc. We were very relieved indeed to arrive after such a long journey.

On our arrival it was necessary for us to stay at Galetamar for a short while, pending the builders putting the last finishing touches to our villa; furthermore, we had to await the arrival of our furniture and belongings etc. We had certainly motored a lot of miles from Cherbourg through France and Spain to reach Calpe and we found it very restful just to get out of the car and relax a little. Our apartment was very nice and we were happy to stay there for a week or so. Later we went down for dinner, but I have to say that in this respect we were quite disappointed. It was not a good meal we had there – the meat we ordered was as tough as old boots! But since we didn't know where else to eat at that time, having only just arrived, we simply had to put up with it as there didn't seem to be anywhere else in the vicinity of the hotel; we learned later that there were indeed other places not too far away in the direction of the seafront that we could have gone to, but of course we didn't know that at the time.

The following day I thought it would be a good idea for us to go along to La Empedrola to see how our villa was progressing. I had already seen it in a partly finished stage on my earlier visits, but Lynne had never seen it at all – not at any stage of its construction. So off we went back to the main road and then turned right into a road leading up to the hills where Empedrola was situated. Unless you knew it well it was a tricky little journey with lots of turnings to the left and then to the right. We came to a rather steep hill and saw some people walking by, so we stopped and asked them if we were on the correct road for La Empedrola and they nodded and pointed straight ahead. We kept on climbing and then we saw our plot of land and our villa.

I will never, ever forget the look on Lynne's face when she saw it for the first time; it was a picture of disbelief that this lovely building before us belonged to us. At that moment I felt very proud and so pleased that I was keeping the promises I made to Lynne when we were both young. I told her then that we would be going places and I promised her that a nice life lay ahead of us – far removed from the dirt and grime of the East End. Well this was it, and I think we both felt so lucky that this terrific villa before us was ours.

Two or three workmen were still there. We entered the porch, then the lounge, kitchen and utility room. We looked at the downstairs toilet and noticed that instead of the tiny washbasin you normally find in English toilets it was a large one like you would expect to see in a bathroom. The tiling on the floors was quite amazing and made the rooms look so palatial. Everywhere we looked – in the lower part of the villa, the stairs themselves and the whole of the upper part of the house – all was tiled immaculately. We walked through the bedrooms, which were spacious, and the bathrooms were just out of this world; the family bath was large enough to swim in! The en suite bath was not quite as big but both bathrooms had a bidet in true continental style. I was especially impressed with the bathroom fittings, which seemed to me to be superior in quality and more efficient than English fittings. For example, every tap had a fitting underneath which enabled you to isolate it if you needed to work on one tap only. So we completed our first inspection and we were extremely pleased and very satisfied with what we saw.

And so we enjoyed a few days of rest at La Galetamar while we waited to be advised that our goods and chattels had arrived, and we appreciated that break very much indeed. We had been out to buy some drinks and it was very pleasurable to sit out on the verandah in the evenings sipping our cool gin and tonics and savour the wonderful fragrant night air. In this way we got to know a young couple in the next apartment who had the same idea and sat out on the adjoining verandah. We chatted with them quite a lot and found that she was a doctor from Yorkshire; I can't recall what her husband did. Anyway, she thought we were very brave to commit ourselves lock, stock and barrel to a totally new life in a foreign country. But we took them up to see our villa and we could see that they were very impressed. As far as the hotel is concerned, we did eventually discover one dish that their kitchen could cook remarkably well and that was Spanish omelette. We were sorry we only made this discovery shortly before we were leaving.

And so the time came at last when we were advised of the day our furniture would be delivered and we just could not wait for that wonderful day to arrive. It eventually did and we were there at the villa waiting for the lorries. Unfortunately, the electrician had chosen the same day to install our internal and external lights, which I had selected and which were mostly, or perhaps completely, of the black wrought iron type. And equally unfortunately, the builders either were there already or came later to carry out a forgotten piece of work in the en suite bathroom, and worse, to carve out the marble top in the kitchen to make space for the cooker hob to be fitted. When carving or cutting the marble, clouds of white powder were produced, which went everywhere. The cleaners had done a wonderful job beforehand and now their work was completely spoiled.

And then, as if there were not enough people around, Michael Ratcliffe and his lady, Maria, called in. It was utter bedlam. I am not sure if Manolo called in that day too. Of course, as Michael Ratcliffe himself said, the cutting of the marble was a task that should have been carried out before the cleaners came to do their job – a job they had done extremely well, as I have remarked. But now the whole kitchen, plus a good part of the lounge, was in a mess and I recall it took simply ages to get completely rid of that white powder, which seemed to penetrate every nook and cranny. Whilst all this was going on the removal people were unloading carton after carton until we stood there totally surrounded by boxes in the lounge. The heavy things they of course carried upstairs and the items of furniture were put roughly into place. But everything else we told them would be unpacked by us later that day and in the days to follow. However, although we had been looking forward to it I think I would like to forget that day and erase it from our minds. So there we were, completely surrounded by large cartons with people coming and going – it was like Piccadilly Circus on a busy day. It was certainly a day of absolute chaos and mayhem from which it seemed no possible order could emerge. Too many people doing too many things, and all on the day we were moving in. We could have done without that trauma.

So we were very glad when everybody had gone and Lynne and I were by ourselves. I should have mentioned that earlier one of our neighbours from down in the valley, about 300 yards away, came to our villa and welcomed us. Her name was Dorothy Beevers; she was alone in her villa because her husband had business connections in Nigeria and at that moment he was out there. She spent her time partly in Nigeria and partly in Spain and so we became quite good and close friends over the coming years, and with her husband Ron too. She was pleased that we were English and she gave us some news and information about Empedrola; but frankly we were so tired and worn out that I don't think we absorbed very much of what she said. No matter, we were to see a lot of Dorothy in time to come.

Well, by now it was evening; we managed somehow to find some glasses, a bottle of gin and some tonic and sat down to enjoy a refreshing drink and try to relax a little. It was obvious that we could not cook anything to eat and so later on we locked up, took the car and drove down to town to find somewhere to have a meal. One must remember that we knew very little about the place at that time – we were strangers then. Of course, all that was to change in time; we eventually became experts in knowing where to eat in the locality, but for now we just wanted to find a decent restaurant – any restaurant. Manolo had advised us of a place on the seafront so we made for that and found it – Pedro's, I believe it was called. It wouldn't rank high on my list of Spanish restaurants, but at that moment we were past caring. We just wanted a meal and a bottle of wine and then maybe have an early night to refresh ourselves and prepare for all the work that lay ahead the next day and the days thereafter. And that is exactly what we did.

The next day we awoke to blue, cloudless skies. I opened the double doors downstairs and walked out through the porch onto the patio and breathed God's good air deeply. I looked around me, and what a sight it was. There were at that time no buildings in front of us at all and so we could see the town and the sea beyond without any impediment. It looked very calm, peaceful and inviting. Then I looked towards the right at the Sierra Bernia Mountains, which had, it seemed, several kinds of blue graduating into a mauve colour towards the tops. And behind us even more hills and mountains. Up there at the top of the first immediate hill behind, we were told, a hotel would eventually be built – it never was, and as far as I know, it never has to this day.

Anyway, the point I am making is that on that first morning one could not fail to be enormously impressed by the lovely views we were going to awake to every morning over the coming years, and the beautiful, fragrant air. Give me ten years of this, I thought, and I really wouldn't care what happened afterwards!

Lynne somehow, but God knows how, managed to find cups and some food – maybe it was only cereals – and she prepared some breakfast for us after which we got cracking unpacking carton after carton, but where to put it all? Well, eventually everything found a place, but thank goodness we were sensible enough to include a utility room in our plans. And so we plodded on, emptying carton after carton; we thought they would never come to the end. I cannot remember how long it took us to get shipshape but it was quite a while. We concentrated on the lounge and kitchen first of all, for they were of most importance, and eventually it began to look like a home. All the empty cartons were, of course, eventually collected by the removal people when we called them.

On that second day during the morning we were visited by a lady named Velma. She lived in a villa about eighty yards away – only scrub and some bushes separated her villa from ours. "Are you English?" she enquired. I was unpacking a carton containing photographs in frames just then and I held a photo of our marriage ceremony in my hands. So I answered, "Yes, we are English, and look, such memories," as I showed her the photograph. She was very pleased at that and also very pleased indeed that we were English because Velma was an Anglophile from the tips of her toes to her hair – she loved everything English, especially old-fashioned English style and old-fashioned manners, as indeed I did and still do. She spoke with a curious accent which puzzled me. I am usually quite good at recognising accents but this one defeated me. Velma became very friendly with us over the next weeks, months and years. She was mostly on her own, although her two daughters and her small grandson came out to visit her from time to time.

Velma told us she was married previously to a gentleman who was some kind of executive for a well-known bank and in that capacity they had visited and lived in various countries as and when her husband received instructions to do so from the bank that employed him. I believe he was killed in some kind of accident.

But Velma became something of a mystery to us. She claimed to come from Alsace and she told all kinds of stories about wartime and being there under German occupation. She had a scar on her leg and also claimed that this was a German bayonet wound, which she suffered whilst hiding in a cart of hay when she was running messages for the French underground, the Maquis. However, she spoke neither French nor German, which all Alsatian people do. We caught her out in a number of fibs and soon learned to take anything that Velma said with a large pinch of salt. For example, she came to our villa one evening just as we were finishing dinner. We were drinking a bottle of Hugo's Gewurtztraminer, an excellent white wine from the Alsace, the name conveying that it is a peppery or spicy wine made from the Tramin grape variety. As she walked in I said to her, "Hello, Velma. I am just enjoying a glass of wine which is from your country." Velma looked at the bottle and said, "Oh Yes, I know it well. My father and Gewurtz were very good friends for years!" In such ways those who tell fibs are found out.

But we tolerated Velma despite the fact that you could not rely upon very much that she said. However, it remained an intriguing question – where did she come from? What was her real country of origin? She most certainly was not from the Alsace. She gave a clue one day that might throw some light on that puzzle. One early evening we were sitting in our porch looking out towards the sea; we were enjoying a cool glass of wine and discussing the war. At one point the conversation centred upon concentration camps. At a busy point in the discussion Velma suddenly blurted out, "I Know – once in Ismalia–" and then abruptly stopped. We looked at her to encourage her to continue but she would not say another word about camps and clearly wanted to change the subject. But the fact of the matter was that a large refugee camp was situated in Ismalia, Egypt, during and immediately after the war.

We may be quite wrong, but Lynne and I added two and two together and came to the conclusion that she was most probably a young Egyptian or Arab refugee, perhaps even Israeli, although I don't think so, for she had that kind of classical Arabic appearance. However, she was a very sophisticated lady and met her first husband when he was serving in the British army. Sometime afterwards, we learned, they married and she returned with him to Britain after the end of the war. He was a milkman in 'Civvy Street', or something like that. But then, we assume, she must have divorced him for some reason and then met another man named Short; he was, or became, a bank executive on the foreign section. So she not only became accustomed to English ways, but also travelled with her husband to various foreign localities as and when he was posted abroad. That is our summary of the puzzle of Velma – we may have been right, we may have been wrong. But whatever may have been true, we accepted her at face value and forgave her fibs.

Velma adopted the habit of coming over the grass and scrubland separating her land from ours when she saw our external lights on and us sitting out on the patio catching the cool evening breeze. We then had coffee and liqueurs and long, long periods of conversation which went on sometimes into the early hours of the morning. They were very enjoyable occasions and I recall them very well.

After we had been there three days Manolo came again to our villa. He had a statement with him that showed that an amount was outstanding and he requested a cheque, which we immediately gave to him. But I thought it strange that up to then we had not a received a proper invoice showing and detailing what had been done and what this or that had cost. Such an invoice should have accompanied a statement showing what amounts had been paid and what was still outstanding. That is quite normal procedure in any business and in any country – apart from Spain, that is! As an ex-businessman myself I should have insisted upon such a proper procedure, but I didn't. All that I ever had from Manolo were statements which showed little or no detail at all. Therefore, it was unclear and somewhat confusing to know what had been charged for what and how much each item had cost. I suppose that was the Spanish way back then. But I can say that I knew to the last peseta what I paid him and when totalling up everything we were well satisfied. We had acquired a wonderful villa for a very reasonable sum.

Anyway, we made use of Manolo's visit because he asked us why we had no water in our swimming pool. We replied that we had been told it was forbidden to fill swimming pools from the mains water supplies and that water for pools had to be ordered by tankers from an organisation which specialised in that service. At that Manolo snorted, immediately went down to the pool room and turned on the water from the mains supply! I believe it took at least two days for the pool to fill properly, but when it was full it truly looked beautiful because the reflection of the coloured pool tiles through the water was something rather special and we looked upon it with pride. Having also heard some horror stories about frequent water shortages in Spain we had also ordered, and had built next to the swimming pool, a huge 20,000 litre underground emergency tank, which Manolo also filled. I was very pleased we did this for there were water shortages from time to time and our emergency supply was more than useful. Of course, you could not drink this water, even if it were boiled, but for showers, baths, toilets and washing etc it was quite OK, of course.

We had not been there more than a few days before yet another lady came to our villa, introduced herself as being English and invited us to an English resident get-together which they were holding the following day. It would be a barbecue and wine affair. Well, having only recently moved in we were up to our eyes with various tasks to perform, but we thought that we had better show a friendly response – also it would give us a chance to meet some more people. So we gladly accepted their invitation. Their villa was the very furthest point on the urbanisation away from us, way down in the valley and No. 1.

It was a pleasant gathering of people and the face of the man of the house looked vaguely familiar to me; however, I couldn't place him. So I asked him what he did back home and it transpired he held a position with Landauer & Co. of Eastcheap – importers of various items including dried and canned fruits – and he traded with my old boss, Harold Frost. So that is where I knew him from and why I thought I had seen him before, because Harold Frost used me in every possible capacity from making the tea to fetching and carrying samples of goods here and there. Landauer's place in Eastcheap I had visited on a number of occasions for Mr Frost. What a very small world this is! He did not live on Empedrola permanently but visited his villa there from time to time when he could get away from business.

As I have mentioned, Velma had two daughters, one of which, Amy, was an editor involved with the BBC and had something to do with various popular programmes of that time. The other daughter, named Fran, was connected with the film world, although precisely in which capacity I am not sure, but I believe she was something to do with PR work.

DAVID MITCHELL

She showed us photographs of herself with various film stars – maybe just to prove she wasn't telling 'porkies' like her mother!

But then the situation changed somewhat because a family, who also lived on Empedrola, entered the picture. I should point out that opposite the entrance to our villa was the post house, which consisted of a small brick and tiled building in which one complete wall was almost covered with individual metal post boxes. Every resident had keys to their own box and we all labelled our box with our address details. The postman then came to the post house, pushed the letters into the various boxes and then later on the residents would come to see if they had any post to collect. Any post that had a bad address and which the postman could not decipher he placed in a pile on the side for people to examine and try to recognise.

And so it followed that we had quite a lot of visitors, especially if and when I was playing the organ. The music would attract people to pop over the road to see what all the commotion was about. We met a lot of people that way and so I invented a low alcohol drink consisting of 33% chilled rosé wine, 33% Casera (a fizzy drink something between tonic water/soda water/lemonade) and 33% soda water. This I topped up with ice cubes, and a two-litre jug of what I called 'David's guaranteed cough mixture' was always to be found in our refrigerator. I must admit that sometimes I threw in a small glass of Spanish brandy to liven it up. It became well known by all our neighbours, as well as friends away from the urbanisation, because sometimes our debates about various things of interest went on for ages and we all needed to lubricate our throats from time to time. The beauty of this drink was that it was low in alcohol content and so you could drink glass after glass and not feel tipsy at all. And just as soon as a jug was emptied I refilled it immediately. We never ran short of 'David's cough mixture'.

Anyway, one day a chap had been to the post house and either we or I met him there and invited him over for a drink, or perhaps he came over of his own volition – I really can't remember. But anyway, we met him. He seemed to be an affable kind of man and he claimed that he owned in fact three plots of land, each adjoining the other right in the centre part of the urbanisation. On one he had built his own extensive and immaculate villa. He was married and had two sons and a daughter. So we invited them round for a drink sometime and that was how they became introduced to Velma, who as usual came over when she saw something was going on.

During our chats and from what was said it became clear that the father of this chap, I shall call him Simon, was a mid-European and left his country at some point before the war to come to England as he was Jewish;

174

with him he brought a number of very historical and ornate documents and books from Eastern Europe which had been passed down to his family and he claimed to have these precious documents in his villa. Hearing of my own connections with that part of the world, Simon promised he would show them to me, which he did eventually and although I am no expert in old documents, I would say they were quite valuable. The snag in this story is that Simon had a brother who was abroad somewhere quite far away and when the father died I heard that Simon had assumed control of a number of items from the estate. I do not know if it is true but I was told that there was a bone of contention between the brothers about who was entitled to what, as there often is in many families about inheritances. Casting my mind back I seem to recall that this was told me by Simon himself!

Anyway, we had a jolly nice get-together at our place and inevitably the conversation got around to food, at which Simon said they had found a really good restaurant in Calpe and invited us to sample it. We accepted and duly went to the restaurant with them. We found the restaurant to be OK, but nothing very special in our view, although politeness forbade us to say so. When the bill arrived I asked what our share was, but Simon refused to take even one peseta from me. We found this to be a little embarrassing because we always preferred to pay our way and sharing the bill was the custom whenever we went out with other neighbours. However, never let it be said that we did not have a reasonable degree of grace and so we accepted the situation, vowing to have our 'revenge' at some point in the future – and we did ! So it seemed that Simon acted as though money was plentiful and no problem to him. We had introduced Velma to Simon and his family around our patio table and as far as Velma was concerned she, under the impression that this was quite a rich family indeed, regarded them with a degree of respect that in due course appeared to be perhaps unwarranted although I must stress that we had no actual knowledge of anybody's financial status – except our own.

Our very first visitors from England were our youngest daughter Debbie and her husband, Cliff. On their day of arrival we motored from Calpe to Alicante Airport, a journey we were to do so often we could almost do it blindfold. There were two ways you could go: by the ordinary route through the towns and villages, or by the motorway, for which you had to pay. Mostly, unless time was of the essence, we chose to go by the ordinary route, which made for a much more interesting journey anyway. I believe, thinking back, that their plane was slightly delayed but not badly so. Delayed flights and hanging around the airport was something else we were to get quite used to in the coming years. Anyway, they arrived and they were as pleased to see us and we were pleased to see them – our first of many visitors, and all of them were very welcome indeed. They were our link to home. Debbie wanted to know if our swimming pool was ready for swimming and we were able to tell her it was.

As I have already written, we had Manolo to thank for that; he also gave us very useful information on keeping one's pool healthy, hygienic and clean, for we, of course, knew nothing at all about how to do that as we had never had a swimming pool before. We also received good advice in this respect from Michael, the agent, who told us where we could purchase the necessary materials. Fortunately, a vacuum pool cleaner came with the pool, together with a long-handled brush, both of which I of course used and I made it almost a daily practice to get up in the morning and vacuum the pool, whether necessary or not; the water drew any dust or dirt with it and went through the filter, was cleaned and was then returned to the pool. Apart from the addition of chlorine, which one tested and topped up at least twice per week for the purpose of hygiene, it was necessary to control the pH, or the acidity level, of the water, which was achieved with another powder.

I, like most people who had never had a pool in their lives before, mastered pool care quite quickly and we all became experts in the procedure before long. But anyway, we were able to satisfy Debbie that the pool was open for swimming.

We had also arranged for a cold-water shower to be installed on the far end of the patio and we requested guests to take a shower to wash off the worst of any sun oils etc that they may have on before entering the pool. We did this in a diplomatic way, but it was necessary that this be done otherwise you would find a rim of oil scum all round the tiles after a while, which was rather hard work to eliminate. Also we found that some guests would strip off down to their bathers, oil themselves and then sit on our lovely patio chair cushions, which were of a burgundy colour; or maybe on the small velvet-cushioned sofa we had in the porch. It was really quite embarrassing how thoughtless some people could be and although we never wanted to nag – it shouldn't have been necessary to do so – we didn't want our lovely new furniture and cushions, of which we were quite proud, to be spoilt and I am glad to say that most people understood that.

Anyway, we arrived back at the villa and Debbie and Cliff were very impressed with what they saw. We ate mostly at home, of course, but we did go to a few nice restaurants, including a special one in Altea, a town along the coast in a south-westerly direction, where Jack Charlton, the famous footballer, has his villa, and where at the top of a hill, reached by climbing a quite long stone-stepped alleyway, one would find this medium size restaurant. It was run by a Swiss gentleman who, we were told, used to be a theatrical man some years previously back in Switzerland.

The food there was more expensive but very good indeed. But without doubt the main attraction was the proprietor himself who performed various acts for the amusement of his clientele. For example, he would dress himself in a special costume which made him look like a woman from one angle and a man from the other. He would stand there on the stairs looking over the clients so that he could be seen by everybody, and then he would begin to sing an operatic aria. When he turned as a man he sang in a deep voice and when he turned and showed himself as a woman he sang in a falsetto tone. It was truly a brilliant act and well worth paying the extra to be entertained like this. And then he would play tricks on various people, which made everybody laugh – even our Debbie, whom he approached; I do not know how he did it, but somehow he made it appear as if he had robbed her of her bra! The laugh was that she wasn't even wearing one! Then he would serve a customer with a nice steak and give him a steak knife which promptly bent when the customer attempted to cut the meat; and spoons which bent too – there were lots of tricks and all the time you were kept amused by this artist. I doubt very much if this particular restaurant exists now, for the proprietor was not exactly a young man back then in the 1980s and at the time of writing this it is now sixteen or seventeen years or so ago! Time flies.

Well Debbie and Cliff had a very enjoyable holiday with us, but it is surprising how quickly two weeks go by when you are having a nice time. They swam, we explored the Penon de Ifach and, if my memory serves me correctly, Cliff and I, at least, reached the top; and we visited quite a few restaurants, so all in all it was a nice fourteen days. I would also like to say that whilst he was there on holiday Cliff did a number of jobs around the house and garden for me. I did not expect this of him and told him not to worry but to enjoy his holiday. However, he seemed to like being occupied and so I let him get on with it. But I was truly grateful for his help.

We had a small disaster during their stay when after Debbie took a bath one day, she emptied it and suddenly water began to gush from the external stairs leading down to the pool room. Being out of town we had a septic tank arrangement for sewage. It should have consisted of at least two tanks, preferably three, and for usage by just Lynne and myself this worked quite well and without any problem. But it seemed that with a greater number of people and, therefore, a much higher usage of water, the system was inadequate. However, the builders were very good about it all and after digging down to examine what had happened they found the fault – only one septic tank had been fitted. I was told by the Spaniards that if you have the three-tank system the water in the third tank is almost pure and could almost be drunk – not that I would wish to drink it!

Our builders could not give me a satisfactory explanation for this error but the problem was solved when they told us, after some lengthy discussions between themselves, that the new terraced villas they were building in a road almost opposite to our plot would have a different system in that a sewer pipe would run from the development, down the hill and away into the countryside somewhere at the other end of the valley – I didn't particularly want to know exactly where! So they said it would be a simple thing to connect us to that system via a pipe running from our villa underneath the road. They eventually carried out this work and we never had any further trouble at all. It was just like having a main sewerage system.

After the return home of Debbie and Cliff I heard from Ray back in England that one of our customers in the Midlands had been enquiring about further supplies of a bubble gum line I handled whilst in business. He could not take a whole twenty-ton lorry load, which was the only economical way to shift goods from Italy to England, and so I got cracking with other clients by phone and soon we were able to make up a full lorry load. With the kind help of our builders, who had a telex machine in their Benisa office, I was in touch with our Italian suppliers, agreed price levels with them, organised a lorry to collect the goods with instructions where to drop the goods off – I believe it was just two drops – and Ray oversaw that part of the operation for me for which I, of course, gave him a cut of the profits. So, it seemed, we could still operate even when sitting round our swimming pool! It was a healthy transaction which earned us a few thousand welcome pounds, but to be frank, I did not encourage any more business. Rightly or wrongly, I decided that retirement means just that. It was time to put Confectionery Marketing Services to bed.

Our next visitors would be Jackie and Ray, Lynne's mother and our two grandsons, Darren and Grant. They were coming from Gatwick Airport and of course I was there, at Alicante Airport, to meet them. Lynne stayed at home for two reasons; firstly, there would not be enough room in the car, and secondly, she wanted to prepare something to eat for them when they arrived. So off I went to the airport, but I asked Lynne to listen out for a loud honk from my car and that when she heard it she should switch on all the lights of the villa, including the pool lights. We knew that it shone like a brilliant beacon high in the hills, almost like a palace, and we also knew that our guests would be very impressed. You could call it showing off if you like – and I would agree! But why not? We were, after all, very proud of our villa.

As far as I can recall there was no great delay with their plane and so we were soon on our way to Calpe. It was rather late at night, I think, and when I approached La Empedrola I gave a loud honk from down in the valley as arranged with Lynne – I was about a half mile away but sound at night carries much more easily and Lynne heard it without difficulty. So we drove up the hill until we came to our driveway and as I drove in Jackie cried out, "No, Dad, you can't drive in here. You'll get into trouble!" She just could not believe that this lovely place before us could be ours. But I assured her that it was and all I can say is that she and Ray and Lynne's mother were all quite astounded. And that made us feel very good. It was half term, but Jackie and Ray had to obtain special permission for Darren and Grant to miss a few days' school so they could stay for two weeks. To be truthful, I cannot recall much of those two weeks, but I am sure we all had a nice time and, like all our visitors, we were sorry to see them go back home. I ran them to the airport, of course, but we knew we would see each other again quite soon because I had to return to England with my Santana car, as the permitted six months on my English licence plate was drawing very near.

10

SETTLING DOWN IN SPAIN

And so the time went by and it was necessary to arrange the return of my car to England. Of course, we spoke of our intentions to go home in December, at which Velma expressed her sorrow that we would not be there for Christmas. So Lynne and I considered that it would be a pity for her to be on her own and therefore we decided to run the car home to England and return by plane before Christmas. This was just as well because Lynne's mother expressed a wish to come to visit us at Christmas once more, and our son Philip decided he too would like to join her and see this villa that all the family was talking about. So there was a double reason for us to return and to be there for the holiday period.

In the meantime there was no question about it, Velma was becoming more and more enthralled by Simon and his family. She was now so sure they were a rich family and that is something that impressed her enormously. She seemed to have a great respect for apparently wealthy people and Simon, with his large and very attractive villa plus his additional plots of land, certainly gave the appearance of being wealthy. Similarly, Simon and his family seemed to become very attached to Velma – they too perhaps assumed, by the way she spoke, that she was a very wealthy woman and similarly, therefore, they also respected her. In due course we were to find out that perhaps none of them appeared to be very wealthy people at all! We neither gave the impression that we were poor or rich – we just didn't speak of it, feeling that it was uncouth to do so, and neither did wealth, nor the lack of it, affect any degree of respect we paid to anybody. Anyway, what is rich? It seems to me that it means different things to different people. Once upon a time it seemed to be really something when referring to being a millionaire – but today that is nothing special. In my life I have met many wealthy people and in my knowledge of them many seemed to have something in their past activities of which they were, or should be, ashamed. In my experience of all kinds of people, both rich and poor, I truly believe it is perhaps difficult, although not totally impossible, to become rich without resorting to methods that most of us would shrink from. Very few truly nice people become rich in my considered opinion!

Anyway, our plans for the Christmas period were made and we decided to go home to England via the Valencia-Pamplona-Bordeaux route and then on to Roscoffe to catch the boat there to Portsmouth. I booked a complete service for my car, which, as I have written, was a VW Santana – one of the nicest cars I ever had – at a garage in Calpe. They were VW agents so I thought all would be OK in their hands. I collected my car a couple of days before our departure and when the day came we made a point of starting very early in the morning, about 5.30, I think. Of course, during the early stages of our journey the traffic was sparse, but as the time went by so the traffic increased. Our first problem was Valencia, because there were no ring roads at that time, but by going carefully and with Lynne peeling her eyes for signs we managed to get through without too many problems.

Not too long after Valencia we knew we had to take a turning to the left which would take us up in the direction of Pamplona. We found that road without bother and soon were winging our way through countryside and climbing all the time. This was just a normal winding road and we noticed that we were going up and up, seemingly for miles. When we reached a part of the road which had a clearing on the side we thought we would stop to have something to eat and drink, as we had had very little breakfast before our departure. So I drew over, parked and turned the engine off. I got out to stretch my legs and noticed the bitter cold. We were up very high and soon it began softly to snow. Fortunately, it was not that heavy kind of snow and so there was little drifting or anything like that.

We finished our snack and were ready then to resume our journey, but when I turned the ignition key on nothing happened. I tried again and again – nothing. So what on earth could we do now? We were stranded on a country road, miles and miles from anywhere, not a soul in sight and with a car that didn't function. We could not even keep warm because by now in those low temperatures the engine was stone cold anyway. We must remember that this was December.

My first thought was that although I was not at all suitably dressed, for I had never expected to encounter snow in Spain, I would walk back in the direction we had come from, because I thought I remembered seeing some buildings and maybe even a garage back there, but how far back I had no exact idea.

There were no cars on the road that I could stop to ask for help. But wait – wasn't that a car in the distance coming towards us? It most certainly was, so I hurried to the opposite side of the road and flagged down the approaching car. I just prayed he would stop. Actually, they did and there were two men in the car. I explained as best I could that we had a problem and that we were on our way to England etc, at which the driver brought out a mobile phone – glory be! But my immediate sense of triumph quickly changed back to despair when he failed to make any connection. I was now getting worried that poor Lynne would be frozen sitting in our car and I just didn't quite know what to do, when suddenly the very nice man in the car told me to wait there (as if I could go anywhere anyway!) and he promptly turned his car around and went back in the direction he was coming from.

I returned to Lynne, who was bearing up to our predicament quite bravely, but we were getting colder and colder. However, before long we saw our friends approaching us in the distance once more. I hastily got out of our car, ran over to the other side of the road and they pulled up beside me. He gave me to understand that all would be OK and that help was on its way. I thanked him over and over again for his kindness towards us and they drove off.

About five minutes later a breakdown vehicle arrived. They had a look in the engine compartment, connected up my battery to theirs and my car started. But they said, if I understood them correctly, that I must follow them. I did so for about two miles or so and we came to a small conglomeration of buildings. On one side was a café and on the other was a garage workshop. They indicated then that we should go to the café and that they would examine my car and check on the trouble. We did so and at least we were in the warm with a nice cup of hot coffee to keep us going. The café was filled with lorry drivers and they were a noisy lot, but never mind, we had been rescued and we were happy at that.

Whilst we were sitting there I began to try and fathom what could have possibly gone wrong. How was it possible for us to travel all this way, I would estimate about 200 miles or more, with our car behaving perfectly and then have our battery give out on us just like that? It just didn't make sense to me, but then I am not a motor mechanic. We had to wait for a while; probably they had checked the battery and put it on rapid charge.

But eventually they came to tell us our car was ready. So I paid their bill, thanked them very much for all their help and on we went, but although I didn't say it at the time I wondered if the same thing might happen again. However, it didn't and we sailed through to Pamplona and then on towards the French border without further mishap. That was a mechanical mystery for which there was no logical explanation.

Crossing the border was no problem at all and now we were on the main road to Bordeaux, but we had been seriously delayed and so we thought we had better try to find somewhere to eat, drink and sleep. So we began looking and after a while we saw an exit from the main road. It was not signposted but we could see some bright lights a few hundred yards ahead and we hoped it might be a hotel. But it wasn't – it was a restaurant. However, it looked to be quite a homely-looking restaurant so we thought it was worthwhile asking if they had any rooms, and to our great relief the lady there told me she had one.

Once again the problem we had to face was unloading all the items we had in the back of the car and the boot. We remembered our experience at Roquefort and didn't want a repeat performance of that. But I found that I could back up with the end of my car deep in the thick bushes; nobody would be able to touch anything in our car boot because they wouldn't be able to get to it. So with that we went to our room; to be honest, it was pretty ghastly. Yet again, nice restaurant, lousy rooms. But we were both so tired. It had been a very long day. Neither of us felt like looking for some other place. And so we decided to rough it for the one night. However, there was dinner to consider and so we went downstairs to the restaurant and as I recall we had quite a nice meal there and a bottle of wine to buck up our spirits, which, considering everything, were remarkably high, especially after the wine!

The next morning we had breakfast and then began our journey to Bordeaux. I was a bit nervous of that city, bearing in mind our experiences there when first making the journey through France to Spain. But on this occasion we found the ring road quite easily and before long we were on the northerly side of Bordeaux and racing along in the direction of Rennes. At some point south of Rennes we thought it was time to start once again looking for somewhere to eat and to sleep. The memories of Lynne and myself differ somewhat about what happened after that because we did quite a number of similar journeys and it is easy in one's mind to mix up one journey with another. But I must write according to my memory and as far as I can recall we were directed by a sign on the opposite side of the road, which simply said 'Hotel' with an arrow.

But as it was a dual carriageway I had to wait until there was a break in the road before I could turn round and go back. I did so, followed the sign and eventually came to what was a restaurant rather than a hotel. I walked inside and they were clearing up with not a client in sight. That was our first indication that in the countryside of France you will be jolly lucky to get anything to eat after 9 p.m. I spoke with the people there and they told me to return to the main road and go back a little further where I would find an Ibis Hotel. So we did that and sure enough there was the Ibis Hotel before us. I went in, asked for a room – they had one – and I then asked if it we could get anything to eat, but they said that wasn't possible, as the kitchen was closed! Don't, for goodness sake, get hungry in the French countryside after 9 p.m! At least we were able to get a couple of bottles of beer and we still had some sandwiches left over from the previous day – they were a little bit stale by now, but well, it was all we had so we ate them.

We arrived at Roscoffe quite early the following day and so had some time to burn before our ship sailed. We found a restaurant where although I had to keep popping out to check on our car we had a nice meal. Lynne saw crab salad on the menu and ordered that. She was quite perplexed when served a whole crab, still in its shell and with claws intact. That was a nonsensical meal because it was a fight to reach the flesh of the crab and it should never have been described as crab salad. But somehow Lynne managed it, but I could see she was disappointed. I offered to order something else for her but she declined. And so off we went to get in the queue to board the ship. I know we had a cabin but my recollection of that sailing and our arrival at Portsmouth is not particular for any reason and so I can only think that nothing remarkable occurred.

At that time Jackie and Ray were still living at Purley and Lynne's mother lived at Wallington. So we decided to arrange our accommodation at a place not too far away which used to be a restaurant called El Pirata, which we had previously frequented but which was now a small hotel. And so, after disposing of our car and attending to some affairs concerning the winding up of our company, we took a plane at Gatwick and returned to Alicante. At the airport we found that Simon's three children were there and were booked on the same plane as us, evidently returning to Spain to spend Christmas with their parents. At Alicante Simon and his wife were there to greet them, but we seemed to notice a degree of coolness when they said hello to us.

This puzzled us and later we discovered why; Velma told us that Simon had had a word with Manolo, who in the course of conversation is supposed to have warned him against getting too friendly with us, as we were 'troublemakers'. I am not at all sure I believe this nonsensical story, for what had happened was quite innocent as all kinds of rumours were going around about new taxes for this or that. We learned later not to take too much notice of the rumours that used to sweep Empedrola from time to time because some people with not a lot to do found solace in gossiping and exaggeration of stories. But, for example, there were a number of stories going round including one about a property tax that the authorities were going to levy on urbanisations such as ours. But nobody really knew if they were true or not. So to some it was perhaps worrying.

It so happened that Michael Ratcliffe was driving through Empedrola one morning with a prospective client and stopped when he saw me walking up the hill. His client in the back of the car, a rather odd person, began to bombard me with all kinds of questions, which I answered as truthfully as I could. He then asked me if we had engaged a solicitor when buying our property and I told him that we didn't because we had checked that both the landowners and the builders were bona fide people. He then asked me if I wished I had used a solicitor and with all those rumours of taxes flying around I replied that on reflection I probably wish now that I had. At this Michael appeared to take some offence at my remarks and began to drive off with his client shouting out of the window, "You are putting me off!" in a somewhat effeminate voice. In fact, I was attempting to put nobody off – I had been asked some questions and had answered them truthfully and in a forthright manner. It seems that Michael's client eventually decided not to buy and he used me as the reason for the failed sale; I can only assume he told Manolo about the incident, hence his conversation with Simon, and only then did we find out that as true friends, Simon and his wife rated quite low in our estimation from that point on. They did not even bother to ask us our version of what took place but just gave us the cold shoulder to some degree.

Anyway, we took a coach to Calpe at the airport and as we passed through the various towns and villages we saw Christmas trees and various other decorations, even though it was only early in December and strangely, I began to look forward to spending that holiday in Spain. I was already beginning to feel at home there and that was a very nice and comfortable feeling.

I had previously ordered a new car from a garage in Benisa and I simply had to collect it some time before the holidays, as I would, of course, need it. All I needed was for some kind soul to give me a lift over to Benisa from La Empedrola, and I had no trouble in this respect at all. Generally speaking, people were very helpful and anxious to assist.

We had of course told Velma that we would be returning for Christmas in Spain and that we would be around, but when we got back to our villa we found that her daughter Fran had arrived, together with her boyfriend. Due to objections from Velma, however, the boyfriend had to sleep in a villa down in the valley, which was available for letting now and again, and this had led to words between Velma and her daughter, which was rather unfortunate.

Then, to our considerable surprise, we found that Simon's family, together with Velma, Fran and her boyfriend, had all booked to go to the Swiss actor's restaurant over at Altea on Christmas Eve. It had been our intention to ask Velma over, probably both on Christmas Eve and on Christmas Day itself, for we didn't want her to be on her own, and her solitude, and possible loneliness, was the only reason we had come back to Spain for the Christmas holiday. We did not want her to be alone at Christmas. Had it not been for that we would have preferred, of course, to spend Christmas in England with our family. The situation had changed somewhat due to the arrival of Fran and her boyfriend, so they were unable to accept our invitation because of their arrangement to go to Altea. Lynne and I had not been included in this arrangement, although with Lynne's mother and our son Philip coming to us for Christmas we could not have gone anyway, but it would have been nice, we thought, to have been asked. We would never have dreamed of arranging such an evening without asking Velma at the very least, and very probably Simon and his lot too. But we were totally unaware of the stories about us that Manolo and Simon et al were circulating.

But we announced to Velma, Fran, her boyfriend and other near neighbours that we were having drinks at our place on Christmas Day morning. Velma didn't come, which we thought was a little curious, but Fran and her boyfriend did. We noticed a coolness on the part of Velma too in the period that followed Christmas, which puzzled us at the time, but when we eventually knew the whole story it was clear that even Velma was being influenced by Simon and his family. Nobody, it seemed, wanted to upset Manolo or the developers or the builders, and it seemed I had done so because I answered questions put to me in a truthful manner. We totally ignored this rather silly situation. We thought it was all very childish.

However, Lynne's mother and Philip returned home on New Year's Eve on quite an early plane. We took them to the airport to wave them off and then returned to Calpe quite quickly because we had much earlier arranged to take Velma and her grandson to a restaurant in Benisa, which was holding a special dinner on New Year's Eve. Evidently, Velma had thawed sufficiently to want to keep to this arrangement. The clientele were a mixed bunch of Spanish, German and English guests; the food was quite good and the atmosphere jolly. We were all glad we went and we enjoyed it.

Our next family visitors were going to be our two grandsons, Darren and Grant, once again, but this time on their own, and they were going to spend the main part of their school summer holidays with us. The intention was to place them in the care of the airline staff, who were very good indeed and looked after them very well. By this time Jackie and Ray had moved down to Devon, Ray having been offered a transfer there by his employers, which he accepted. So now they had to come all the way to Heathrow from their village, Tedburn St Mary, so that the boys could fly to us in Spain.

But a near disaster occurred because on arrival at Heathrow Airport and on presentation of their passports it was observed that Grant was only four and a half years old and to travel alone, even if under care of the airline, a child had to be five. So a crisis developed at Heathrow and at one point it looked very much as if they would not be able to come. Of course, everybody was upset and wondering what to do when after waiting ages for some resolution, a kindly member of the airline staff, after hearing about this situation, decided to overlook the youngster's age and accept responsibility. So Grant was able to go together with Darren after all. Of course, we had travelled to Alicante Airport not knowing anything of this situation, but when we arrived there the arrivals board told us that the flight from Heathrow was delayed – as is often the case; nothing unusual about that. So as we were rather hungry, Lynne and I went upstairs to the restaurant and ordered something to eat. We were about half way through the meal when we heard our names being paged on the loudspeaker. We left the half-eaten meal and rushed immediately down to arrivals where we saw a very anxious older brother Darren and a smaller Grant, who looked as though he could not have cared less; they were glad to see us and off we went homeward. I would just like to say that back in the 1985-6 period parking at the airport was so easy and far less crowded so you were near to your car when you exited the airport building. I have been back to Alicante Airport since, which is now much larger, much more busy and absolute bedlam compared with the relative peace and simplicity of the 1980s.

Soon we were winging our way to our villa at Calpe and when the boys saw the pool they went crazy, pleading to be allowed to swim immediately. We of course said they could and so they rushed upstairs to their bedroom to change into their bathers. To see them frolicking in the lovely blue water, laughing, shouting and having a whale of a time was worth every single penny we had paid for our villa. It was one of those precious moments that one always remembers.

That evening we took them to a very nice restaurant on the sea front called Alfredo's. It was an offshoot from the owner's original restaurant, the Capri, which was situated at the bottom of the main road in Calpe – Avenida Gabriel Miro – and also only a few yards to the beach. It was, without doubt, the best restaurant in Calpe and it had won some golden awards in the past. The owner, also named Alfredo, ran this superior restaurant and then also decided to open a place further along the same beach. This was to be a restaurant which was going to be on a lower level than the one in town, and where you could get a three-course menu for 1,000 pesetas, including wine – about £4.40!

But better still, clients would also get entertainment there for no extra charge. It had been the pleasure of Lynne and myself to witness some wonderful Spanish classical dancing there after it first opened, and as well as flamenco, excellent singers, and it seemed to us to be always crowded – sometimes it was difficult to get a table there, but we usually succeeded as we were known by the head waiter, who had transferred from the main restaurant to which we used to go from time to time.

So this was the spot where we took the boys on the first night, and just as we finished the meal an explosion of fireworks began over by the fishing port. It was the annual celebration of the fishermen's fiesta, but we pretended to the boys that this wonderful display of fireworks was especially for them to welcome them to Spain! Of course, they believed every word that we said, even though they knew I was quite a practical joker, and I'll never forget Grant's great big eyes when he stared up into the blazing sky. He really thought that this most impressive display was for him.

We had a great time over the next weeks. By this time I had our half tennis court laid, which was done when we had our patio barbecue house and bar built, and we had many a great battle, especially between Darren and myself. Of course, being only half size we could not play to the proper rules, but I devised special rules. Darren tried desperately to beat me but couldn't; however, I knew that if he had patience, then one day he would be the winner; all he had to do was wait until I got older and not so active and he got taller and more active. In due course that day would arrive – sad for me, great for Darren; but I was pleased for him, for he just loved to win, especially against his old grandpa!

During their stay we managed to obtain a video of the well-known Disney film *Pinocchio*. The boys sat there totally enthralled; as the film went along I made an occasional remark to heighten the drama. The next day I went out to clean the pool and there sitting on the edge was a cricket! I quickly went inside and called to the boys to come and have a look. They hurried outside and I told them, "Look! Jiminy Cricket has come to see you!" Darren, being older, was not to be taken in, but little Grant knelt down and actually spoke to the cricket saying, "Hello, Jiminy. How are you?" What a polite, dear little boy he was! I have a still photo of that moment, but how I wished I had a video camera then. As a matter of fact, we found many different types of insects on our patio from time to time as well as in our porch, and even inside the house, including a type of scorpion, praying mantis, various strange flying insects as well as a snake. Once, in the folds of our large sun umbrella we even found a bat sleeping. It had evidently taken refuge in there thinking it was a safe place to hide. I did manage to get that on video. I am very surprised that Lynne, who shrinks from contact with normal insects let alone the extraordinary animals we encountered in Spain, put up with all of this. But she gradually got used to it and bravely accepted the situation.

Unfortunately, all good things come to an end and on the night before their return to England we had the 'last supper' on the patio where we mostly had our meals. I think we were all a little bit sad then and even more so the next morning when we set off for the airport. There we had to hand them over to representatives of Iberia Airline, who were really excellent. They put the boys at ease immediately, hung their special identification packs around their necks and then we had to say goodbye to them. The boys were very sad, although they were looking forward very much to seeing their mum and dad again quite soon. Lynne and I returned to our car and drove quite silently back in the direction of Calpe. When we arrived back at our villa the place was so quiet and I believe we both yearned to hear the voices of the boys enjoying themselves. It did not seem the same without them. They were such wonderful boys, well behaved and great fun to have around the villa. But we had to get used to it, and we did after some days, for we knew there would be further visits.

Meanwhile, we had joined The English Speaking Club. We had to be vetted and we received a visit from the lady who ran it – Jean. We enjoyed our membership of this organisation and for quite a while we went to their Saturday evening dinner/dances down town in Calpe. We also went on their planned walks to various places of interest that otherwise we may never have seen. Usually the walks were planned for the morning period and the programme included lunch at some restaurant or other chosen by Jean. She was quite a card really, for behind that first headmistress impression one got when meeting her she was a very amusing lady and after a couple of gin and tonics she was quite funny and entertaining when you got to know her.

We had a lot of pleasant Saturday evenings with the club but, as one often finds, they retained the same couple playing organ and drums, with both singing, and for week after week they played virtually the same repertoire. In time we got a little tired of the sameness of the occasion and we first of all cut down our attendance and then cut it out altogether. I believe this coincided with some crisis or other in the club, which meant it was inactive for a while. But I understand it did resume later on.

One of the club activities I really did enjoy and appreciate was the art classes and I became quite wrapped up in that. We painted in oils and of course my first efforts were quite hopeless; but I gradually got better, although I doubt if I would ever be a Gainsborough! I loved it when they brought in experts who would explain to us how to calculate perspective when planning to paint. This was very important, as was demonstrated, if for example one was painting a house on top of a waterside cliff with some trees in the garden. That meant the shadow of the house and trees would fall on the water below and we learned how to project objects like that. I found it absorbing and of great interest. I was very flattered when an elderly lady sitting by my left side whispered to me that she didn't understand what the art teacher was saying; so at a suitable interval I explained it to her and she said, "Thank you very much, but why is it I can understand you when you explain it but can't understand it when he talks? You should have been a teacher." I recall that dear lady very well; she used to come out every year for the winter and every time she came said the same thing to the effect that when she was in Calpe she sometimes thought that she had died and that this was Heaven! What a very lovely thing to say. Later on she stopped coming to the art classes and I never saw her in Calpe again; maybe she had found her real Heaven at last. If so, I do hope she is as happy in the real Heaven as she was in Calpe every winter.

But eventually the art classes too died out as the club continued to deteriorate. When it stopped activities during the crisis I referred to above, which I believe had something to do with a number of things, including an illness suffered by Jean, both Lynne and I were extremely sorry, for we had appreciated very much the comradeship of the club, which included our Belgian doctor, Joseph, by the way. Once at a Saturday night dinner dance he came over to our table and playfully kicked our friend and neighbour, Terry Pollard. Terry voiced a mock protest at which Josef said, "Well, I have to get patients somehow!"

And so the summers and the years passed. We made the discovery in the winters that our lovely tile-covered floors were not so lovely at all. They looked very nice indeed and were wonderful in the summer when they produced a degree of coolness inside; but in the winter they attracted a lot of dampness. It is not true that Spanish winters consist of wall-to-wall sunshine every day. Yes, you can indeed experience some nice days or even short periods of good weather, but generally speaking the winters there can be damp and cold too. Therefore, we realised too late that the Spaniards seemed, back then at least, to build villas only for the summer conditions, forgetting that those of us who had chosen to live there all the year round would suffer from this dampness in the winters. Of course, in our innocence and inexperience we did not even think of perhaps installing a type of underfloor heating, for example. That would have been expensive but would have cured the problem of dampness and black mould appearing in places, especially places where it was quite difficult to get to. It would have been too expensive to use electric fires in every room all the time and so we bought canisters of liquid gas and gas fires. But these were quite ineffective against the dampness because that system of burning liquid gas for warmth only produced even more moisture in the atmosphere. It remained a continual problem every winter.

Another point that I failed to think of, because I had never built a villa before, was always to ensure that the exits to any outside point were higher inside than outside. I believe British regulations provide for a difference of about six inches, thus making it far more difficult for rainwater to penetrate inside. I did not even give matters like that a single thought because I assumed it was not only a matter of commonsense but of good building practice everywhere. Not in Spain, it seems. As I have remarked above, let nobody ever say that the sun shines all the time in Spain; it rains too. And oh boy, when it rains it sure rains. I would often describe such rain as equatorial and torrential. Up on our sun verandah there were three doors, each leading to a bedroom. But as the internal floors were exactly the same height as the external floors, when it rained the water simply poured under the doors into our villa. We also had one entry from the exterior to our lounge where the same problem existed. And then we also found that almost all the windows, which because wrought iron security grills were fitted outside the windows, of course opened inwards. Beware windows that open inwards because in storm conditions the kind of windows they fitted back then leaked very badly. I am sure this doesn't happen today when most fitted windows are, I understand, of an immensely improved standard. But this was a great disappointment to us and proved to be quite a problem.

And as for our sun verandah upstairs, which we had planned and fitted out with table, chairs and sun umbrella, this was a complete and utter waste of money; we tried to sit up there on a number of occasions, but each time we had to retreat inside because of the heat. Each bedroom had an exit door which led out to the sun verandah; we thought it would be rather nice for us, and our guests too, to be able to walk out there each morning to greet the day and look at the lovely views all around, but it was not a very practical idea. Those experiences taught me that if I was ever to do this again, I would insist upon a six-inch difference between the outside and inside levels, as in England, and have this written into the contract with the builders. I would also insist upon totally different windows; ours were lovely to look at but useless in rainy conditions. Also I would have underfloor heating to eliminate dampness and black mould in the winter, or even air conditioning, perhaps. I am sure that today with all kinds of builders, including British that have started up there, the kind of problems we had to contend with do not apply to today.

We complained bitterly to the builders, who came to examine both the floor levels and the windows. It was obvious that nothing very much could be done about the floor levels and not much about the windows. To the Spaniards it seemed as though we were complaining about nothing and that a little drop of rain is to be expected from time to time. But that was a ridiculous attitude; we were not complaining about a few drops of water, for when it rained heavily we were virtually flooded out! And as far as having different levels from outside to inside, Lynne seems to recall that they said that would be dangerous as people could trip over! What a stupid response! We tried very hard to get somewhere and I think that if the problems we had were surmountable in a simple manner they would have made some alterations.

All they could suggest to us were slatted door blinds for the verandah doors and the main entrance double door, which, by the way, was also a waste of money because nobody ever used it. Everybody entered our drive and simply walked round to our porch or patio where we would invariably be sitting. In the design of our villa we had thought, like most people may have, that a front door entrance was necessary; in point of fact it was entirely unnecessary. We had seen Spanish homes with these blinds, which they called persianes; we thought they were there to keep the hot sunrays out or maybe even insects. Maybe they served a double purpose, for they certainly helped to keep out the rain. So we found a shop over at Moraira which specialised in these persianes, gave them measurements and collected them about a week later. After fitting them we never had any further problems with rain coming through under the doors whatsoever.

But we could not fit them to the windows because all windows were arched at the top. However, sitting in our lounge one day when it was raining I noticed that the rain hit the window at a point two-thirds from the bottom and below that point, so therefore the leakage was at the bottom part of each window. Although I am not at all clever at DIY stuff – I have always employed others to carry out such jobs for me – in this case it was a matter of necessity, for if I didn't find the answer to the problem of leaking windows then nobody else would. So, I reasoned, if I could find a way to prevent the rain from hitting the lower parts of the windows by deflecting it, the problem might be solved. Anyhow, it was worth a try.

I knew a shop in the street in Calpe where they held the Saturday market, and this shop would probably be able to cut some thick clear Perspex sheeting to my measurements. I could then screw them on to the surrounding frames and, with a little bit of luck, we wouldn't have leaking windows any more. So that is what I did and as we had the boys with us at the time, Darren helped me to install them. I am very pleased to say this completely stopped any further leakages via the windows. Problem solved! But how was it possible that an ignoramus like me could find the answer to this problem and fully qualified builders could not?

And so we gradually settled down there and ironed out all problems, and to us Spain was home. We returned to England from time to time, sometimes for the Christmas holidays and always for the birth of any new baby. I think that young mums like their own mother to be in the vicinity at such times. So we got quite used to travelling backwards and forwards. We also tried different routes and different ports of embarkation and arrival. Although it was a long way I always liked those trips both going and coming back. Once I had the crazy idea that I could drive non-stop from Cherbourg to our villa in Calpe and actually attempted it. It was a silly idea and I was sorry that I ever thought of it. We managed to get home without mishap, but after eight hours or so I was getting very tired and sleepy and that is not a good condition in which to drive. I never did it again.

11

MORE STORIES OF OUR LIVES IN SPAIN; OUR TRIP VIA FRANCE, SWITZERLAND AND AUSTRIA TO CZECHOSLOVAKIA; AND WE MEET ALENA FOR THE VERY FIRST TIME

The months, and then even the years, seemed to slip by very quickly. We were thoroughly enjoying our lives and continued to have more visitors and also making new friends. On one unforgettable day at our place we invited Margarete and Tom Gray and their guests Debbie and Stan. We got to know Margarete and Tom because Michael Ratcliffe, the property agent, had told them that a couple, which was us of course, had moved out from Old Coulsdon and would be living in Spain permanently. They were also from Old Coulsdon and both were curious to meet us and to ask us some questions about living in Spain. They had a very nice villa built by the same builders as ours and it was situated very high up in the outskirts of Moraira. They had really lovely views from their patio and pool area and their pool was exactly the same as ours, i.e. thirty-three feet long with a Roman end. Margarete was of German origin but both Tom and she had held positions with British Telecom. They too were contemplating full retirement and considering the prospect of moving out to Spain permanently. But on this day they brought their guests Jackie and Stan with them. Jackie we already knew because she was a receptionist at the surgery we attended back home in Surrey and she soon recognised us when she saw us.

We sat chatting away over a glass of wine and then I did the barbecue. At that time my barbecue house had not yet been finished. But never mind; I was able to manage. So we had, I hope, a tasty lunch with more wine, after which I brought out a couple of bottles of Spanish champagne I just happened to have in the refrigerator. We polished those off during the conversation which followed and then we all began to feel a little hungry again. So I suggested a fish and chip supper downtown to finish off the day and said we knew the very place – it was called Pinocchio's, a restaurant down near to the fishing port. Everybody agreed and so down we went, and I have to say that the fish and chips there were very good indeed. Of course, we had yet another bottle of wine and at the end I went up to the bar counter to pay the bill, but Tom, seeing what I was doing, came up, pushed me out of the way and insisted on paying the bill himself.

Now, dear reader, from my description of that day – and there were many not quite the same but very similar – you may have gained the impression that we did nothing else in Spain but drink. To that I would say – yes. Without question, the cheap prices of alcoholic drinks there, plus the fact that Spain is a wine producing country and the fact that many people have nothing else to do except meet and socialise with each other and have long conversations, does encourage a higher level of drinking than is normal back home, for example. In Spain if anyone came to see you it was the custom to ask if they would like a glass of wine. However, most sensible people realised that it was somewhat unwise to carry out this pleasant pastime in excess and after a while most of us learned how to pace ourselves. It was not as bad as it may sound, but admittedly there were some who got so accustomed to continual drinking they couldn't stop. We developed the habit of taking one day a week on which we consumed no alcohol at all. I believe that if one is sensible and uses commonsense then it is OK to drink within reason, and it certainly helps the conversation along.

At this point I have to return to our friend and neighbour Velma. One day she announced that she had decided to sell up and return to England. Despite everything we were indeed sorry to see her go. She was part of our lives from the first day we were there and we enjoyed her company. She asked us to keep in touch with her after her return. She then sold her car to Terry Pollard, our neighbour, and with that she returned to England. She gave us a contact address and phone number in Oxford somewhere, which was the address of her daughter Amy with whom she would be staying. On our next holiday to England I tried to contact her at this address, but was very short of time and when I began to encounter difficulties I gave up and vowed to try again. I was not able to on that trip but I did on subsequent trips and was told that Amy and, I suppose Velma too, had moved. Apparently, they had been living only in rented accommodation. The person on the line was not very helpful but he did give me a slight clue where I might find them; however, in that particular village or town I was referred to Amy was nowhere to be found and so in that way we completely lost touch. I have tried to locate her via the BBC and did succeed to log on to a web page where her name was mentioned, but there was no option for communication. On the other hand, neither did Velma nor Amy attempt to communicate with us in Spain in any way.

But one day, not too long after Velma's departure, her other daughter Fran turned up at our villa together with her gentleman friend. We, being hospitable people, of course welcomed them and served them the usual glass of wine and toasted cheese and ham sandwiches out on the patio, which they thought were delicious and were much appreciated. Then Fran began to tell us why she had come to Calpe and a very surprising story then emerged. From what we were told it seems that Fran had put the money up to buy the plot of land, also paid for the pool, part of the money for the building of the villa and paid for the car that Velma used. When she heard that Velma had sold the car and the villa she was beside herself with fury, because, she maintained, her mother had no right to sell anything without her permission. I asked what she proposed to do about this situation and she said, but whether she meant it I do not know, that she would take her mother to court. Fran promised to keep in touch, but that was just another meaningless promise, for we never heard from her or any of them again. I would imagine that Velma, who did not enjoy the best of health when we knew her, is probably no longer with us, but Amy, her son and Fran no doubt are.

I should also like to tell the story which we heard about Simon and his family. We had virtually ceased all contact with this chap and his family so it is possible that what we heard may or may not be all true We had not fallen out with them, we just decided they were not our cup of tea, despite the fact that Manolo and Michael Ratcliffe et al had also completely forgotten about our being so-called 'trouble makers' and the stupid issue that gave rise to it, and so we were all friends again. But we had not forgotten about the odd attitude that Simon and co had shown towards us when they thought we had been 'blacklisted' by the developers/builders. However, a few people stayed attached to them, we were told, including a very nice fellow who lived in a terraced villa down in the town – his name was Thomas. We had known Thomas from The English Speaking Club, of which he too was a member.

Well, one day, according to what we heard, it appeared that Simon and his family had moved lock, stock and barrel from La Empedrola and had gone to live in a village somewhere up in the mountains. In such places it was still possible to buy properties of a kind quite cheaply, especially run down properties that needed a lot of rebuilding and refurbishing. Whether they bought such a property we had no idea and frankly we were not at all interested. But those people remaining on Empedrola who knew them were quite puzzled when these stories reached us. During the time we were still friendly with them I believe Simon mentioned that he intended to have a villa built for each of his children. So what had happened to the grand plan? It seemed to be a mystery to all; all kinds of rumours were floating around, to which we paid no attention whatsoever. We were simply not interested and after a little while we dismissed the matter, and them, from our thoughts.

Some months passed by and then we heard a horror story concerning Thomas. Apparently, so the story went, during his continued association with Simon it appears he was asked to act as guarantor for some financial transaction, which may or may not have had to do with property, in which, so we were told, Simon was involved. However, in some way the transaction had backfired and failed. Thomas, as guarantor, was called upon to make good the deficit, one can only presume, because Simon was unable to. As a consequence we heard that poor Thomas lost everything, and we were told that also included the terraced villa in which he and his wife lived. Spanish law is very tough and harsh indeed.

If this story were true then how one friend can do something like that is something that people like ourselves simply cannot comprehend. Thomas was a nice, inoffensive chap, but one who was perhaps so nice, to the point of being naïve, that you could ask anything of him and if he could he would do it. We felt very bad about the whole situation and even worse when, somewhat later, we heard that Thomas had sadly passed away. We cannot be certain, of course, but if what we had heard were true, we wondered how much this whole unsavoury affair had to do with his death. If someone had asked me to act as guarantor, then offend or not, I would have refused; people should not ask such things of friends. I would never dream of doing such a thing. You can always ask good friends for their advice or opinions, but not for money or any kind of financial commitment.

All of this, of course, occurred after Velma had sold up and returned to England. So it was natural for us to wonder what her reaction would have been when hearing of this drama about her so-called 'wealthy' friends. It is possible that Velma herself had experienced a lucky escape, although as to whether she actually had any money or assets remains an open subject. It is more than possible that her apparent grandeur and the impression she gave of having money behind her was just a pose. However, relations between Velma and Simon had cooled and eventually broken off completely much earlier – we think it is possible this happened when Simon realised that Velma was not the gay, rich widow he had thought she was. And who knows, maybe Velma came to the conclusion that Simon did not have a lot of money either. To people like ourselves who accept people at face value and do not have a deep love for money and do not differentiate between poor friends or wealthy friends, such attitudes are hard to understand. It is people and their actions that are of the most value to us, not their money.

One Saturday I went to the street market in Calpe. I like the atmosphere of street markets and always have. In Spain they were a noted feature of Spanish life and most people went to buy fresh vegetables, new laid eggs, fruit bargains and anything else that might catch their fancy. The two best street markets in Spain I ever went to were in Benidorm and Altea. Lynne would come with me quite often, but on this occasion I was alone.

I had reached the top of the market and turned round to make my way back to where I had parked my car when I heard a female voice calling out, "Kolik stoji, kolik stoji?" which is Czech for how much does it cost? So I approached this lady and asked her if she was Czech. She replied that she was and enquired if I was Czech too. When I told her I was English she was surprised and called her husband over to say hello to me. We stood there for some minutes talking and I invited them to our villa some time for a glass of wine and to continue our chat.

It was the worst thing I could possibly have done, for after a day or two they turned up. And their visits became more and more frequent. Not only that, but they seemed to call at the most inopportune times, i.e. just before lunch, during lunch, just before dinner etc, and once there it was very hard to get rid of them. Added to which the husband was a near alcoholic and every time I gave him a drink he would gesticulate to me to fill his glass to the top. No sooner had I done so than he drank it in one and was asking for another. Never let it be said that the Mitchells were not good hosts and we prided ourselves on this fact, but this was ridiculous, and to be perfectly frank we preferred not to have an alcoholic as a friend.

In fairness, I should say that they also invited us to their villa and we occasionally went to them. They lived about a mile and a half from La Empedrola on a quite large urbanisation called Maryvillas on the other side of Calpe. We could see Maryvillas quite clearly from our patio, and its biggest handicap was that the beginning of the Sierra Bernia Mountains was just behind them. This meant that they lost the setting sun quite early in the late afternoon as it disappeared behind the mountains. In the winter they got almost no sun at all – quite different from us on Empedrola, where if the sun shone we both saw it and felt it the whole day long.

The story told to us was that Maryvillas was a gift from General Franco to noted members of the German military and SS people during the war. I have no idea if that were true or not but the story was told to me by various people. However, one must make allowances for the gossiping and exaggeration that is rife among the foreign residents in Spain. So I neither believe it nor disbelieve it – although it's funny how Maryvillas was mainly populated by German people.

But to go back to our Czech couple. We tried every way we could, without being rude and impolite, to discourage these people from visiting us at such inconvenient times, or at all, and eventually I think they got the message; I stopped feeding him with drinks and slowly their visits died down and then died out.

One day, not very long before Christmas, I went into town and was just leaving the post office when I saw the lady – or rather she saw me. She called to me and I had no choice but to stop and respond. She told me I should come to their villa as she had a big surprise for me. I told her that it was very kind of her but right then I was very busy, for we were preparing to go back to England for Christmas. I left her with a promise that upon our return we would call upon her, but not before she gave me an indication of what this big surprise was all about. Apparently, she had the sister of my very good friend 'Georgie' Jiri Trnka of Prague, whose name was Alena, staying at her villa. I was both shocked and intrigued by this surprise news.

So we went home for Christmas, had a nice time in Tedburn St Mary, Devon, where our eldest daughter Jackie and her family lived. We returned to Calpe, but I cannot recall if we went to the Czech couple's villa of our own volition or whether I met her again and she repeated her invitation. One way or another, we went over to Maryvillas and there, for the very first time ever, we met Alena and her husband Vaclav. Their surname was Hrdlicka, a right tongue-twister to pronounce properly, but more easy to say after a glass or two of wine! Well Alena made a big fuss of us as her brother had told her about us many times over the years and it was evident that she and Vaclav were also pleased to meet us – and indeed we were pleased to meet them. This occurred, as far as I can recall, about 1987–88, and as one of my best friends' sister, we welcomed them to our villa and went out to lunch or dinner with them on a number of occasions. But Vaclav was a very generous host and kept paying the bills, which embarrassed us a little; he was a very insistent person. But that was rather a change for me as I was usually the one who ended up paying the bill! And then Alena told me that she had invited her brother to come from Prague to Calpe for a holiday, which was wonderful news for me. I should explain that the villa of the Czech couple, which they had let to Alena, consisted of two parts, i.e. the main villa and an annexe, which was fully self-contained. It was this annexe that she had offered to George and there he would be alone, if he wanted, and could look after himself there if he so wished.

Eventually, the day of George's arrival came and I volunteered to pick him up at the airport. He had to fly via Zurich before being able to catch his flight to Alicante, as there were no direct flights from Prague then. I was very pleased indeed to see George again and he was also very pleased to see me. I took him straight to Maryvillas and there he was re-united with his sister and Vaclav. But I noticed a small degree of coolness on the part of Vaclav. He had, of course, met and known George previously and I got the feeling that he was not 100% in favour of him. It turned out that my impression was correct – Vaclav had little time for George. I can understand that to an extent, because George could sometimes give the impression that he wants this and wants that all the time and that he was somewhat selfish and even a little greedy. It is true that George was a self-centred person, and just like an artist he could be temperamental. But I forgave George all his weaknesses, because we all have weaknesses ourselves – who can claim to be lily-white? I grew accustomed to George's faults and had known him for a very long time. However, others were not as tolerant of George and all his faults as I evidently was.

During George's stay we went over to Maryvillas often; we went out to eat and I thought he was having a very nice time. But towards the end of his stay he took me to one side and asked if he could spend his last week with Lynne and me at our villa. I was surprised but of course immediately said that would be fine, but asked him why. He replied that although his accommodation was separate from Alena and Vaclav he could still hear them quarrelling, and that after three weeks of that he was quite fed up with it. On that basis Lynne and I agreed that he should move over to us and he did. Alena seemed to understand and was not annoyed about this in any way.

One of the first things I did was to open the bottle of Charles Heidseck 1957 Vintage Champagne, which I had been keeping for years to drink when George and I would meet again, and this was a perfect opportunity to do so. And so with much grandeur and pomp I opened the treasured bottle, which had been an item of jest between us for a long time – every letter I wrote to George ended with the remark, "Charles Heidseck is still waiting!" And George would respond, "I am just waiting for the chance and I too am very keen to taste Charles Heidseck." This was in the period following the Warsaw Pact invasion, during which exit visas in Czechoslovakia were very hard to get as the political situation had deteriorated considerably once again.

So here we were, drinking Charles Heidseck at last! But as I brought my glass to my lips I could tell that it was badly corked and tasted horrible. George, trying to be polite, said, "Mmm, that really is nice." But I took his glass from him and poured it all away – it was impossible to drink! – and opened another bottle of wine instead. What a total disappointment, and after all those years too, during which I had guarded that bottle with my life!

During the week that followed we entertained George; we took him to restaurants, he swam, he sunbathed, and it looked as if he really were enjoying a nice rest. I even went with him to Altea Golf Club and there we played nine holes, which was very pleasant. I should mention that George claimed to be an Honourable President of the World Senior Golf Association, an honour, he said, which he accepted on behalf of his country because there was still an international sympathy level for Czechoslovakia after the invasion in 1968. Anyway, George claimed that this title enabled him to play at any course in the world as a guest and so no green fees were applicable. So he spoke with the people there at Altea, we played and we didn't pay! Some years later when talking about George with his ex-wife, Helena, she said that he was never president of this organisation and that he wasn't telling me the truth. He did receive some honour from them, she said, but he was never an Honourable President. So there you are – I always knew that George was apt to exaggerate and sometimes even tell 'porkies', but if Helen was correct this was indeed a giant 'porky'!

You never knew whether to believe George or not. He was a very good actor and I remember one of my visits to Prague when West Ham, the London football club, was playing against Sparta Prague in the European Cup, or maybe it was the Cup Winners' Cup. I had already seen the first match at West Ham's stadium, Upton Park, which was good, so I badly wanted to see the return match in Prague.

I needed to go to Prague sometime anyway to straighten out a few problems and so I chose to be there for that return. I managed to get two tickets somehow – it was not being held at the Sparta Stadium, as it was too small and they expected a much larger crowd, so it was held at a large stadium called Strahov. Everyone was talking about this big and important match; Prague was buzzing because they do like their football, especially when a foreign team was playing. Anyway, the day before the match I met with George and as we were strolling up Vaclavske Namesti he took me by the shoulder and said we were going to visit a famous students' coffee or wine bar which everybody was talking about. It was in a turning on the right at the top of the square. We arrived there but were told at the door that the place was full. George then said to the man in charge, "What! Are you even full to the Captain of West Ham United?" looking at me. The man also looked at me and his attitude changed completely. He ushered us in, found a table from somewhere, placed a clean cloth on it, plus the usual Union Jack, and asked us what we would like to drink! As all this was going on I could hardly contain myself and laughter was just bursting within me. I was both highly amused and very highly embarrassed when it spread like wildfire throughout the place that the Captain of West Ham was with them that evening! People began to look at our table, smiling at us, lifting their glasses as if to say 'cheers!' So for one very delightful evening George made me Captain of West Ham United, and it was a good feeling even though it wasn't true. We went to the match the next day when West Ham won by 1–0, with Johnny Byrne scoring the winner. Johnny and I were to become friends in later years; he visited my home in Old Coulsdon and I visited his in Coulsdon.

And yet another story about George and his antics, this time back in England when George was on a trip there at my invitation. We went to a wine auction over Banstead way somewhere. When you go to these auctions you are given a card with a number on it which you hold up if you are bidding. At the prior tasting of the various wines on offer we were jostled a few times by an ignorant and very rude man who evidently had no manners. We both took an instant dislike to this chap; we noticed that his number was sixty-nine and ours was ninety-six, so during the auction George urged me to bid for a simply terrible wine, of which there was just one case, but, he said, hold your card upside down so it looks like sixty-nine. Laughing away, and as I too had taken a dislike to this ignorant fellow, I went along with this prank, held my card upside down, and then we quietly left the premises. I often wondered how that fellow got on when trying to deny that he had bid for this lousy case of wine.

NOTE: During editing it has been pointed out that the number 69 looks the same either way up. This means that the bad wine was in fact bought by us but we walked out without realising this ! Thus the nasty man escaped the punishment we thought we had inflicted upon him!

So that was the kind of relationship between George and me. We were jolly good pals and he was fun to be with. I would like to say that we would do anything for each other and that certainly applied to me, for over the years my dear friend cost me quite a lot of money in one way or another. But I have to say that he could be generous too and was certainly a good host to me on some occasions when eating out in Prague or Marianske Lazne, where I would sometimes meet him at the golf club there. Once George told me that he spent the previous Christmas alone, as he was separated, and ultimately divorced, from his wife Helena. I was concerned to hear this and suggested he could come to us in England for the next Christmas. He then said something about it being too expensive, so I dipped into my pocket and peeled off £50, which I gave to him. In those days £50 sold on the black market would fetch an awful lot of Czech crowns, and most people, if they could get hold of foreign currency, did this – it became a part of life under communism. I left it to him to either use it as a contribution towards his flight in sterling or sell it on the black market and pay in crowns. He took the money but never came to England that Christmas, despite my letter of invitation, to which he never replied, and he never gave me the money back! That was George. But for all his faults, I accepted George for what he was. Later on I will relate the end of our friendship and the tragic end of my dear pal.

We visited Czechoslovakia again in 1991 by car. We made a great journey from Calpe up through to Valencia, Barcelona, then over the French border, following the route northwards up to the Swiss border. There the Swiss border control people asked us to purchase a special sticker that went on the inside windscreen and which entitled us to drive on Swiss motorways. They explained that it was an offence to drive on motorways without this sticker and that if caught, the fines were very heavy. I think that is a wonderful idea; all users of the road should contribute towards the cost of maintenance, even tourists. We stayed overnight in Switzerland at a small but very nice hotel-restaurant and made our way the next day through the remainder of Switzerland and over the Austrian border.

What a truly lovely journey that was. We passed through a number of small villages on both sides of the border, seeing one or two we wished we were staying at instead of going on to the one recommended to us by neighbours on Empedrola and where we planned to stay and rest up for a few days. But we decided to keep to our original plan and eventually reached our target village; there we immediately started to search for a hotel. The actual hotel, recommended and described to us back in Calpe by this couple who had been there some years before, was nothing like the small Alpine type of hotel we were led to expect. Now it had a quite modern frontal facade and not at all what we had imagined. In any case, it was under repair at the time so we preferred not to stay there.

But further along we managed to find a small tourist office open and although they warned us that this being the end of the summer season and too early for the winter season many hotels were closed for their own holidays, they gave us details of one or two places we might try. The first one appealed to us and so we located it and spoke with a young lady inside, who explained that they were closing down too, but she reflected and then said that as we wanted accommodation only for several nights, maybe she could arrange something. So she showed us a room, which was quite OK in an old-fashioned way, with a view over the village sports field, which we were amazed to find illuminated at night and teams of young boys playing football – not the sort of facilities one might expect in a mountain village.

We had a very happy holiday there. Lynne especially liked Austria very much and so did I. We went to the top of the mountain by ski lifts and made the mistake of walking down virtually from the top to a tiny little village called Saint something or other. There we found a little restaurant where we were quite alone and had a nice small meal there. It wasn't all that far from where we had parked our car but when we got down below, we found we could hardly walk as the effect of walking down all that way was devastating on our leg and stomach muscles. But we managed it somehow and returned to our hotel. We went to quite a lot of places in the Austrian Alpine region and one can only say that the scenery there is totally fabulous. The food we sampled wasn't bad either.

But soon it became time for us to wend our way towards Czechoslovakia. We went in a northerly direction, bypassed Salzburg, which was a pity as we would have liked to have seen something of that charming city. After that we went very briefly into Germany, where we saw a sign to Berchtesgarten, another place where I especially would have liked to dally for a while. We found the road to Ceske Budevice and from thence we intended to travel across country onto Marianske Lazne, where I had asked my good friend there, Slavek Svinger, to reserve us a room at Hotel

Palace, which I knew and which was OK, although I am bound to say that today there are much better hotels. As we crossed over the Czech border I reflected how it used to be in the bad old days, but now it was a piece of cake, totally unlike the days of communism. We were welcomed with a smile and no questions at all about money or anything like that. Then we continued north to Ceske Budevice, after which we followed our journey plan and proceeded toward M. Lazne.

On our way we stopped at a small town or village and had a bite to eat. I warned Lynne not to eat too much because we wanted to go to a special restaurant that evening on our arrival at M. Lazne where we could have delicious venison or wild boar steaks etc, and our mouths watered as we thought of the wonderful meal we were going to have later on. I ordered Prague ham for us both, but they didn't have any. It's funny; in the bad old days of communism you could get delicious Prague ham everywhere, but now you could hardly get it anywhere. They served ham, but it wasn't as good as the Prague ham I used to love years before. However, the café we stopped at offered a kind of sliced sausage, which wasn't too bad. But why no Prague ham, I wondered? Anyway, we carried on and finally reached M. Lazne; but something was wrong and I felt it immediately, because the whole place was buzzing and crowded with people – grossly overcrowded, in fact. There were people everywhere; I had never, ever seen M. Lazne like this before. I later discovered that these were German people who now needed no visas and were taking advantage of the possibility to cross the border for long weekends, and often much longer than that, and this traffic increased greatly after the fall of communism in Czechoslovakia when visas became an annoying procedure of the past. And of course it was very cheap for them compared to the prices in Germany; the Czechs, on the other hand, appreciated their business – and their Deutschmarks! In my day Germans were not liked at all and it was people from the West who were most favoured. Now it seemed totally different. How times and attitudes change.

Anyway, I found a spot to park and went immediately to Hotel Palace as I had asked my friend Slavek to reserve a room for us there. I spoke to the receptionist, but she looked all through her register and said she had no reservation for us, and neither did she have a spare room to offer. I returned to Lynne, who was waiting in the car, and we decided to go up the hill to Hotel Golf. They used to know me there quite well as a regular guest and I was sure I would get a room. When we arrived, however, we found a brand new hotel, very modern and nothing like the hotel I used to know; neither were the people the same. Nobody knew me from Adam. I went to reception and enquired about rooms; they had one but quoted such a preposterous price that I said I would think about it. Meanwhile, I asked if we might enjoy a meal in the restaurant. The receptionist replied in a haughty manner that she was sorry, but "The restaurant is reserved for our German guests only." With that, and with an obvious show of disgust on my face, I walked out. I wouldn't stay at that place again free of charge. Once upon a time they were very glad of me and the money I used to spend there some years ago. But as I have remarked before, times change.

So again I returned to Lynne and told her the bad news, so we returned down to the town; luckily, I found a place to park, but with much difficulty, left Lynne there and walked over to Hotel Crystal Palace. I was getting rather desperate now, because Lynne was tired, hungry and thirsty. There, to my great surprise, I found Inge, the daughter of my friend Slavek, working at reception. I asked her where her father was and she said she wasn't sure, but she thought he was at his cottage outside M. Lazne. I asked if she had a room to offer us but unfortunately they were full too. Our German friends were everywhere, it seemed, and there wasn't a room to be had in the whole of M. Lazne! Not being too sure what our next step should be, I asked if I could use the telephone. First of all I phoned my dear friend Jiri Stepan, with whom we would be staying in Prague for a few days, but he had already told me he would be away until the following Tuesday, so although I tried in my desperation, I knew that I would probably get no reply. So then I phoned our friend Alois Zich, also in Prague, to ask him if he knew of somewhere between M. Lazne and Prague where we might get a room, and he told me not to bother looking for a hotel but to come directly to Prague where we could stay with him.

I felt horrible imposing ourselves on people like that, even if they were friends; but I was in trouble and to me it was a very nice gesture on their part which we appreciated very much. So whilst we did not relish yet another journey, we went on to Prague, about 100 km, where we met Alois at an agreed point and he guided us to his house, which was situated in an outskirt of Prague called Slivinec; it would certainly have been difficult for me to have found it myself. There we were welcomed by his wife Irena, whom of course we knew, and it was so wonderful to sit down, relax, have a drink and not to have to worry about where we were going to sleep that night.

We were dreadfully hungry but temporarily forgot about that. It was now midnight and so we were very surprised indeed when Irena called us into the kitchen area, where they also ate, and served us a lovely roast chicken dinner. We had no idea she was cooking; who would expect to be served a chicken dinner at midnight? But we tucked in and enjoyed every morsel, for Irena was and still is a very good cook – just as a reminder, she was the one who prepared all that lovely food years before in 1966 for my Sugosa World Cup Willie parties at Brent Bridge Hotel.

The next day Slavek phoned me at the home of Alois. I had no idea how he obtained the number; I can only think it was Inge who told him what had happened and gave him the number I rang, because she would know that, of course. He said he was coming to Prague that day and would come to see us. Alois gave him some directions and later on he duly arrived. But I think he was a little tipsy – and even more tipsy when he left! But it was OK, for he wasn't driving. He explained that he thought Lynne and I would prefer to stay at a small cottage by his own out in the country rather than in crowded M. Lazne and that he had left a message at Hotel Palace about how I could contact him. He was quite angry when he heard that we had received no such message. Anyhow, he evidently had not taken into account our long journey from Austria and the fact that when we arrived in M. Lazne we would be tired, hungry and thirsty. I told him it would have been better to have kept to the original plan and booked us in at the hotel.

The next day was Tuesday and we had an obligation to call George Stepan, with whom we were supposed to be staying, and although he was sorry to hear our story of the hotel mix up in M. Lazne he was glad that Alois and Irena had stepped in to help us. Of course, we had to go to the Stepan's, which we did later on after thanking Alois and Irena many times for their kindness and hospitality. In a small way we had a chance to repay this because we held a dinner for all our Czech friends and of course Alois and Irena came to that. And as I will tell later on, Alois and Irena were our guests for a very short time at our villa in Spain.

I would like to mention that during their holiday with us in Calpe I had asked George Stepan if he would be so kind as to call my old friend George Trnka to maybe find out what is bothering him and why he had gone silent on me for so long, and lastly to invite him to the dinner I was holding. For some reason George Trnka had stopped writing to me and I wanted to know what was wrong. George Stepan told me he did speak to George Trnka, somewhat reluctantly, for the two Georges did not like each other too much (quite peculiar that, because I liked both of them), and that he had promised to write to me; however, he said that he couldn't accept my invitation as on that day he would not be in Prague. George Trnka never wrote to me and neither, of course, did he come to the dinner. I pondered over whether to call at his flat/studio in Revolucni Street and, by chance, I found myself actually walking right past it. I hesitated, looked at my watch to see that I had little time just then and, to my very deep regret, I walked on. I now realise that it was my mistake to do that and that I should have made a quick call, but the fact was that I was on my way to have lunch with John Vokac (the former captain from the Czech Embassy in London) at Dum Potravin (the House of Food) and I felt I may be late if I experienced any delay.

Anyway, I met John; I was very glad to see him, for at that point I had no idea what had happened to him and I asked Alois, when staying with him, if he would kindly look in the phone book to see if a Jan Vokac was listed there. He was and I phoned him, and I shall never forget his response when I told him who it was calling. He said, "David, after all these years. I am so glad to speak with you again." And so it was then that we made an arrangement to meet and have lunch together. And it was also then that I heard for the very first time his story of betrayal by Major Macek and the fact that he was dismissed from his commission as a captain in the army and made to work for five years as a labourer, helping to build the Prague underground railway. He described that period as being the worst of his whole life. However, I was very glad to hear from him that he was now OK and was involved with a glass factory, which had completely sold their output for the whole year and so he was doing well. I am still in touch with him now and then.

And so on the next evening we held our dinner for our other friends in Prague. It was extremely pleasant for Lynne and I to be able to see and to entertain old friends like this and we enjoyed their company very much indeed. But now it was time for us to return to our villa in Spain. George Stepan very kindly led us to a point just outside Prague where we could easily connect with the road to the Austrian border, as it was apparently a somewhat tricky journey from his flat to find it. And so we said goodbye to George and went on our way. Knowing that we had a long journey before us we wasted no time, although we did stop for breakfast just over the Austrian border.

We motored on through Austria, always heading west, and finally, only a few miles after we crossed the Swiss border, we found a very nice and extremely elegant place. We considered that it would probably be unlikely that we would find a hotel as nice as this one, so we decided to stay there. It was indeed an excellent hotel in every way and although we were there only one night we thoroughly enjoyed our stay.

The next day we made our way through Switzerland, got bound up in very heavy traffic in Zurich, but eventually found our way to Lichtenstein, a small principality that you hardly know you had been to, because no sooner have you entered it than you are leaving it! And so we went on to France, crossed the border and continued our journey in a south-westerly direction. This being October, many places were closed, but we managed to find a kind of motel which looked reasonable and stayed overnight there. But it was way out in the country, and the motel kitchen, if indeed they had one, was not functioning. Very few places to eat existed there. We managed to find a restaurant a mile or two along the road; it wasn't at all marvellous, but it sufficed for one night.

From there we had a sporting chance to reach Calpe during the next day, and we did. After a gruelling journey it was very nice to be home again in our own surroundings. We reflected on our whole trip and Lynne and I agreed that we had had a nice and interesting journey and that we liked Austria very much. We promised ourselves to return one day, but I am sorry to say we never did.

12

WE LOVE SPAIN BUT DECIDE TO RETURN
TO ENGLAND

Now we were back in Spain and I have an unpleasant story to tell in connection with Alena and Vaclav. Somehow I didn't think that Alena and the Czech lady who owned the villa she was renting would get along with each other for very long, for they were both strong-willed ladies. Matters came to a head when they had a big row concerning the deposit that Alena and Vaclav had put down, which, I believe, is normal practice when renting a property. Anyway, the upshot of this row persuaded Alena to go to the bank and somehow she managed to convince the unfortunate young female cashier to return this deposit to her, which I believe had been left with this bank in the mutual names of both Alena and the Czech owner. It was, of course, quite illegal for Alena to draw this money on her signature alone.

When the Czech lady found out what had happened she immediately reported the matter to the Spanish police – La Guardia – which was really quite a nasty and unfriendly thing for one Czech to do to another. At the very least they should have made their intentions known before going ahead with such drastic action. Lynne and I arrived on this day at the villa to find the Czech owners and Alena and Vaclav, plus two members of La Guardia standing outside the villa and a furious discussion was going on. I didn't like the sneer on the Czech lady's face; it wasn't at all nice and she seemed to be gloating at Alena's obvious discomfort.

Alena appealed for us to help her as the police wanted her to go with them to the La Guardia station to explain herself and make a statement, and she didn't want to go. In our limited Spanish we spoke with the police-men and they said quite clearly that if Alena refused to go with them they would place handcuffs upon her and force her to go. So I advised her to go quietly with the policemen, and told her that I would take Lynne home first and then come directly to the La Guardia station. Alena was absolutely boiling with rage but saw sense, thank goodness, and agreed to go with the policemen. I quickly took Lynne home and left straight away to join Alena. It was a relief to find that they had someone who could translate there; she made her statement and I was able to take her back to her rented villa. I do not exactly know all the details and what the basis of the row was, and although Alena should not have done what she did, I think the Czech owners should not have gone to those lengths; that was somewhat over the top. To me it seemed much ado about very little as the sum in question was not a large amount.

After a period of questioning, Alena was allowed to go and then asked me what further action she should take, because having been denounced by the Czech lady a charge was still outstanding against her; she felt that her point of view should be taken into consideration too. I could advise her in no other way but to consult a Spanish solicitor. She was reluctant to do so because she thought that she should not be placed in a position whereby she would incur even more expenditure; but after consideration she decided to accept my advice. I accompanied her to this consultation. I cannot recall details of the conclusion reached, but it was eventually settled to the satisfaction of all concerned. Alena repaid the money into the bank and just as the solicitor said, La Guardia forgot about the whole thing.

However, Alena and Vaclav were in no way prepared to stay at the rented villa in Maryvillas any longer and managed to find a small flat on the third or fourth floor of an apartment building right on the beach. This suited Alena even more, because she could take her beach chair downstairs anytime she wanted and sit on the beach, which she liked to do very much – however, not in the nude as she liked to do at the villa! After some weeks they decided they had had enough of Spain and they informed us that it was their intention to return to their adopted home in Sweden. We were sorry to see them go, for we had enjoyed some good times with them.

On their departure they left us a number of things they didn't want to take with them, including a bottle of red wine with a special crown design in gold on the label. Vaclav told me that it was indeed a very special wine and extremely expensive to buy. He had acquired it whilst living in the Canary Islands before coming to Calpe. Someone who saw it in my lounge also told me the same, i.e. that a wine with that particular crown imprint on the label denotes a very special and very exclusive wine indeed. So I looked for an opportunity, i.e. a special occasion or a very special dinner perhaps, to try it, and I have to say that it was one of the most perfect red wines I have ever tasted – anywhere. I am sure it was a Rioja wine and quite fantastic, and I was very grateful to Vaclav that he had so kindly given it to us.

After the collapse of communism in Czechoslovakia there was no reason now for Alena and Vaclav not to return to their country of birth and with their two Swedish pensions they would be quite wealthy people there, and so after some time they did exactly that. However, I cannot understand them, because of all the lovely places they could have afforded and gone to, they returned to live in a flat in a town called Teplice in northern Bohemia, which is an industrial and fume-ridden area. Alena is most unhappy there and she has told me this on a number of occasions. For some reason Vaclav insisted upon living there.

Oh Alena, Alena; what a puzzle and a conundrum she really was – and still is. She is forever trying to fall in love with somebody new, even though she is well into her eighties, and every year goes to the Canary Islands hoping to meet a fresh sweetheart with whom maybe to have an affair. Of course, she is old now, but the last time I saw her, which was in 2004 when Lynne, Jackie and Ray and I went for a nostalgic visit to the Czech Republic, about which I will write later on, she was looking very good for her age. Lynne is certain that she has had plastic surgery, because to look at her one would never believe she was well into her eighties. I have written a short story about her because her life was very interesting and I will include that in some future publication.

We had other Czech visitors too. I had always wanted my old friend George (Jiri) Stepan and his dear wife Jarka, from Prague, to come to Calpe and stay with us. But although they could get the permission, obtaining the necessary foreign currency was a problem. Also, in his little old car it would have been a terribly long journey. So I told George I had discovered that if he could get across the border in his car, just to Nuremberg, it was possible to pick up a coach there which comes all the way directly to Calpe, and we would pay their fares if there was any problem obtaining the necessary foreign currency. George immediately refused and would not accept my offer, and neither would he use his position in the bank to acquire such foreign currency, which he could easily have done. George is a very honest and straightforward man. But I thought I knew the way to get him to change his mind and so I wrote to him and said that if the boot was on the other foot I am certain that he, George, would be willing to pay my fare, and if that were so then I have a right, as an old friend, to expect him to accept my offer, because we wanted to see him and Jarka in Spain. That did the trick. To our great pleasure George and Jarka accepted our invitation. So I booked and paid for the coach tickets in Calpe and sent them by registered post to Prague.

On the day of their arrival I went down early to the seafront, where the coach dropping point was situated, and just as I had parked my car and walked back there they were, standing on the pavement, having got off the coach just moments before I appeared, looking around them. They were both pleased and I think a little relieved to see me, as I was to see them. It was excellent how smoothly everything had gone. So George and Jarka spent a fortnight with us and I would like to think they had a good time. We took them here and there but we also dropped them in town so that they could be independent, explore and have a good look round on their own, and then picked them up later by arrangement. Whilst they were with us Lynne and I celebrated our fortieth wedding anniversary. We decided to have a luncheon party out on the patio, as the weather looked OK. We had a sun canopy fitted to cover that part of the patio some time earlier, because sitting out in the hot sun without any cover was not only very uncomfortable but also rather silly. So a table was set for ten people and it looked a picture; in fact it looked so nice I took photographs of it.

Of course, George and Jarka were already with us, but the others duly arrived and we served drinks at the table. Lynne took care of the first course, which was smoked salmon; she also took care of the vegetables and dessert, whilst my job was to cook two whole legs of lamb on my barbecue, which, if I may say so, were done to perfection, and I also had to look after wines etc. It was a lovely party, but just before the end of the meal it began to rain. Normally we would welcome it, but not then. Fortunately, the sun canopy kept us all dry – except me at the end! So I went inside and found our hand umbrella, which I held over me. Thank goodness the rain did not last very long. But like many parties, and after drinking some good wine, someone broke into song and so I suggested we sing properly and I would tape it for posterity, not that posterity would be likely to preserve our humble rendering of the famous tune and song 'Danny Boy'! However, I like it and sometimes I play it to remind me of that occasion, which proved to be a very enjoyable time and a wonderful way to celebrate our wedding anniversary. Three of the people who sang and who were recorded on that tape have now sadly passed away.

Then Alois Zich and his wife Irena asked if they could come to see us, as they were driving down into Spain. Of course we welcomed them, but sadly they were only able to spend one night, or maybe it was two nights, with us before continuing their journey right down to Granada and then returning through the middle of Spain via Madrid and then towards home. They wanted to see as much of Spain as they could during their trip, which was understandable, but we wish they could have stayed longer with us.

We were also very pleased to see Carole, daughter of my sister Elsie, together with her husband Roy. They came by coach, as Carole does not care for flying. It must have been quite a journey all the way from England. I tried to find out where along the main road the through coaches made their stop, but it seemed difficult to get precise information. One person told me here, another said it was there, therefore I didn't quite know where to pick them up. So I had to cruise up and down and luckily I spotted them just as they alighted from their coach. As a young baby almost, Carole was sent away from the bombs falling on London and was fortunate enough to go to Lord and Lady Cottesloe at their stately home in Bedfordshire. Indeed, they wanted to adopt her. My sister pondered over that for some time, wondering and weighing up what would be best for Carole, but I don't think it took her long to decide that she would be better off with her own mother. However, one cannot help but wonder what might have happened if Elsie had allowed Carole to be adopted. For sure she would have lived a fine life and would certainly have had a wonderful education.

Her husband Roy was a professional boxer and retired as Undefeated Southern Area Heavyweight Champion. Roy is bigger than me, so we don't argue very much. I agree with everything he says! Anyway, I believe they had a nice holiday with us and we were very pleased to see them.

Our final guest from Czechoslovakia was Helena, former wife of George Trnka, my artist friend who, it seems, had forgotten all about me or was angry with me for some unknown reason. Anyway, he had stopped all communication with me and it was a total mystery why, for when I took him back to Alicante we parted the best of friends. Helena came by air and I of course collected her from Alicante Airport. It was nice to renew acquaintance with her. Once again, we showed her around but left her to enjoy her own space, which she appreciated, because she liked to wander round and about to explore the town for herself. On this occasion we had departed from our policy of not having single visitors, as they are always more of a problem to us, as they seem to need more care and attention. If we only had one visitor a year that wouldn't matter, but when you have an almost constant stream of visitors, as we did, then it does get a little tiring. But I am glad to say that Helena was no trouble at all and she maintained an independent attitude.

Whilst Helena was there we discussed the strange situation with her ex-husband Georgie, but she could offer no explanation for his behaviour. Maybe, she said, it was jealousy on the part of George, who had seen our villa, having stayed with us for a week. But in my knowledge of George I just could not imagine him allowing jealousy to spoil a friendship which was over thirty years in length. No, in my view there had to be another reason, but for the life of me I could not fathom out what it might be, and neither could anybody who knew George; it was a complete mystery to us all. Anyway, Helena agreed to take back a letter from me to George in which I asked him to tell me what was wrong between us, and if I had said or done something which has offended him in any way, and I pleaded with him to write to me. Helena told me afterwards that when George came to the shop, where she worked for a friend from time to time, she handed him the letter from me; she said he reached out his hand to take it from her, hesitated, but quickly withdrew it and refused to accept it. Such strange behaviour was, and still is, beyond comprehension, but perhaps it may have been partially explained by his sister, Alena, who thought he was on the borderline of the dreaded disease of many old people – Alzheimer's. Alena said that in her opinion George was ashamed of this and that is the explanation for his odd behaviour and apparently I was not the only old friend he ceased to have contact with. He acted in a similar manner with others too.

If that was so, then George grossly underestimated the value of my friendship, because had I known he was seriously ill then without doubt I would have flown to Prague to be with him, if only for a short time, because that is what I believe true friendship is all about. I had made the same offer to my old friend Alan Root, our neighbour from Caterham Drive in Old Coulsdon, who had moved to Purley, some three miles or so away. Sadly, he fell victim to cancer whilst in his sixties and he knew his number was up. Now Alan and I always had a good laugh together, for we both had a good sense of humour. We had been to innumerable football matches together and made that unforgettable trip to Czechoslovakia together by car; on some Sundays he would come to play my piano and I would accompany him on the accordion; we spent some nice times with each other. So if I thought that I could have cheered him up, if only for a few days, then I would have gladly come home for a spell and sat with him. I offered to do so but he decided not to accept my offer. At least I know I made him laugh when I sent him a postcard from Calpe showing about eight young men, all naked, lying on their fronts on the beach with their bare bottoms being very prominent. On the back I wrote: 'Hello, Alan. Here I am on the beach with a few of my Spanish pals – guess which one am I!' I must have sent this before he became so ill, because my memory tells me that I did see him for the final occasion when on a visit home. We laughed about the card and he said, "I couldn't say which one was you – it has been a long, long time!"

But to return to George, I believe Helena visited us in 1992 or thereabouts and not very long after that I received a letter from her telling me that George had apparently gone berserk in his studio having suffered a brainstorm, was taken to hospital and there my old friend passed away. I was very sad indeed that I never had the chance to say goodbye to an old pal. I do not exactly know what he died from. When hearing this I was of course upset and since then I have spoken about my relationship with George many times with both Helena and Alena, and what possible reason there could be for his very strange behaviour. Helena is as puzzled as I am and can offer no explanation. I have no idea if Alzheimer's really was the cause, or perhaps it was some kind of mental condition. I shall never know now, for George has taken his secrets to the grave with him. But how I wish, over and over again, that I could have repaired my friendship with him before he passed away. How many times have I relived the occasion when I passed by his studio in Prague but walked on? I truly wished I had made a decision to be a little late for my appointment if necessary and I am sure that on a face-to-face basis I could have broken the ice and found out what was troubling him. Later on, had I known he was that ill, then I would gladly have made the journey to Prague to be with him for a short while if only to say goodbye and maybe reminisce over some of the good times we had enjoyed together if he remembered them, that is. I miss George a lot, no question about that.

As we approached 1994 I was diagnosed as having some non-malignant growths which needed to be removed surgically, and so I had to go into hospital, one recommended by the specialist. I was privately insured and so imagined this would be a very nice hospital. Our neighbours, the Pollards, drove us there and when I saw it I was rather disappointed – it wasn't as nice as I had hoped. But I was there and so it was too late now to start being fussy about whether I should go to this hospital or that one – I should have checked beforehand. I was shown to my room, which was en suite, and I think that's all one can say about it, for it was nothing special. There was no point in Lynne hanging around so she returned to Calpe with Terry.

Later that afternoon I was duly removed from my room to the operating theatre; I remember that I was covered with a dingy-looking thin cloth. Downstairs, where the operating theatre was, a group of doctors, including my specialist, were standing around gossiping. They were alerted on my arrival there and one doctor, I think he was the anaesthetist, explained to me that I would have an epidural injection into the spine. Well, they tried and tried to get this needle into my back, but it seemed to be just impossible – they called me 'el toro', 'the bull'! They asked me to try and relax – not easy in a foreign country in a strange operating theatre, not quite knowing what was going to happen to me (an awful feeling), but I tried and eventually they succeeded. Just to make sure the injection was working I kept wiggling my toes – and I succeeded! How was this possible? Well, my recollection of what followed is very sparse. I recall they placed a cloth barrier in front of my face so that I shouldn't see what was going on and I swear they gave me some form of gas, because I remembered nothing until I came to in my room once again. I have no other explanation.

Meanwhile, Lynne was worried because she did not drive herself and had to rely on friends and neighbours to get to Alicante to see me. But I have to say that they were quite fantastic and so I did not lack visitors, despite the difficulties. Later, on the first night following my operation, the drip in the back of my hand became dislodged and came out – probably because I was tossing and turning. This started to bleed quite profusely; I reached for the emergency button, which was on a cable just tied in a knot to the rail of my bed (which shows what class of hospital it was), but in my drowsy state I only succeeded to untie it and drop the whole contraption on to the floor. Try as I may I could not reach it; it was much too painful.

Meanwhile, the bleeding continued; in fact it was pouring from me and I could see that if I did not do something about this situation I would bleed to death. So I made one last super-human effort and although it was very painful, this time I succeeded and pressed the button. In a couple of minutes the night nurse came in, saw what had happened and re-attached the drip. But my sheets were by now soaked in blood, but to my surprise she didn't change them. Maybe she was reluctant to move me as I had only had my operation a few hours ago. But the next day they did change my sheets and so then all was well again.

But I have to say that was a very frightening experience and one I would not care to repeat. Even our NHS hospitals are much better equipped than that one in Alicante, although I have to say that my experiences of Spanish health treatment, generally speaking, had been very good and I held a high regard for them and still do. But should it ever have happened to me again I would be wary of the chosen clinic and certainly check it out before agreeing to anything. The Benidorm Clinic, for example, where Terry Pollard had his much more invasive and serious operation, was quite fantastic and I would have been quite content to have gone there. It was modern, clean and bright – also much nearer to Calpe. After all, I was a private patient and as I was paying for my health insurance I had a right to approve the place where they intended to operate upon me. After four or five days or so I was allowed to go home. Terry once again volunteered to collect me and Lynne came with him. I was already waiting downstairs for them; I just couldn't wait to get out of that place.

Back at our villa I tried to return to normal activity, but soon realised that was the wrong thing to do as I developed an inflammation on the site of my operation and had to contact the hospital in Alicante. They prescribed some anti-inflammatory medication; I rested more and soon everything was OK.

But then Lynne and I sat down to have one of our long chats and to talk about where we go from here. Of late, Lynne had become exhausted by the often oppressive heat. I had felt it too but to a lesser extent. We spoke of having air conditioning fitted, but as Lynne said, that would hardly answer the problem because you cannot live inside all the time and as soon as you open the door the heat hits you like a hot blanket. Next we thought about the last couple of weeks during which I was in hospital in Alicante, some 70 km distant. As I have explained, Lynne, who does not drive, had to rely on help from friends and neighbours and we both agreed they had been terrific and gave her all the help she needed. We were both very grateful and of course, if ever necessary, we would have done exactly the same for them.

But fantastic as our friends were, we also both agreed we could not be fully dependent upon the very kind help of friends in the event that I might become immobile once more, and therefore, something had to change. And then, and as it proved quite wrongly, we had the idea that our family would tire of coming to the same place to holiday year after year and that we could expect to see less and less of them in the future. And finally, the Spanish tax system is quite different to ours and we had heard some horror stories of couples in dire straits when one passed away; it seemed that the Spanish tax authorities automatically freeze all joint accounts until they receive their pound of flesh in terms of tax applicable when a death occurs!

Putting all these factors together we both agreed that we had enjoyed a wonderful time in the last nine years or more and agreed that it had been a wonderful experience, but sad though we would be, it was perhaps time to consider selling up and going back home to England again and finishing our days there. And so we made that decision there and then. Therefore, we immediately contacted Manolo Aniorte, who by this time had left the building company and was now a successful independent property agent – by all accounts he was doing quite well – and placed our villa with him for sale.

To be quite frank, I would have preferred to use another agent, because the system followed by property agents in Spain was very poor both for buyers and sellers. It is – or perhaps I should write was, because perhaps it has changed now – a poor system, because there appeared to be little or even no control. The system worked like this: having decided to sell your villa or apartment you then went to the agent and told him what price you wanted; he then put on top of that whatever sum he thinks the property can stand and then offers it at the highest price level he thinks he can get. Unless one is a Sherlock Holmes and has the means to find out these things, often the seller has no idea of the price his villa is being offered or sold at and the buyer has no idea of what the seller receives. In other words, it is not an open and above-board procedure, such as we have in England – in Spain the agents work on the largest profit they can make rather than a commission. But although I spoke with other agents there is no doubt about it; Manolo was the best and if you wanted positive results then it was preferable to go to him because he got things done.

I should mention at this stage that in the period following my operation I suffered a depression. I would not describe it as a very deep depression and as it was explained to me, was understandable, for every operation one has is an attack upon the nervous system and a lot of people suffer such depressions after operations. Those people who know me and know that I am mostly a cheerful fellow might find it surprising that I would suffer in this way, but as I discovered, it can happen to anybody. In my case I was very thankful to my dear wife who gave me a lot of TLC, which I desperately needed at that time when all and everything around me seemed to be filled with doom and gloom. I spent a lot of time in bed; it is maybe understandable that when you are in depression you want to lock yourself away and speak to nobody – except to Lynne, of course. I was, and still am, very grateful to Lynne for her understanding and the excellent way she handled my temporary setback. I think I was slowly beginning to get more back to normal as we approached the time of our return, but it is a fact that I was still in depression when I drove back through Spain and France to England. Perhaps I should not have done that, but we succeeded in arriving home quite safely and without mishap.

At around this time we began to try to dispose of some of the items which we would probably not need to take back home. We advertised our table tennis table, which was brand new when we went to Spain, also our billiards/snooker table and other items. All sold very quickly at the attractive prices we were asking. And then, one evening during a dinner over at Moraira at the villa of our friends Tom and Margarete Gray, Tom told us of the predicament of his cousin who had come out to Spain to live bringing with him the 'car of his dreams' – a Citroen BX Turbo – only to find that the Spanish authorities would not give him an MOT certificate for continual driving in Spain on the basis that it had right-hand drive. His six months, during which every visitor is allowed to drive a foreign car there, was up and so there he was with a car he couldn't use and there I was with a Spanish Renault car that I would prefer not to take back to England for the very same reason. His car had only 17,000 miles on the clock and was one year old, whilst mine, which was also only a year old, had only 18,000 km (just under 11,000 miles) on the clock. So Tom suggested we make a swop. It sounded like a very good idea to me, for I had been to the Renault agent who sold my car to me only to be told that he could not give me any more than the equivalent of £4,000, despite the fact that it was in perfect condition and almost new.

So through Tom we arranged for his cousin to come to our villa with his Citroen when we could compare notes and, if possible, make a deal. When I saw his sky-blue car and noted that it really was also almost like brand new, I imagined he would say that he would make a swop but that he would require a cash amount in addition, as the two cars obviously had different values. But to my surprise he didn't! He agreed to a straight swop, at which I was delighted. So we went down to town to regulate the insurance covers of the vehicles. My requirements were rather more complicated because I would be making the trip home quite soon and I needed cover until I was able to organise new cover in England. But Tom's cousin's transfer was just a simple task, for he was remaining in Spain. I looked forward to driving this very nice car home; it is now 2007 and the car is still running very sweetly and the bodywork remains immaculate. I have thought several times about buying a new car here in England – but why? My Citroen runs very well and is quite adequate for the limited amount of motoring we do now that we are getting quite old; it is comfortable and very economical and in all probability should last longer than me! So I have to say that it was one of the finest deals I ever did.

As far as the sale of our villa was concerned it was not all that long before a gentleman – a Danish man who worked somehow in harmony, perhaps as a sub-agent, with Manolo – together with a rather elderly Swiss couple appeared on our patio and asked if they could look at our villa. We liked him but we were not at all sure about the woman who was an unsmiling and rather severe lady. But they were prospective buyers and so we jumped into action and showed them around, and we could see that they, especially the man, were impressed. As the gentleman was a computer expert he wanted an area where he could carry on his work. This seemed to be a problem but then he looked again at the integral garage and, if I recall correctly, spoke to us about converting that into a computer workshop. Anyway, without talking about price they agreed to buy, and even made the small boy who accompanied them, their grandson we presumed, take down the For Sale sign we had placed at our entrance. They promised to be in touch with Manolo the following morning. They did and we heard from Manolo quite quickly. He told us that the Swiss couple had placed a deposit with him and that they wanted to move in as soon as possible and asked when we could make the necessary arrangements. We agreed a date about four or five weeks hence and worked towards that.

With two agents involved, I have no doubt that it was the most expensive way to sell on our part, and very probably for the buyer too. But to be frank, we were not in the mood for a lot of messing about; here was a chance to sell without any quibbling and it meant we could be home before long. So although such a situation was irksome, especially to me as a businessman, we put such thoughts on the back burner and went ahead. We obtained a good quote for our goods and chattels to be removed back to England from a firm situated in Okehampton – near to where we were probably going to live – and in the weeks that followed we slowly prepared as much as possible in readiness to be packed.

On our very last day we awaited the removal people, who came quite early. But from the already sultry atmosphere we could tell that this was, unfortunately, going to be a scorcher – and we were right because for most of that day the temperature was above 100 °Fahrenheit. How those chaps worked during such heat one can only imagine. We of course kept them as cool as possible by serving them, and ourselves, with plenty of cold drinks. We were given cardboard wardrobes in to which to place our clothing so we were kept quite busy too. I believe Lynne made some sandwiches at lunchtime and afterwards the chaps resumed. Fortunately, we were leaving a lot behind us – although many times subsequently we wished we hadn't – and in the late afternoon all had been packed into cartons, which were numbered and a rough description of the contents of each scribbled on the outside, the paperwork was attended to and finally the two vehicles were ready to leave. I am sure each man had lost at least a stone in weight from perspiring. It must have been very difficult to have done such work on a day like that. But finally the job was finished and the two vehicles drove away with all that we possessed in them. What a strange experience it was, and what a mixture of feelings we had when seeing our possessions vanishing down the hill out of sight. We would not see our belongings again until October.

Well, the big day had ended and we were totally exhausted. So we went down into town to have our 'last supper' and invited our friend and neighbour from down in the valley, Dorothy Beevers, to accompany us, but as I recall it was rather a solemn supper. It is seldom a happy time when you are saying goodbye.

Afterwards we returned to La Empedrola, Dorothy went home, Lynne went to bed (we left all beds and bedding behind) but I, for the very last time, sat out on the patio, turned on the pool lights and watched the fishing boats setting out – you could easily see them, for every fishing vessel had a lamp on its mast. Sitting there in the moonlight on that balmy evening, sipping a glass of wine and listening to very nice soft music from my barbecue house I thought about the last nine years and just how very lucky we had been to have enjoyed such a marvellous experience. Without doubt, we had witnessed possibly the very last of 'good old Spain' – the Spain of unbelievably cheap prices, of flamenco, of classical Spanish dancing, of bullfights and fiestas and a very special kind of atmosphere which belonged to that era and before, but began to vanish, in my opinion, from around 1990 when Spain was admitted into the EU. From 1990 one could detect a perceptible air of change. It was becoming a little bit 'ordinary'.

There was a light breeze that gentle night and the ripples on the pool reflected against the villa and made it shimmer; it really was a very impressive sight. Our old friend Velma always said that from her kitchen window our villa looked like something out of Beverly Hills; in fact she forecast that our urbanisation, La Empedrola, would become a European Beverly Hills – she was wrong, for on a nostalgic return visit in 2002 we found that Empedrola had in fact deteriorated quite a lot from our days. We would not choose to live there today, for it seemed to us that the gardens were not being cared for as they once were and the floral bushes that were planted when we were there were untidy and growing all over the place. It is sad that such a beautiful urbanisation as La Empedrola was being neglected in this way. I believe much of the problem lies with those people who have bought villas there as holiday homes only and so are not there all the time. However, that is no excuse, as arrangements for garden care can quite easily be made in the absence of the owners

And so we spent the last night in that way; later on I thought that I too should go to bed for it would be a long journey the next day. So I did, but sleep was beyond me and also for Lynne.

As far as I can recall that final day I believe we were both still awake long before dawn and so I suggested to Lynne that we might as well get up and make an early start to the long journey ahead of us rather than just lie there wasting time. And so that is what we did. We had a nice cup of tea and a small breakfast and got on our way as quickly as we could. I could not help feeling a great sad wrench when driving out of our driveway for the very last time – and God bless her, even at that unearthly hour there was Dorothy standing on her verandah with her little poodle in her arms waving us goodbye! I gave a short honk to acknowledge her and drove down to town to join the main road towards Valencia.

On this particular journey we had to be rather more careful than usual because it had been widely reported that on the road from Calpe to Valencia, in a number of instances, foreign cars especially were being persuaded by con artists and thieves to pull over for one reason or another, occupying the driver's attention, and then stealing from them whatever they could. The favourite scheme was to drive up to the side of you and gesticulate wildly that something is very wrong with one of your wheels; this led many drivers to be alarmed and they stopped. Then the con artists got to work, and whilst one pretended to help you and occupy your attention the other would steal from you. Sometimes the robbery was effected in a more direct way – motorway mugging, in fact; in some instances I believe they became rather violent if you didn't cooperate with them fully.

In our case we were carrying with us a bank certified cheque for a considerable sum of money, this being part of the proceeds of the sale of our villa, payable of course to anyone who presented it. If we were robbed of that we would have been in very serious trouble indeed. I think our very early start helped a lot, but in any case I had made up my mind that if anybody tried to stop me I would just keep going and ignore them. I am glad to say we were not bothered by any of these criminals. But just to be safe I placed the cheque in an envelope under the rubber mat on the driver's side.

The road going north east to Barcelona and on towards the southern French border was another danger area, but this would not bother us too much, after Valencia, as we were striking through the middle of Spain making our way towards Zaragoza, Pamplona, on to the Spanish-French border, bypassing Bordeaux and getting as far as Saintes in France, where our neighbours, Terry and Pam Pollard, had recommended a nice hotel where they had stayed on a previous trip.

We got to Saintes in the late afternoon and by asking for directions, half of which I could not understand, we nevertheless eventually found our hotel. The Pollards had recommended this particular hotel because there was an option to have your car locked up overnight and this was very important to us after our previous experiences. Anyhow, we checked in, put our car away and asked if there was a bar. To our disappointment they told us that their bar and their kitchen were both closed for renovations. We were very thirsty so they directed us to the railway station where they said we could get a drink. So we went there and, my goodness, what a very delightful railway station it was. The cafeteria was quite superb, without a doubt the best I had ever seen in any railway station anywhere. My first thought was why couldn't British railway stations be like this? But I soon found out why when we ordered two gin and tonics to quench our thirst – the bill came to around £13, and that was back then! If they charge those kinds of prices no wonder the railway stations are so great! In Spain two G and Ts would cost around £4 by comparison.

We had to ask in our hotel where we might get an evening meal and they directed us to a place just around the corner. It was nothing special; in fact I think we found it rather disappointing. Never mind, we thought, the next day we would get our boat at Cherbourg and hopefully be in Plymouth by the evening. And that really is how it worked out.

13

HOME AGAIN!

Jackie, Ray and our two grandsons, Darren and Grant, were waiting for us, for they knew our expected time of arrival and gave us a nice welcome. We had little choice but to ask if we could stay with them for a, hopefully, short time until we were able to find a house somewhere in the vicinity, and they were quite happy to agree to this request of ours.

So we wasted no time but began to search for somewhere to live more or less immediately. I will not bore you, dear reader, with our escapades during our search, but suffice to say that my dear wife fell in love with almost the first house we saw.

We had decided on some guidelines, although we never thought that any house we might find would satisfy us in every respect. But we were very fortunate and achieved virtually all our aims because it had four bedrooms, three with integrated wardrobes, which enabled us to have a box room as well as a study for me, a family bathroom plus one bedroom en suite, downstairs toilet and washbasin, a small garden, which is exactly what we wanted – although more about that later – it was near to a shop, which might be needed in case of emergencies – the village shop and post office is just a few yards away – it was only 200 yards to a bus stop, in case of need, and it was near to Jackie and Ray, who live in the next village, Tedburn St Mary, some two and a half miles from us. Furthermore, it had an Economy 7 heating system fitted, which was ideal for a couple like us who were at home all day; plus a burglar alarm, smoke alarms and front and side entrances, as well as a fine fitted electric cooker, a washing/drying machine and a refrigerator/freezer; furthermore, it was carpeted throughout, upstairs and downstairs – all included in the purchase price, which, as a seasoned buyer, I negotiated and on which I obtained a reduction.

It was just one house standing on its own on a plot where a total of eight houses were to be built. Ours was the show house and that is why it was so well fitted. Well, it seemed that our developers and builders ran into some financial problems and were not able to complete the remaining houses – we were fortunate enough to view the property at this exact time. The whole eight-house plot was subsequently bought by another company who, would you believe, also had some money problems. They either sold out or were taken over by yet another company. But at last, building of the remaining seven houses was started and completed and when all was finished it made what is now a rather nice compact and small close.

So from 1994 until the present day this village of Cheriton Bishop in Devon became our home and we have been very happy and contented here. We have an excellent surgery with nice doctors and nurses just around the corner – about five minutes' walk – and the countryside around is quite beautiful, enabling me to take part in one of my very favourite occupations – walking. I can walk in a number of directions, but for pure enjoyment nothing can beat the walk from Cheriton Bishop to Tedburn St Mary; the scenery is quite lovely and except for the madcap drivers who use this road as a race track and sometimes travel along it at absurd speed levels, it is peaceful and quiet.

When we first came home and I began to walk in various directions I would invariably see some form of wildlife. Either deer – in fact, before the house opposite to ours was built we could also see deer, with the aid of binoculars, grazing along the hedgerows from our bedroom windows – sometimes foxes, and once I had the wonderful experience whilst walking of a stoat, or possibly a weasel, crossing the road with a big fat mouse in his jaws. Halfway across he saw me, panicked, dropped the mouse and hurried across to the side of the road where there were bushes. But it apparently changed its mind about me – maybe he thought I didn't look such a bad chap after all – and with a more confident look he went back, picked up the dead mouse and rushed back in to the bushes, giving me a sideways glance; he probably thought on reflection that he had nothing to fear from me. And he was right; I didn't want his mouse! You see, for such an experience, or to see any form of wildlife, I would willingly walk any number of miles.

But of late I have not been walking so much, firstly because of the weather, which has been very bad with very cold winds that cut right through you; here in Cheriton Bishop, being on the edge of Dartmoor, the winds blow across the moors and are sometimes very bitter and strong. Secondly, because I have had some health problems in the last months – especially with my heart – and I have become somewhat breathless as well as a lot less energetic. So whereas I gladly walked five miles a day I am now down to two miles only; but I haven't given up and remain hopeful that when the better weather arrives in the springtime I will be able to walk my five miles a day once again, which, incidentally, I could do in less than two hours; at least I will try my best. Not too bad for an old chap who celebrated his seventy-ninth birthday this year!

> **STOP PRESS:** Matters have improved and I am now walking five miles per day as I used to, weather permitting of course, but now it takes me a little more than two hours.

What concerns me, however, is the lack of wildlife at present. I have not seen a deer for a very long time, certainly no foxes, and not even a nervous stoat. I find this to be a worrying factor as a person who is very interested in wildlife. We have had rumours that we have a large black cat, possibly a panther or leopard, roaming around our countryside, and even wild boar are heading this way they say. They have certainly reached Exmoor, I have been told, and that being so it will not be long before they will spread to Dartmoor and the surrounding areas. But I have seen nothing of these yet – if I do suddenly confront one of these then I can assure you, dear reader, that there will be a new half mile British running record!

Not all that long after our return home and our establishment in this village, in 1996 in fact, Lynne and I were invited to go to Scotland for the New Year. It was a long way to go but we thought that it would be another new experience to enjoy. Before setting out we made sure that the radiator on the upstairs landing was on but we turned the water heating off. So off we went in the direction of Scotland. Actually, it did not take as long to get there as I thought; the roads to Scotland are very good and fast. We had to head for the Loch Lomond area and find the De Vere hotel there, which we managed to do without any problems. There we found the lodge where our youngest daughter, her partner at that time, Gary, who had a time share arrangement there, our two grandchildren and Gary's two children were staying. It was a very nice lodge and we occupied a basement room. We had a very enjoyable Scottish New Year and we were very glad we had accepted Gary's invitation. The previous year Paul Gascoigne, the football player, was there enjoying himself and they all met and mixed with him during the evening. The year we went I don't think there were any famous people, but one young man who was roaming from table to table in a very friendly and jocular manner looked to me very much like Ally McCoist, and to this day I am sure it was him.

Back at the lodge everybody had become rather disturbed at seeing some rather large mice running suddenly from place to place and the cupboard where the children were keeping all their Christmas sweets had been entered by something which had chewed some of them up, especially the chocolate. I did not like the look of it myself but one evening, when we returned from having supper out, Gary's daughter went to her room and all of a sudden we heard a most terrible scream. It appears she had opened the door and a rather large rat was poised just above it, evidently climbing to seek a way out. It jumped from there onto a chest of drawers and from there to the floor where it hid. Gary closed the door immediately to trap the rat inside whilst Debbie and Lynne tried to pacify the little girl, who was understandably terrified.

As I recall, Gary phoned reception and they promised to send someone immediately. A man soon came along and Gary and he went into the room. They began to move the furniture around when, suddenly, we heard a commotion. Apparently, the rat went from its hiding place and began to climb up the back of the window curtain. Gary saw the curtain moving and smashed and smashed it with the broom he was holding. The rat, of course, was killed by this very strong attack.

But nobody was prepared to sleep there any more because, as everyone knows, there is never just one rat. So the hotel staff, who were full of apologies, offered accommodation at the main hotel. But unfortunately, they did not have sufficient room for Lynne and me. They offered us the option to move to another lodge, but by this time we were both tired out. We were going home anyway the next day and we didn't feel like moving lock, stock and barrel just for one night. So bravely, rats or no rats, we decided to stay put. I had a packet of chocolate biscuits by our bedside, which I thought it would be prudent to place in a totally inaccessible place – if there is such a place, for rats are amazing climbers.

I was very surprised indeed that Lynne agreed to this plan, because normally she would rather run a mile than get involved with rats or mice, or anything like that. But she was very brave. Come to think of it, so was I for that matter, as I am not exactly in love with rats either!

Before leaving home we had arranged that Jackie and Ray would go over to our house on the Saturday night, the day before our scheduled return, and switch on the radiators so that we would have a nice warm house to return to on Sunday, as we had previously arranged to stay overnight on the Saturday during our trip back home with Dorothy and Ron Beevers, our friends and former neighbours in Spain, who had also returned to England and now lived in the Birmingham area. We looked forward to seeing them again and as they lived at a place quite near to Birmingham, it was not far out of our way. We found them all right and spent a very enjoyable evening with them and the following morning we made tracks towards Bristol and then on to Exeter and home.

Our house was a very welcome sight. I still had my car in the drive-way when I heard Lynne cry out. I thought for a moment we had been burgled, but it was even worse than that – the whole house, it seemed, was completely soaked with water pouring everywhere. Lynne and I looked at each other and we could quite easily have burst into tears – our lovely new home was seemingly ruined.

I cannot remember now the actual sequence of our actions, but we phoned Bill Strutt, who lives in the next village and who helped us out and did some work for us from time to time; we then phoned the insurance company and thank goodness someone was on duty – at least they were there in the midday period, but not in the afternoon. We also turned off the water and emptied the loft tank as quickly as we could; at least that stopped the pouring water cascading down. Bill Strutt and his wife Lynne are good and kind people and rushed over straight away; what we would have done without their very kind help I cannot imagine and we were most grateful to them.

They were certainly a great help to us and tore out the material in the loft placed there for heat conserving purposes. It was now soaked through and of no use whatsoever. And then various people began to arrive; firstly an electrician, a gentleman representing the insurance company, and so on. Then later on in the afternoon a lady who lived around the corner in Church Lane called to say she had heard of our terrible plight and that she had a room in her bungalow that we could occupy for as long as we wished. We didn't know her from Adam and so we were very touched by her kindness; but we had made arrangements to go to Jackie and Ray in this emergency and so we thanked her profusely but declined.

It appears that during our absence the winter temperatures had fallen to eight degrees below zero – not at all usual in the UK and certainly not in the southwest. Therefore, the pipes in the loft had become frozen and consequently fractured by expansion, with the result that when Jackie turned on our radiators, the temperature went up, the fractured pipes thawed and water just began to pour from the loft; as we had not turned the water off, the loft tank just kept refilling and it kept on pouring down into the house.

We slept at Jackie and Ray's home for a few nights but we couldn't put upon them for too long. The insurance man had told us that reasonable expenses for accommodation would be claimable and so we went to the nearest place to Cheriton Bishop at Whiddon Down, about five miles away, where there was a Travel Lodge or some such similar place. We could also eat there in a cafeteria-type restaurant. But when returning to our home to see how things were progressing we heard that one of our two pubs had some accommodation available and so I went to The Good Knight Inn, as it was called then, and sure enough they had a small apartment which they could rent to us for as long as we needed it. This was much more convenient for us as we could bring some of our own things there and feel a little more at home. Also I could keep popping back to keep an eye on the workmen, who by this time had moved in.

Our insurance claim was quite substantial, as can be imagined, but on the other hand, we and the insurance company were very lucky we came home when we did and managed to stop further damage, because on inspection we found that quite a lot of things we thought might be ruined were undamaged by the water. We had to have two large wind machines that were turned on all day long for two or three days to dry the house out, and then the decorators came to completely re-paint all the woodwork. There was a brief discussion about whether they should paint the walls and the decorator's view won in the end, for they said that in their experiences of such occurrences it is common in wood framed houses such as ours for cracks to appear in the walls after it had dried out. To simply re-paint them would only mean that such cracks would almost certainly develop. They recommended, therefore, that all walls should be papered with vinyl paper. The insurance agent agreed to this and so, with his approval, we had to rush out to choose paper and bring it back to the decorators as quickly as possible, otherwise they would be sitting around able to do very little. It gave us no chance to order paper we might have preferred. We just had to take what paper they had in stock at the place they had recommended to us in Exeter.

We were out of our house for six long weeks. But eventually we were able to move back in, settle down and resume normal life once more. Of course, such a lesson taught us a great deal, which is first of all try not to go away in the winter, because you never know. Secondly, summer or winter, turn the water off and empty the loft tank and the pipes. I know that sounds very wasteful but if we had done those two things then this terrible experience would not have happened to us.

In the years that followed we had a number of visitors to us in Cheriton Bishop whom we were happy to welcome and see. Alois Zich and his wife Irena came from Prague on a motor tour of England and stopped off with their granddaughter, who was studying in England somewhere; they slept at The Old Thatch Inn, but we entertained them to dinner etc. Anton van Zeyl and his then wife Ellie came from Holland to visit us. Then Pam and Terry Pollard, our old next-door neighbours in Spain, also came to see us when visiting England, and of course we had a number of other relatives and friends too. We were pleased to see and welcome them all.

We also made three trips abroad, firstly to Prague by car with Jackie and Ray. Ray did the driving and he managed very well indeed. On that trip we showed them the church near to the river in Prague where the parachutists who assassinated Reinhard Heydrich, the Nazi monster, took refuge and were all killed; I wrote about this event in my first volume. They also said they would like to see the Terezin (in German, Theriesenstadt) concentration camp and so I arranged that we would meet Alena and Vaclav, as we would be not too far from them. We did not go to their town, Teplice, for they chose to meet us in a nearby town called Luhacovice. Terezin itself, incidentally, was not a killing camp but even so many people died there. You could describe it as a transit camp where people were sent on their way to Auschwitz to be murdered in the gas chambers.

Once I made a bad mistake with Sydney Eagle. He had expressed an interest in visiting one of the factories that produced so much of his goods for the supermarket trade. I was there in Prague already when Sydney arrived by plane and so I took him by car to the Diana Factory, Decin. On the way we passed the camp and I asked Sydney if he would like to take a quick look. It proved to be not such a quick look, for Sydney wanted to see everything. As a devout Jew, before entering the camp, as he did not have the normal skullcap, he placed a handkerchief upon his head, for neither did he have a hat. He paid a lot of interest to every corner of that dreadful place where so many had died, mainly Jewish people, and where so much unhappiness was caused.

He saw the swimming pool built by the prisoners because the Camp Commandant's daughter liked to swim. However, anyone caught looking at the daughter when she did swim was punished very severely, sometimes even by death, I was told. Sydney was all right until at the end and as one exited the camp it was necessary to pass through a small museum. Here, in each of the rooms, were very small plaques individually naming as many victims as they could trace. These plaques were in memory of those who died there either from illness, hunger or from execution, and all the walls of this museum were fully covered by these tiny plaques. But on one pillar there was a letter in a frame and underneath were translations into other languages, including English; it was from a little Jewish boy named Pavel, and it was written to his aunt and uncle in Prague to tell them he was OK and that all the children were very excited because they were going to the forest to pick berries that afternoon. Underneath was a caption to the effect that this was the last letter Pavel ever wrote because the trip to the forest was a ruse – it was a trip to the grave, for all those Jewish children were sent north to Auschwitz and murdered there. At this Sydney began to cry uncontrollably and I could do nothing but pat him on the back and try to comfort him. But once back in the car, when we resumed our journey to Decin, Sydney soon recovered. I could have kicked myself for taking him to this awful place – it was a foolish mistake on my part. However, Sydney himself was very glad indeed that he had experienced this visit to Terezin.

But back to our trip together with Ray and Jackie. On each visit to Prague I made I held a dinner for my friends there, or those I could trace and kept in communication with. They were as glad to see me as I was to see them. But a week passes very quickly and soon it was time to return home. Unfortunately, we had chosen a period during which the European Football Championships were being held in Belgium and so the roads were crowded and so were the motorway restaurants.

But I would like to mention that when going through Germany I noted that the Rasthausen restaurants on the autobahns, such fine establishments as I recall in my day, were not nearly as nice as they used to be years ago when I was travelling so frequently through on my way to Czechoslovakia. It may be that with the growth of traffic these places have become much more used; it only needs a large or increased volume of people to spoil things, and the greater the volume of people, the quicker places become spoiled. But that, of course, applies anywhere, not just in Germany.

Our next visit to Prague was a couple of years later and came about as a result of an idea on the part of Jackie and Ray. They said they were thinking of going again, as there was much of Prague that they didn't get the chance to see on their first visit, and asked if we would like to accompany them. We said we would, but this time we all decided to go by plane. We asked our old friend George Stepan to fix us accommodation and we flew from Bristol with Easyjet. Bristol was very crowded but soon we were on the plane and winging our way to Prague. We were somewhere around the French-German border, I would think, when the captain announced that we would be returning to the UK because the plane had developed a fault, but there was nothing to worry about. The plane, which was holding us 30,000 feet up in the air, had a fault – and there was nothing to worry about? Well sorry, Mr Captain, but we were worried; I would say, however, that the more seasoned travellers accepted the situation philosophically. Personally, I thought it would have been just as well to go on to Prague rather than turn round and go back to the UK. Anyway, we found ourselves back at Luton Airport where we had to disembark and lounge around for an hour or so. Then we boarded the plane again, and as I passed the steward I asked him what the fault was. He said that the engineers were unable to find any fault!

Meanwhile, George Stepan was very kindly waiting for us at Hotel Intercontinental, certainly one of, if not the finest, hotel in Prague. In fact, I would go so far as to say that it was one of the nicest hotels I have ever stayed in anywhere. I gently berated George for waiting all that time. I told him we were very grateful but that he should have gone home. Anyway, we were shown to our rooms and what a great surprise awaited Lynne and me. We found that George's friend in reception, who had arranged our accommodation, had given us what I can only describe as the presidential suite. To the left in the large entrance hall there were toilet and washing facilities for guests, then in the main lounge a long table suitable for a meeting of twelve people, large TV, computer, comfortable furniture and a coffee table with a bowl of fresh fruit, and leading off from this were the bedroom and the bathroom, which was an absolute dream and equipped with everything one could possibly want, including toothpaste and new toothbrushes sealed in cellophane, shampoo, moisturisers, hair dryer, dressing gowns and more! Certainly it was one of the finest bathrooms I had ever seen in my life. This was an apartment fit for a king. It is certainly very nice to have good friends. George, and his friend of course, had really made all these very special arrangements and we were most grateful to them for so doing. Jackie and Ray's room was in the same corridor – very nice, very comfortable, in fact a beautiful room too, but which in no way could be compared to ours. Taking everything into account, and having stayed at many hotels in many countries, I have to say once again that this was one of the very best hotels I have ever stayed in and I was rather sorry to leave it behind.

That evening we ate at a place just off the Old Town Square (Staromestske Namesti) called Cerny Slon (The Black Elephant) and it was a great meal served by very pleasant people and we enjoyed our sojourn there. We strolled through the square and had a look at the restaurant where we would be eating dinner the next evening, which was Restaurace Staromestske (Old Town Restaurant), and where we had invited our friends to join us. Sadly, the numbers of my friends were getting fewer and fewer with each visit. Then Lynne said she was feeling rather tired and so we walked her back to the hotel. Jackie, Ray and I returned to have a last glass of beer in the square. We were sitting at a table there when Ray received a text from his son back in England, advising us that the favourite football team of us all, Crystal Palace, had won the play-offs and so was now in the Premiership. That was terrific news indeed for us, as we were all old Crystal Palace fans, and needed to be celebrated, so we had another glass of beer. But what was unsightly were the numbers of young and even middle-aged Englishmen staggering around quite drunk on the cheap beer. The language of some of them was quite appalling. Prague has become a target for stag parties it seems, and I am not at all sure that is a good thing for a wonderful and historical city like Prague, not, at least, from what I saw. When I returned home I made a point of writing to our friends who live in Prague to assure them that we are not all like that in England – I was ashamed of what I had seen. It is very sad to witness such an ancient and lovely city tarnished in this way

The next day I wanted to show Lynne, Jackie and Ray Vaclavske Namesti (better known as Wenceslas Square) and some of my old haunts. First of all I showed them Hotel Alcron, the very first hotel I ever stayed at in Prague in January 1953, which is situated in a street called Ulice Stepanska, just off the square. Of course, the hotel is a quite different place to the one I knew. It has been completely refurbished and modernised – all shine and glitter. We had an aperitif there and I wandered into the restaurant to see my 'lady friend', the naked statue by the table which I always sat at when eating there in the old days, but she had gone. Just then the head waiter appeared and I told him of my past history with the hotel going back half a century; he was quite interested and told me that my 'lady friend' now resided in a museum, because she did become quite famous. Without doubt, the Alcron is a very nice hotel indeed, but call me old fashioned if you like, to me it was cold and non-atmospheric. Give me the old Alcron any day. Now that was a hotel and a half. Ask anyone who knew it back then.

From Stepanska we returned to Vaclavske Namesti and we walked up in the direction of The National Museum. I told our small party that we were going to lunch at a very nice restaurant situated above Dum Potravin (The House of Food). Below the restaurant was the shop, internationally known, which sold every kind of sausage, salami, ham, cheese, caviar – everything one can imagine. Many years ago I always tried to visit this shop before returning home to buy some delicacy or other to take back, and many people I know did exactly the same. As we neared the museum I peered across the gigantic square and to my horror Dum Potravin had vanished! To add insult to injury, it had been replaced by a McDonald's burger bar! This really is a national disgrace – how could they eliminate such a wonderful and well-remembered landmark, a landmark known to so many people all over Europe and perhaps even beyond who had visited Prague? It was a shock to me and brought home the fact that I was looking for a Prague that doesn't exist any more. Just like London, Paris and so many places, my Prague – the Prague I used to know so well – has in so many respects gone. So with that disappointment we wandered down the square and in an alleyway we found a restaurant that looked inviting. But it proved to be nothing special; I ordered one of my old favourites as a starter, Prague ham with Czech gherkins. But what I received was as far away from the Prague ham that I used to eat as one could possibly get. It was not a meal I recall as being in any way memorable except for its unrecommendable standard.

Then we continued window shopping in the square and slowly wandered down to the bottom where it meets the street called Ulice Prikope, but just before leaving the square I walked into one arcade at the bottom of which used to be Vinarna Budapest and where you could sit with a bottle of wine and listen to amazing gypsy violinists for as long as you wished. With a heavy heart I saw that had gone too. In Prikope itself I pointed out Restaurace Pelikan, where I had such a nice experience many years before – that was still there. Then I looked for a small street to the right in which there was a wonderful small restaurant called Restaurace U Markyz, introduced to me by my old friend Jiri (Georgie) Trnka, the artist, but not only was the restaurant not to be seen, even the small street had gone. As a confirmed nostalgic I felt very sad indeed, because it seemed to me that many of the things which represented my old memories of Prague didn't exist any more. By this time Lynne and I were getting a little tired so we told Jackie and Ray that we were returning to the hotel for a rest and to prepare ourselves for our dinner that evening with my friends. They continued to wander among the shops. And so with a final reminder to them not to be late for the dinner we bade them adieu. Being in Prague I should have said Na Shledanou!

That evening Lynne and I got ready and as we had agreed to meet Jackie and Ray at the restaurant we went on ahead. At Restaurace Staromestske we were shown to our table, but to our surprise nobody was there. We were expecting four of our Czech friends to be there. We waited, but after ten minutes I was getting a little concerned, so I wandered outside into the square and found them all there in a small group waiting for us! No matter, at least we had found each other. But of Jackie and Ray there was no sign, so we returned to our table where we all said a proper hello to each other and ordered some wine to sup whilst we waited for them to arrive. They did eventually and so the dinner could begin. As I recall it was quite a nice meal; the company was excellent and the wine flowed. We spoke about everything and included some old memories which were worth recounting. At the end we reluctantly said goodbye to our friends and went back to our hotel to retire. I didn't know it then but because we have decided to bring a halt to foreign travel, it almost certainly proved to be my last trip to the Czech Republic and so it is very unlikely I shall ever see any of them again; that is a rather sad and sobering thought.

The next day we were leaving Prague and had hired a car, which was brought to the front. We loaded our luggage and off we went. Our first call was to have been Plzen, the famous city of beer, but somewhere we must have taken a wrong turning and found ourselves heading for Karlovy Vary (Carlsbad) instead; this was to have been our second call. Just before arriving there we saw a restaurant on the right which looked inviting so we stopped there and had lunch; it wasn't bad and it wasn't at all expensive. Then we went into Karlovy Vary itself, parked the car and strolled through the main centre.

I tried to find Hotel Pup, where many years before, after a hunting expedition in the forest nearby, my old friend Slavek Svinger and I went for breakfast, as were we very hungry. We ordered ham and eggs but were told, and this at the finest hotel in Karlovy Vary, that they were very sorry but they had no eggs! Breakfast in the best hotel in the town and they have no eggs? Whatever next? So on this trip I wanted to pop my head in and ask them in the restaurant if, after half a century, they had any eggs now! But I couldn't find the hotel and it was pointless asking anyone because the name Pup would most certainly have been changed by now. At a café we sat down at a free table to have a drink. After some time had passed we were still sitting there so I asked the passing waiter in English if he could serve us, as we had been waiting for quite a while; but although he acknowledged my request it was another several minutes before he deigned to serve us, and even then with a rather surly attitude. However, we noticed that his attitude towards his German clients was quite different – full of smiles and jokes and evident pleasant repartee. In our earlier days it was quite the opposite. It was people from the Western countries that were popular and interesting; the Germans, of which there used to be very few back then because of the difficulty in obtaining visas during communist times, were thoroughly disliked. So rather disappointed, we were quite pleased to leave Karlovy Vary behind us. What had happened to those lovely people of Karlovy Vary who were so nice, friendly and so helpful to us back in 1960? To me the change was remarkable. I promised our small party that we would have a quite different reception at our next stop, which was Marianske Lazne (Marienbad).

The trip from Karlovy Vary to M. Lazne is a lovely trip – full of winding roads and hills and valleys. But it is only forty-five minutes or so by car and before we knew it we were there. We were staying at Hotel Excelsior, once recognised as the best in M. Lazne and at one time a Trade Union Hotel, reserved for the workers not only from Czechoslovakia, but also from other communist countries. But it is far from being the best hotel now, as other newer and better hotels have sprung up, whilst other older ones have been completely refurbished and which are greatly improved. But I did not know that before I made our reservations. Slavek came to the hotel in the late afternoon and so we invited him to stay with us and have dinner. We went to some Balkan type restaurant along the road, but it was nothing special and the service was sluggish. Again I noticed that people seemed to be going about their business in a rather sad and some-what melancholy manner, and this is a psychological question that puzzles me. How is it possible that back in the old days when the Communists ruled, when life was grim, living standards were poor and people were often denied the possibility to travel abroad, and so on, they nevertheless seemed happy and always ready with a smile and quite willing to share a humorous joke or remark with you; and yet now, when they are free, have a much better lifestyle, better standard of living, more money and can travel abroad whenever they like, they are looking unhappy and fed up ? It seemed hard to extract a smile from anyone let alone a small humorous quip? Can anyone answer that question, because I cannot. If I had the time I would like to have befriended a normal, typical Czech family, and requested their view on this for from past experience I found that was the best way to gain accurate information of what life was really like for them.

But I would not want to say that people were miserable everywhere we went. In Prague we found people there quite normal with no sign of their spirits being low. But in Karlovy Vary and now also in M. Lazne too they are a quite different people compared to my experiences years before. However, it is worth remarking that the next day we went outside M. Lazne to visit Lazne Kynzvart, the place where in 1963 I shot my stag. On the way Slavek asked if we would like to have some lunch and as we were rather hungry we agreed. So we stopped at a roadside restaurant that he knew and there we received a very nice welcome that reminded me of the old days. The lunch was good and the service quick and pleasant and, by the way, it was cheaper than a comparable meal in town. So the sort of people I remembered still existed; maybe the best idea is to go outside the main towns and eat and drink there.

At Lazne Kynzvart we visited what the Czechs call a castle but which we would call a stately home. Lynne and I knew it because we had visited it many years before and so had Jackie when she was a little girl, but she could not remember it. But now the whole building had been completely renovated and looked palatial and magnificent, all courtesy of an EU grant, by the way. It is used more as a kind of museum these days. After that, Slavek invited us to his home quite nearby. I had previously asked my family not to speak to him about his second wife, Draha. I had the chance to speak privately with Slavek on this sad subject a little earlier. He was quite willing to talk to me, an old friend, but he said that afterwards he did not want to discuss the matter again. He admitted to me that in his anxiety to earn as much as possible for his family his dealings and work took him away quite a lot. He had a nice business importing used agricultural machinery from Germany and reselling in the Czech Republic, which it had become by then, the Slovaks having decided they wanted their independence some years earlier. I think that was a mistake but the Slovaks had a strong nationalistic feeling and preferred to be on their own. I think they would have made much more progress and it would have been better for the people had they remained as part of Czechoslovakia. Anyway, I had the feeling that Slavek was genuinely sorry that he had neglected his wife somewhat and that she had become lonely. I had a strong feeling that if he could have turned back the hands of time he would have done things differently. Anyway, it seemed that Draha began to act strangely from time to time and in various ways and one day Slavek came home to find that she had committed suicide by hanging herself in the garage. Of course, it was a terrible thing to happen but quite obviously she was mentally disturbed. And so nobody mentioned the matter, as I had requested, and I didn't talk about it any more with Slavek either.

The next day Jackie and Ray decided that they would like to see the sights of M. Lazne by taking one of the horse and carriage rides, so Lynne and I went with Slavek up to the golf course where our Prince Edward, Prince of Wales, in the early part of the twentieth century, and myself many years later enjoyed some very pleasant games of golf; in fact I still hold the King of Drivers Championship there, for I have never been notified that the exceptional drive I achieved during that contest has ever been beaten. To be fair I should add that I have never made another drive like that – ever – so it truly was exceptional. We drove up the long hill out of town and when we arrived at the clubhouse I was extremely surprised to see a grand, palatial building; the old clubhouse evidently had been completely demolished and this terrific building erected in its place. Before the clubhouse was a grassed area with very good quality tables and chairs, and this was, and still is, where one can sit and obtain refreshments. I looked around me and I must say that this was a club of which any country would be proud. I wondered what my old friend Jiri (Georgie) Trnka would have thought of all this, and Johnny Goldscheider, and the doctors from the Sanatorium too, for these were the people who fought so hard for the Golf Club and its continuance. I wandered around the sparkling clubhouse, for I wanted to see if there was a plaque or any kind of commemoration in memory of those people who had fought in the bad times and at considerable risk to themselves to ensure that this club lived on and was not turned into a public park and/or potato fields. I went into the trophy room; I was sure that is where it would be. But there was nothing; not a word. I thought to myself that it is sad to be forgotten.

When I returned home I sent an email to the director of the golf club complimenting him on a wonderful club and course, but suggesting to him that something should be placed there in memory of those who fought so bravely for the continued existence of the club and suggested that without their dedication the club might not have survived at all. He did not reply to my email; he did not even acknowledge it. Nobody, it seems, cares much about our yesterdays.

We came back down into town and got to our hotel just as Jackie and Ray had finished their horse and carriage ride, which they had enjoyed. Then Slavek said he would like to invite us to dinner that evening, our last evening, as he was almost seventy, a special occasion which needed to be celebrated. He had also been successful in a good business deal that day, so he asked us to come along and be his guests. We were very pleased to accept and especially delighted to know that Jarka (which is the familiar case of the name Jarmila and which we, as very old friends, could use), Slavek's first wife, had also been invited and would be there. We looked forward tremendously to seeing her again.

It is perhaps interesting to note that in English we do not consciously have cases in our language, although they do exist and we say them unknowingly. But in Czech there are in fact seven cases, the names of most of them I have forgotten many moons ago. In addition, in the Czech language, and maybe some others too, they also have a polite form and then the familiar form of addressing people and the difference between the two is rather important. This is often a problem to anyone learning Czech, for sometimes you are not sure which to use or at which stage to change. But I learned after a while that when one friend permits another to address him in the familiar case it is always a matter of some celebration and is carried out by lifting one's arms, linking them and taking a sip of wine or whatever. One of the problems when meeting in a group of people is to remember how to address each of the people there. If you have met someone for the first time you will always use the polite form of address. But if they are, or become, old friends you will use the familiar form. This evening would present no problems like that because they were all old friends.

We agreed to meet in the bar lounge of Hotel Crystal Palace, today a very nice hotel where I wish we had stayed instead of the Excelsior. They arrived before us and so we all greeted one another; it was really nice to see Jarka again after such a long time. Of course, like us all, she had aged. But I will always remember the young bride we met first of all in 1960, over forty years ago. I sat by her because I wanted to speak with her; her English was not as good as it used to be. No doubt, like my Czech, it had deteriorated due to lack of practice. But between her poor English and my poor Czech we got along fine. After a couple of drinks Slavek led the way across the road to the restaurant, where he had reserved a table for seven. It was called Mon Ami and Slavek had booked it personally and phoned to confirm the booking afterwards, but when we arrived there it was almost as though they didn't expect us.

However, they did show us to a table and we waited for the waiter to come to our table so that some wine might be ordered while we chatted and decided what we were going to eat. But we waited and waited until Slavek got up, went to the waiter and asked him for a little service. He eventually brought one bottle of wine – between seven people! So Slavek asked him to bring some more wine but we had to wait quite a time for that too. Meanwhile, we remembered that nobody had come to our table with menus to ask what we would like to choose. Once again, Slavek had to get up and we could see he was talking somewhat furiously to the waiter. This was very poor service indeed. Eventually, a girl came with the menus and we placed our orders.

During the mealtime our wine had run out and Slavek wanted more. Now, Slavek has never been known for his patience and I could see he was getting more and more angry at this disgraceful lack of service. It seemed to me that having made ourselves unpopular with the waiter he was getting his own back by making us wait. There came a time when

Slavek's temper reached its breaking point and so once again he left the table and collared the waiter, and we could see them having another furious argument. This was spoiling the whole evening and I felt sorry for Slavek, who wanted it to be nice for everyone. After a while the waiter appeared with two bottles of wine, but served it in a very hurried manner as if he could not care less.

Later on, I found he had spilled wine on my lovely brand new fawn jacket. Our main meal was eventually served and it was OK, but I believe that there was a mistake in one or two of the dishes ordered. I would not have made a commotion about it but Slavek berated the waitress who served us. By this time Slavek's patience had completely deserted him and so he suggested to us that we leave this restaurant and have our moucnik (dessert) somewhere else, to which we all agreed – none of us wanted to stay in that ghastly place for one moment longer than necessary.

So we left and crossed over to the other side of the road, where Slavek saw a restaurant which specialised in palacinky, or pancakes as they are known to us. I remember I had pancakes with ice cream, which I thoroughly enjoyed. When we had finished it was time to say our goodbyes. It was sad to think that quite possibly we would never meet each other again. I couldn't imagine Jackie and Ray wanting to come once more and we were getting past the age when we could travel alone and involve ourselves in queues and delays and humping cases around, as we used to quite easily when younger. Neither would I be prepared to drive in the Czech Republic, or indeed Europe, again. That is no longer possible.

The next morning we left sharp and early on the road to Prague and it did not seem all that long before we began to see signs to Letiste – just as an example of Czech pronunciation, that word is pronounced Lettishtyeah, because there is a hook over the 's' and I think there is another over the 'e', but in any case, where 'e' follows a hard consonant like 't' you must pronounce it as 'tyeah'.

Soon we were driving into Ruzyne Airport; we dropped off Lynne and Jackie with the luggage and Ray and I went to return the hired car. The man responsible walked round the car inspecting every square inch and then triumphantly found a scratch. He demanded that Ray sign a document admitting liability, but Ray refused to do that. We argued and argued that this scratch was there when we collected the car from outside Hotel Intercontinental, but we were getting nowhere. Unfortunately, they had Ray's credit card details and could still debit some unholy amount if they so wished. But nevertheless, we walked away from this unreasonable man and I hoped that George Stepan's friend at the hotel, through which we had reserved the car, would see that the matter was overlooked in our favour – and it was.

So we entered the airport, which was absolutely milling with thousands upon thousands of people. We looked for somewhere to sit whilst Ray went to see about the tickets and find out if there was any delay, but it was hopeless, and we had better not even think about trying to get a cup of coffee or a last beer. I have never seen an airport so crowded in my life. It seems that many people are travelling both in and out of Ruzyne Airport and it urgently needed enlargement to cope with such numbers – maybe by now that problem has been fixed. I seem to recall there was a slight delay, but nothing serious and soon we were in the air winging our way back to good old England and Bristol. The stewardess came round asking if we would like something to eat; we were peckish and so we ordered some sandwiches, but were then told that the last sandwich had been taken by people in front of us – Jackie and Ray! Of course, they offered to share their sandwiches with us but we declined and had a packet of crisps and some biscuits instead. It was truly marvellous to be back again in our own home, and this applied specially to Lynne who vowed there and then that she would not travel abroad again. She says that when we were younger we enjoyed the best, but the travelling conditions that prevail now are the worst. I agree with her, but I don't feel as strongly about it as she does.

I should mention that before this second trip to Prague we also had a family holiday, and for Lynne and myself a nostalgic return to Calpe on the Costa Blanca. They say never go back, and maybe that is good advice. Calpe had also changed almost out of all recognition, but the beaches were much improved.

We had reserved accommodation in a hotel-apartment on the front. The apartment that Lynne and I were allocated was quite poor and I cannot say that we were comfortable during the week we stayed there. We went up to La Empedrola and as I have remarked earlier, were very disappointed to see how this once lovely urbanisation had deteriorated. The gardens, generally speaking, seemed not to be well cared for and bushes that had been planted when we were there had been allowed to grow out of control. To be frank, it looked a mess. In that state I would not particularly care to live there today.

On one of the days we went to the restaurant La Solana and invited our friends Pam and Terry Pollard to accompany us. La Solana used to be a very noisy restaurant where they served very good food in a fast and furious manner, and they were large portions for very low prices – about £5 per person, including wine. It was always busy with people from various countries and it had a special atmosphere, which I suppose was created by the packed clientele and the variety of languages you could hear babbling away and the bustling waitresses serving steaming trays of food. We went there often and always enjoyed it. In fact when Lynne and I tried to start a luncheon club on Empedrola, whereby we went out once per week or month, I can't exactly recall now, together with our friends and neighbours, with every person having a choice of restaurant when it was his or her or their turn, we had the first choice and we chose La Solana. Everyone agreed it was an excellent choice, but unfortunately our Luncheon Club, which we thought was an excellent idea and which brought us all together once in a while, died out because some people just could not be bothered.

Anyway, it was now years later and we were very surprised when entering the restaurant to find that it was almost empty. There was no packed clientele, no noise, nothing. We were almost on our own. Also, the system had completely changed, because now what happened was that the waitress gave each table a list which contained details of every course available that day. It was quite a good and varied menu with columns to indicate what each person wished to have. So somebody had to take charge of the task of asking each person what their choice was, enter it on the list, which, when completed, was handed back to the waitress. It was certainly a different class of restaurant, in an upward direction, than the one we remembered and frequented so often years before. We thoroughly enjoyed it but we missed the old atmosphere very much indeed.

What we could not understand is why the place lacked the old crowded, noisy clientele, because even with all the changes we, if we had still been living there, would still have been regular customers. It was a mystery to us that we just could not understand. Neither was it anything to do with the prices – they were not as cheap as they were, of course, but still quite attractive, and the food, if anything, was better than it used to be and served with a higher quality of service. There was no rush and tumble with dishes of various foods flying all over the place; now the food was served in a calm and, I suppose, more normal atmosphere. But anyone who had experienced the old La Solana, as we had, will know and understand what I mean when I say that it was a very special place to go to, but you always needed to go there in a crowd.

One theory for the lack of clientele that has occurred to me is that a free and easy lifestyle existed when we lived there and therefore provided you were not stupid and overstepped the mark, you could have a glass or two of wine with your meal and not worry about it; however, if you had a crash or were involved in an accident and found to be drinking, then, quite correctly, you were punished heavily for it. Back then, when sitting in a restaurant, a couple of La Guardia would often come in, light a cigarette and order a Soberano brandy, which they would drink and then go on their way and nobody would take the slightest bit of notice. Well, those days have gone. I understand that today the Spanish Policia, or La Guardia, are not so adventurous or tolerant – no doubt because of the influence of the EU. As one who endeavoured to drink only sparingly if I were driving, and also as one who has had the experience of being hit (in England) by a drunken driver, I agree wholeheartedly with this change, even though it has perhaps spoiled the old atmosphere of places like La Solana and many outlying restaurants.

What we found very enjoyable during that holiday was that every evening we selected a different restaurant to go to and we all went out together. How I enjoyed those meals with all our family, except Philip our son, around us.

I should also mention that during our visit to Empedrola we called upon the Swiss couple who bought our villa, Casa Patrice, from us. I had written to say we would be coming, suggested a day and time and asked them to write back to me if that would not be convenient to them. I did not hear from them in reply but our welcome was very poor, especially from the woman. They did not even offer us a chair to sit on or a cool drink on what was a very hot day. The patio had been cleared of the table and excellent chairs we had left them. We could clearly see that we were not welcome and so we made our excuses and left. We are hospitable people and when they came to us when buying our property we invited them to sit with us and, knowing us, we certainly offered them refreshments – in the shade. I think the man appreciated it, but we had not taken to his unsmiling wife from the first time we met her. However, there was no excuse for their bad manners when we called upon them. If they did not want us to call they should have replied to my letter and said so.

But we would have been very alarmed had we still been living there to see on the plot below, which Pam and Terry Pollard had sold to a German, that there was a construction of what seemed to be three garages. But they had been built with dark stone and the whole looked like a grim miniature prison. It was a ghastly view from the patio above and completely spoiled the beauty of the scenery. Personally, I would have had the strongest possible objections to such awful buildings had I still been there. The actions of some people are really hard to understand.

So these were the only foreign trips we made during the period between 1994, when we returned home, and now in the year 2007. Lynne has no objection to my going anywhere I want to by myself, but first of all, who wants to go anywhere at my age by themselves? And then there would be the problem of all my medications, which Lynne has taken charge of as she doesn't trust me to take them all or at the proper times. Neither does she think I would behave myself if, just for example, I went to Prague alone; she thinks that I would overeat and drink when with my old friends. Me? Well, she is probably right – in the company of old friends I always like to celebrate and be happy. But in any case, I think it is impractical at our age for us to travel by ourselves whether alone or together. We have become old and so cannot do the things we used to when younger; this year Lynne will be seventy-seven and I am seventy-nine. In any case, we have had our share of both good and bad travelling experiences over the years; that's enough for one life.

Coming back to the matter of languages, I would like to describe a rather pleasant event which happened to Lynne and me a little while ago. I had a dental problem and my GP recommended I go to a dental doctor friend of his who spends two days or so per week dealing with patients and their problems over at a small NHS hospital in Crediton, a small town some seven or eight miles from us. We arrived a little early and were asked to sit in the waiting area. Sitting there already were two girls, who were quite busy chatting at thirteen to the dozen, as girls do. I was not listening to them as such, but I could not help overhearing some words which seemed to be familiar to me; evidently, they were not speaking English. One of the girls was then called into the surgery and so, being a friendly soul, I spoke to the other girl, asking her if she was a student. She replied that she wasn't; she was here in England to visit her friend, the one who had just gone into the surgery, who had married an English boy. I was almost sure I recognised her accent and I asked here where she came from. She said, "From Prague – you know, in the Czech Republic." So immediately I said to her, "Tak, dobry den a jak se mate?" (meaning: "So good day, and how are you?" - a typical Czech greeting). She looked very surprised and said, "Dobre, dekuji – ale jak je mozny ze rozumite Cesky?" ("Very well, thank you, but how is it possible you speak Czech?") I in turn replied, "Protoze jsem byl reditel v Anglii pro Ceskoslovenske Cokoladovny pred mnoho let." ("Because I was Director in England for the Czech confectionery organi-sation many years ago.") She then said, "Ale, mluvite Cesky velmi dobre – a vas vyslovnost je pekny." ("But you speak Czech very well – and your pronunciation is fine.") I of course thanked her and we spoke further in Czech for ten minutes or so about her country and the situation now as compared to that which applied in the days when I knew the old Czechoslovakia so well. Lynne, who was sitting by my side, was amazed I could speak Czech so well after such a long time without any practice. But I told her that I was just as amazed as she. It is, I find, a fact that there are some days when with the utmost effort you can hardly put six words together and then there are some days when almost without any effort the words come tumbling out. Or maybe it is the type of person one is talking to that makes the difference. I found that when I was younger, and still learning, there were certain people I could talk to in Czech very easily, but with some it seemed rather more difficult. On the whole, although my grammar and sometimes my usage of words would probably make a Czech teacher cringe, I only ever wanted to be able to converse and be understood. I never set out to learn all the many intricacies of the Czech language and its complicated grammar; that could follow later. And I am sure that the way I tackled the task was the right one, for by 1968 I was speaking very well, so friends told me, and I did pick up a lot of useful knowledge about Czech grammar along the way. Anyway, meeting those Czech girls was a very nice occasion and they couldn't believe that in this small country town, miles from anywhere, they would meet an Englishman who could speak Czech and who knew their country so well. It was a very nice experience.

I wrote earlier that I would return to the subject of our small garden. I am not a gardener and never have been, so our small garden suited me very well; it was just what we wanted. Just as well, because there came a time when my back pains made it hard for me to cut the two small lawns we have, so we obtained the paid help of a gentleman who lives in Tedburn St Mary, the next village, and he only charges us a moderate fee. However, opposite to us lived a man called Les Brown together with his wife Margaret. Sadly, Les passed away leaving Margaret on her own. From time to time Margaret had some problems and so, being alone, she obviously required help, which, as good neighbours, we were glad to give. Well, eventually poor old Margaret passed away too and we were absolutely amazed to be informed that she had left us a sum of money in her will! We never expected this and neither did we need it, so Lynne and I thought very carefully about what to do with the £400 she had left us.

On the one hand, we neither needed nor did we want this money, but on the other hand we felt we should accept Margaret's wishes grace-fully. Finally, we came to the conclusion that we should buy a quantity of expensive and ornate shrubs and flowers for our back garden, so that when we looked out from our patio windows we would look at the display of colour and this would remind us of dear old Margaret. So this is what we did and I, not realising this would turn me into a reluctant gardener after all these years, found myself trapped by the attention that a nice and colourful garden requires. And do you know what? I rather enjoy it! So every springtime we go out to buy various new flowers to plant in support of the shrubs and during the summer I am quite proud of our display, which, unfortunately, cannot be seen by anybody except us as our garden is fenced in all around.

When meditating in the quiet hours of the late evening, the faces of long-dead but cherished loved ones keep coming back to me. I can see every one of them so clearly in my mind, as I have a good memory for faces, even the face of my little brother Derek, who died so tragically when so young. What wouldn't I give to be able to throw a big party for all of them right now. And what a wonderful party it would be. Unfortunately, we are only able to recall the past; we cannot relive it.

And so here we are in the lovely county of Devon, and here we shall stay. Although I have been retired now for almost twenty-two years, time is of the essence, for I try to keep busy all the while. If there is nothing to do, then I will find something to do. I cannot understand people who say that in retirement there is nothing else but to just laze around and watch TV. Such people often say they are in 'God's waiting room'. But there is always plenty to do in this life if you have the right mental attitude. I try to keep very busy by walking in the countryside, playing the piano, writing to and phoning friends and relations in this country and abroad, going out to eat now and then, preferably with our family, but sometimes with friends and, of course of late, I have tried every day to spend some time writing this autobiography. I have only one ambition left and that is to be a great grandfather before I die. Please, grandchildren, hurry up! Oh – I forgot – there is a further ambition I have, which is to visit the new Wembley Football Stadium, just once, which has been built in place of the old one, which I visited many times in past years. (The best visit? Without doubt – 1966 when we won the World Cup. I was there and I saw it, and it was a wonderful experience!) But somehow I doubt this will be realized.

> **STOP PRESS:** We have just recently heard that our grand-son Grant (whom I nicknamed 'Tinribs' a long time ago) and his partner Claire have announced that they will have a baby in the spring of 2008. By the time this book is printed the baby will have been born, so one of my wishes has been granted (no pun intended!). Now, which is the way to Wembley?

And so it only remains for me to bring this book to an end. I want to express what a wonderful, interesting, adventuresome and exceptional life I have had the pleasure to experience – a life that I truly never, not even in my wildest dreams, ever thought I would be lucky enough to enjoy. I have been very pleased to share it with you and I hope you have gained some pleasure by reading about it. I would also like to thank the many people, too many to name here, who have helped me in the past; especially those who gave me the opportunity to progress in the way I did. The very first person of all must of course be my wife, who had every confidence and belief in me and who has cared for me all these years, and still does. I thank my family who have given me much happiness and, in later life, much encouragement. And finally my relatives and friends, for what is a man without friends? I realise that I have been so very fortunate and that Lady Luck has been perched on my shoulder through all of my life. And I am proud that despite the fact that I came from 'the wrong end of town' and the handicaps with which my early years presented me, I managed to overcome them and climb to an acceptable level of success, for I was most certainly only…

A BOY FROM NOWHERE!